THE
COMPLETE
MARRIAGE
BOOK

THE
COMPLETE
MARRIAGE
BOOK

Practical Help from Leading Experts

Edited by
Dr. David Stoop
and
Dr. Jan Stoop

Revell
Grand Rapids, Michigan

Published by Fleming H. Revell
a division of Baker Publishing Group
P.O. Box 6287, Grand Rapids, MI 49516-6287

Paperback edition published 2005
ISBN 0-8007-3047-X

Printed in the United States of America

The Library of Congress has cataloged the hardcover edition as follows:
   The complete marriage book : collected wisdom from leading marriage experts / (compiled by) David Stoop and Jan Stoop.
         p.   cm.
      Includes bibliographical references.
      ISBN 0-8007-1810-0 (cloth)
      1. Marriage—Religious aspects—Christianity. I. Stoop, David A. II. Stoop, Jan.
   BV835 .C63 2002
   248.4—dc21   2002007525

Contents

Part 3 The Challenges of Marriage

Part 4 Keeping Love Alive

Introduction

The process of building a satisfying, intimate marriage is seldom a smooth journey. Even though the early stages of a romance are stimulating, affirming, and enjoyable, once a couple moves from courtship to marriage, the very nature of the marriage relationship demands that a couple has the strengths and the skills necessary to make a marriage relationship work. Marriage shows us how good we are at negotiating issues and how adept we are at resolving conflicts. And we discover that what works at the early stages of a marriage may not work as well at later stages as a married couple grows and develops new relational skills.

Every couple is going to encounter new pressures along the way. These may come from outside the marriage, from inside the marriage, or even from long-dormant issues deep inside each person. The adjustment of living with someone intimately, balancing the tasks of developing careers, raising children, and supporting each other is a very complex task.

Many couples are surprised when they learn that the old unresolved conflicts they had with their parents and/or siblings will be brought to the surface in a marriage relationship. Each of these represents great demands on couples as they struggle to work out the issues of balancing control and learning the meaning of sacrifice at new levels and how to trust the person they love.

Marriage hasn't always made so many demands on its participants. Our great-grandparents didn't worry about all of these tasks. To many of them, marriage was part of survival. The husband made the money, and the wife took care of the home and the kids. After all, times were tougher back then, and those earlier generations weren't as demanding as we are about marital intimacy.

We want much more from marriage these days. As a result of these higher expectations, the marital state has become far more complex. So if we are going to succeed, we will need a lot of help and a much wider range of resources. This book aims to be one of your treasured handbooks on building a marriage that lasts. For that reason we have recruited a number of counselors and pastors who have worked with marriage issues for many years. We asked them to cover most every topic you will need to understand to enrich your marriage relationship. Each of these experts then refers you to added resources if you want more than can be provided in a single book.

As you read through the chapters, you will find some themes are repeated. We left these in because we felt they represented each author's perspective, and that might give you a different slant on that particular subject. We also thought that you, the reader, would like to know their thoughts. Here's an overview of what's covered.

In part 1, we begin by looking at the mystery of marriage. How two people can come together and form a lasting relationship is really a mystery. But it is a mystery that can be understood. So in the first chapter, a pastor and his wife provide the basis for building a secure foundation based on Genesis 2. We then look at the role of "attachment theory" as part of the foundation of marriage, and then at the theological basis for marriage.

Part 2 looks at the skills a couple needs to maintain a healthy, growing relationship over the years. We look at what a person's relational needs are and three critical ingredients for intimacy. We then look at the role of communication in marriage, followed by a chapter on building healthy boundaries together. Next we look at sexual intimacy, the role of money, how to set goals and priorities, how to keep playing together as a couple, and finally a chapter on building traditions together.

Part 3 looks at the special challenges two people face as a couple. We look at why couples have problems, then we have a chapter on the unique problems a couple can face sexually. Following that we will examine the two basic fears that can destroy intimacy, how anger can be harnessed for good, how you can unpack the baggage from your past, what the unique issues are that you will face when children arrive, the special task of loving your in-laws, and what to do when a crisis hits home. Finally, we will look at the special issues faced in second marriages.

Part 4 provides the help every couple needs to keep love alive. We describe how to divorce-proof your marriage, how to keep the passion alive, and how and where you can find a mentor couple to guide you. Finally, we will look at what you can do to develop the kind of spiritual intimacy that builds a foundation for a lifetime.

You will find either a list of questions at the end of each chapter or a series of questions throughout the chapter. We hope that you and your spouse will spend time discussing many of these together. In addition, there is a list of important books at the end of each chapter that the author recommends to provide additional information on his or her specific topic. Also, you will find the biographical information about the authors in the following section on contributors. It's interesting to note that combined together the thirty-four authors have over five hundred years of experience in marriage.

Read, reread, discuss, question, explore, but most of all, enjoy your marriage together! Our prayer is that it will last a lifetime.

Contributors

David and Claudia Arp are the founders of Marriage Alive International, a groundbreaking program providing marriage- and family-building resources and training for the church and community. They are popular speakers, seminar leaders, columnists, and authors of numerous books and video curricula including *10 Great Dates* and the Gold Medallion Award–winning *The Second Half of Marriage*. Frequent contributors to print and broadcast media, the Arps have appeared on the NBC *Today Show, CBS This Morning,* and *Focus on the Family.* David and Claudia have been married for more than thirty-five years and live in Knoxville, Tennessee.

Denny Bellesi is the pastor of the Coast Hills Community Church. In 1985, the Bellesis arrived in South Orange County to plant a new venture, now known as Coast Hills. What began as a spark with 10 people in the living room of their home has ignited into a weekly attendance of over 4,000 members. Denny is a graduate of Denver Seminary and has served in a variety of churches and parachurch ministries in Southern California and in Denver, Colorado.

Along with her active participation in several women's ministries at Coast Hills, **Leesa Bellesi** is known for her accomplishments as a choreographer and dance instructor, including the career development of several Christian music artists. She is a seasoned speaker with a conversational, contemporary style appealing to women's groups.

Denny and Leesa are the parents of two grown daughters and recently became grandparents. They are the authors of the best-selling book *The Kingdom Assignment,* and can be reached through their web site, www.kingdomassignment.com.

Tim Clinton is president of the thirty-five-thousand-member American Association of Christian Counselors. A licensed marriage and family therapist and an ordained minister, Dr. Clinton has served as Pastor of Caring Ministries at Calvary Church in Charlotte, North Carolina, and is an adjunct professor of counseling at Liberty Baptist Theological Seminary. A columnist for *ParentLife* magazine and host of *Christian Counseling Today* (a daily national radio program), he has authored such works as *Before a Bad Goodbye,* and with his wife, Julie, has authored *The Marriage You've Always Wanted.* He is also the executive editor of the *Soul Care Bible.*

Julie Clinton is the executive director of Light Counseling, Inc., a multidisciplinary Christian counseling and mediation practice in Lynchburg, Virginia. She was formerly the director of the Liberty Godparent Home, a home for unwed mothers. Before that, she taught middle school for six years. A graduate of Liberty University, she holds an M.Ad. from Lynchburg College and an M.B.A. from Liberty University. Tim and Julie have been married for over twenty years and have two children.

David Congo is a licensed psychologist, licensed marriage and family therapist, certified life planner, and ordained pastor. He and his wife, Janet, are the cofounders of LifeMates, an international marriage ministry and are in partnership with Cook Communications, Colorado Springs, Colorado. Together David and Janet have authored eight books, the most recent being *LifeMates: A Lover's Guide for a Lifetime Relationship.* They are currently producing resources to enable a local church to implement a LifeMates Celebration curriculum program for engaged and married couples. They have appeared on numerous radio and television programs.

Janet Congo is a licensed marriage and family therapist and a former university instructor. She began her writing with a women's book entitled *Free to Be God's Woman.* Both by herself and with her husband, David, she has presented seminars nationally and internationally. David and Janet have been married thirty years and have two adult children. They can be reached on the Web at www.elifemates.com or by e-mail at lifemates@sbcglobal.net.

Don Harvey is a licensed professional counselor/mental health service provider. He is a clinical member and approved supervisor for the American Association for Marriage and Family Therapy. Don received his Ph.D. in marriage and family therapy from Virginia Polytechnic Institute and State University and has been a practicing therapist for over twenty-five years. Along with a private marriage therapy practice, he directs the graduate marriage and family therapy program at Trevecca Nazarene University, Nashville, Tennessee.

Don has authored nine books dealing with various marriage issues, including *The Drifting Marriage, When the One You Love Wants to Leave, Surviving Betrayal: Counseling an Adulterous Marriage,* and *Living in a Glass House: Mixing Marriage and Ministry.* Don is a leading authority on "crisis issues" in marriage. He is a frequent guest on radio and television and is in demand as a speaker at national professional conferences.

Jan Harvey is also a marriage and family therapist and has a private counseling practice in Nashville where she focuses on premarital and marriage counseling. She also works with the Career and Counseling Center on the campus of Trevecca Nazarene University. She is particularly interested in the preventative/educational side of therapy and enjoys relating with young adult populations.

Together, the Harveys regularly host marriage-focused weekend retreats throughout the country, are media guests, and are speakers for premarital workshops for colleges and universities. They are also therapy "Fellows" at Marble Retreat, a counseling retreat center specifically for clergy couples in Marble, Colorado. They have been married twenty-nine years and have two adult children.

Ron Hawkins is a licensed professional counselor and serves as Dean of the College of Arts and Sciences and Professor of Counseling and Practical Theology at Liberty University in Lynchburg, Virginia. He is a member of the executive board for the American Association of Christian Counselors and has participated in several educational and publishing projects with AACC. Ron is nationally known as a trainer of counselors and a passionate advocate for the application of spirituality to the challenges encountered in marriage and leadership.

Peggy Hawkins is Ron's wife of thirty-nine years. Together they have parented four children. She has deeply enjoyed her role as mother and wife while working in the public sector as an optician. She has traveled around the world conducting marriage workshops with Ron. Her many years in the churches where Ron served as senior minister have given her unique insights into the joys and struggles faced by pastors' wives, and she has often spoken to and coached ministry couples. Ron and Peggy can be reached at rehawkin@liberty.edu.

Carol Kuykendall is director of communications and ministry relations for Mothers of Preschoolers (MOPS) International, Inc. and the author of several books, including *Learning to Let Go* and *A Mother's Footprints of Faith.* She lives with her husband, Lynn, in Boulder, Colorado.

Christopher McCluskey is a licensed psychotherapist, board certified sex therapist, and Christian life coach. He is a cofounder of the American Board of Christian Sex Therapists and a founding board member of the Institute for Sexual Wholeness. He serves on the adjunct faculty of Reformed Theological Seminary teaching human sexuality in its master's in counseling program, and he is a nationally known speaker. Chris produced the highly acclaimed video *Coaching Couples into Passionate Intimacy: God's Intention for Marital Sexual Union.*
Rachel McCluskey is Chris's wife and homeschools their five children. She was a schoolteacher before the couple began having children, and she developed and taught a sex education curriculum for the upper-level grades. Rachel has done extensive research into the development of sexual theology as well as the historical and modern challenges influencing the diversity of views present in the church today. They can be reached on the Web at www.christian-living.com.

Paul Meier is a nationally recognized psychiatrist and cofounder of the Meier New Life Clinics. He is also the cohost of the national *New Life Live* radio program. He has authored over fifty best-selling books, such as *Happiness Is a Choice; Love Is a Choice;* and *Don't Let Jerks Get the Best of You.* He has been a guest on numerous radio and television programs, incuding shows hosted by Oprah Winfrey and Tom Snyder. In addition, he serves on Focus on the Family's Physicians Resource Council and is the medical director of the Paul Meier New Life Day Hospital and Outpatient Clinic in Richardson, Texas.
Jan Meier is a marriage and family therapist with a master's degree in marriage and family development. She has coauthored a devotional for women entitled *The Woman Within* and has helped her husband write several of his books. Together they have raised their own four

children as well as two nephews. They have been married for thirty-five years.

Elisa Morgan is president and CEO of MOPS International, Inc. She has a daily radio program, *MomSense,* which is broadcast on more than three hundred radio stations nationally. She is the author of *Meditations for Mothers* and editor of the *Mom's Devotional Bible.* She lives with her husband, Evan, in Denver.

Sharon Hart Morris graduated from UCLA and received an M.A. from the school of theology and also an M.A. and Ph.D. in marriage and family therapy from the school of psychology at Fuller Theological Seminary. She continues to conduct research on marriage and is the creator of "Hart-Haven of Safety," a marital assessment tool.

Sharon and her husband were married for fifteen years. In 1995 he was killed in an automobile accident. With the strength of the Lord and an incredible support system consisting of her family, Sharon raised her two young sons and rebuilt her life. It was during this time that she returned to graduate school and started her research on relationships.

Sharon is currently a relationship consultant at La Vie Counseling Center in Pasadena, California. Specializing in relationships from an attachment perspective, Sharon travels extensively, teaching students, counselors, pastors/missionaries, and couples on relationship issues in marriage and family.

Gary Oliver received his B.A. from Biola University, an M.Div. from Talbot Theological Seminary, a Th.M. from Fuller Theological Seminary, and an M.A. and Ph.D. in psychology from the University of Nebraska in Lincoln. He is a licensed clinical psychologist in both Arkansas and Colorado and is a clinical member and approved supervisor of the American Association for Marriage and Family Therapy. Gary has over thirty years of experience in individual, premarital, marital, and family counseling. For several years he worked as senior psychologist with a group of family practice physicians and for over twelve years was clinical director of a large counseling center in Colorado. He currently is the executive director of the Center for Marriage and Family Studies and Professor of Psychology and Practical Theology at John Brown University in Siloam Springs, Arkansas.

16 Contributors

Carrie Oliver is a licensed professional counselor with People-CARE Clinic. She earned her M.A. in counseling from Denver Seminary. In addition to her clinical work Carrie enjoys conference speaking, teaching, and conducting small groups. She has been active in leadership for a variety of women's ministries. She is featured as a presenter in a video series, *Extraordinary Women,* produced by the American Association of Christian Counselors.

Gary and Carrie have coauthored *Raising Sons . . . and Loving It!* Gary is also the author of *Made Perfect in Weakness: The Amazing Things God Can Do with Failure* as well as the coauthor of ten books with H. Norman Wright, including *Raising Kids to Love Jesus, Good Women Get Angry,* and *When Anger Hits Home.* Gary and Carrie have been married twenty years and have three sons. They live in Siloam Springs, Arkansas.

Les and Leslie Parrott are codirectors of the Center for Relationship Development at Seattle Pacific University (SPU), a groundbreaking program dedicated to teaching the basics of good relationships. Les Parrott is a professor of clinical psychology at SPU, and Leslie is a marriage and family therapist at SPU. The Parrotts are authors of the Gold Medallion Award–winning *Saving Your Marriage Before It Starts, Becoming Soul Mates, Love Is, When Bad Things Happen to Good Marriages,* and *Relationships,* as well as numerous other books and video resources.

They have been featured on *Oprah, CBS This Morning,* CNN, and *The View,* and in *USA Today* and the *New York Times.* They are frequent guest speakers and have written for a variety of magazines. The Parrotts also serve as marriage ambassadors for the Oklahoma governor's ten-year Marriage Initiative. They live in Seattle, Washington, with their son and have been married seventeen years. They can be reached at www.RealRelationships.com.

Greg Smalley earned his doctorate degree in clinical psychology from Rosemead School of Psychology at Biola University in Southern California. He also holds two master's degrees—one in counseling psychology from Denver Seminary and one in clinical psychology from Rosemead School of Psychology.

Greg is currently the president and CEO of two ministries located in Branson, Missouri—Today's Family, a counseling ministry, and the

Smalley Relationship Center, a marriage and family enrichment ministry. He also maintains a counseling practice specializing in working with couples in crisis and teaches at the monthly *Marriage for a Lifetime* marriage seminar across the country.

He has appeared on both television and radio programs, including *Focus on the Family* and *Hour of Power*. He has published over one hundred articles on parenting and relationship issues for *Living with Teenagers, Shine, Homes of Honor, Christian Parenting Today, ParentLife, HonorBound,* and *Branson Living*. He and his father, Gary Smalley, are the coauthors of a book for parents of teenagers, *Bound By Honor*. He is also the coauthor of the books *Winning Your Wife Back* and *Winning Your Husband Back*.

Erin Smalley has a bachelor of science degree in nursing from Grand Canyon University in Phoenix and a master of arts degree in clinical psychology from Evangel University in Springfield, Missouri. Erin specializes in working with teen moms, couples, and families. She writes a monthly parenting column for *ParentLife*. Greg and Erin have been married for ten years and have two daughters and a son. The Smalleys live in Ozark, Missouri.

Jim Smoke is a pioneer in the divorce recovery field, developing the first Divorce Recovery Workshops while on the pastoral staff at the Crystal Cathedral. Jim has been a pastor on the staff of a number of churches, including Hollywood Presbyterian Church. He has written seventeen books, including the best-selling *Growing through Divorce*. He has traveled and conducted over seven hundred seminars and workshops across the United States. He is currently a full-time Life Coach. He and his wife, Carol, have been married for forty-four years and have three children and nine grandchildren. They live in Cypress, California.

David Stoop is a licensed clinical psychologist in the State of California. He received his master's in theology from Fuller Theological Seminary and his Ph.D. from the University of Southern California. He is the founder and director of The Center for Family Therapy in Newport Beach, California, where he has his counseling practice. He is an adjunct professor at Fuller Seminary and serves on the executive board of the American Association of Christian Counselors.

He has authored over twenty books, including *Forgiving Our Parents, Forgiving Ourselves; Self-Talk: Key to Personal Growth; Seeking God Together; Understanding Your Child's Personality; When Couples Pray Together;* and *Real Solutions to Forgiving the Unforgivable,* and was executive editor of *The Life Recovery Bible,* a unique twelve-step Bible.

Jan Stoop is a counselor, author, and seminar speaker. She received her master's in theology from Fuller Theological Seminary and her doctorate in clinical psychology from the California Graduate Institute. She is the cofounder of The Center for Family Therapy in Newport Beach, California, where she serves as a Life Coach for women. Jan is a frequent speaker at Mothers of Preschoolers (MOPS), women's workshops, seminars, and retreats. She has authored *The Tenderhearted Mom,* and *Balancing Gentleness with Toughness* and has coauthored several books, including *The Grandmother Book.*

Dave and Jan have led marriage retreats across the country and in Australia, Europe, and South Africa. They have three sons and five grandchildren and have been married forty-four years.

Michael Sytsma is an ordained minister in the Wesleyan Church and is a licensed professional counselor. He is president and founder of Building Intimate Marriages, Inc., and cofounder of the Institute for Sexual Wholeness and the American Board of Christian Sex Therapists. Michael provides marriage and sex therapy in the Atlanta area, marriage workshops nationally, and co-teaches sex therapy at Psychological Studies Institute and Reformed Theological Seminary. He received his M.S. in community counseling from Georgia State and is currently completing his Ph.D. in marriage and family therapy at the University of Georgia.

Karen Sytsma has been married to Michael since 1985. She received her B.S.N. from Indiana Wesleyan University and is a registered nurse and a certified hospice nurse. Karen has recently devoted her time to raising their two young sons. She is an active volunteer in their schools and a teacher in their church. You can reach Michael and Karen online at www.intimatemarriage.org.

Roger Tirabassi holds a doctorate degree in ministry and a master's degree in pastoral counseling. He is the president of Spiritual Growth Ministries, a nonprofit Christian organization ministering to singles and marrieds. Roger conducts seminars and retreats for couples and has a private counseling practice in Southern California.

Becky Tirabassi is a nationally known speaker and author who often makes appearances on radio and television. She recently hosted a ten-week series on the CBS *Early Show*. She is the author of eleven books, the founder and president of "Change Your Life," and has coauthored, with Roger, *Let Love Change Your Life*. They can be reached at www.changeyourlifedaily.com.

Tom Whiteman is a licensed psychologist with a large counseling practice in the Philadelphia area. He earned his Ph.D. from Bryn Mawr College in 1987 and has authored or coauthored thirteen books, including *The Marriage Mender* and *Be Your Own Best Friend*. Tom also serves as an adjunct professor at Eastern College and is the cochair of the Coalition of Christians in Private Practice, whose purpose is to encourage and empower Christian counselors throughout the United States.

Lori Whiteman was a special education teacher for eight years before she married Tom in 1985. She now works at home raising their three children. Lori is an assistant teaching director for Community Bible Studies in the Philadelphia area. Tom and Lori live in Berwyn, Pennsylvania.

Part 1

The Mystery
of Marriage

1

A Secure Foundation

Denny and Leesa Bellesi

God, the best maker of all marriages, combine your hearts in one.

William Shakespeare, *Henry V*

"I need to get out of this small apartment," Leesa announced to me late one evening. We had just recently moved from San Diego to a new job at a church in Thousand Oaks, California. We had two small children, and on this particular evening she was losing it.

We had sold our home in our previous location and were in the market for a new one. We found a friendly real estate salesperson, and on a Sunday afternoon we were off house hunting. We drove through neighborhoods that seemed appealing, others that weren't. We especially liked one housing tract we went through. The homes were Cape Cod style with picket fences. From the outside everything looked like this was a place we could call home. The realtor hemmed and hawed and then finally confessed, "This is not a development I would recommend you buying in." We looked at each other, puzzled. *What could be so bad about this place?* we thought. He continued, "Most of the homes here have lawsuits pending."

Sure enough, as we listened to the story, we were convinced that buying in this neighborhood would only be a headache rather than a place where we could feel confident raising our children.

23

"You see," he said, "the builder of those homes started out with good intentions, but as he poured the foundations he decided that he would try and save some money by cutting corners. How he decided to cut corners was the issue. He thought no one would ever know, that no one would ever see. When he poured the concrete slabs he left out one important ingredient—the supporting steel or rebar. You see, you can make something hard with concrete, but if it doesn't have secure fittings to keep it in place, it will eventually sink, begin to break, or just plain crack down the middle, forcing the home to fall in on itself."

Our realtor friend ended the story with a final note that we will never forget. The contractor of the homes had been under so much pressure because of what he had done that just a few months previously he had committed suicide. Sad but true, he had made the mistake of his life.

Start with a Secure Foundation

As in marriage, even though we have the best intentions and may plan the wedding day to perfection, if we don't have a secure foundation we can depend on when the roof feels like it's going to cave in, we're in big trouble.

Over the years we have unfortunately seen too many people come across our path who develop relationships or enter into marriages that are built on rather shoddy foundations. For one reason or another they cut corners. They were willing to settle for a relationship based on feelings and fantasies alone, or on appearances and assumptions that have little to do with reality. They leaned on anticipations and unrealistic expectations that set them up for failure. They developed selfish behaviors and attitudes that often led to some rather disastrous results down the line.

We believe God has some things to say about a secure foundation on which to build a strong, lasting, and meaningful marriage. If we want to know what God has to say about this foundation, we have to go back to the beginning, and that means going back to the relationship of Adam and Eve. Someone once said that the reason Adam and Eve were able to survive a monogamous relationship is because Adam didn't have to hear about all the other men. And Eve didn't have to hear about the way Adam's mother cooked and cared for him. But we know it's more complicated than that.

Genesis 2 sets a foundation for relationships between men and women.

> The LORD God said, "It is not good for the man to be alone. I will make a helper suitable for him." Now the LORD God had formed out of the ground all the beasts of the field and all the birds of the air. He brought them to the man to see what he would name them; and whatever the man called each living creature, that was its name. So the man gave names to all the livestock, the birds of the air and all the beasts of the field. But for Adam no suitable helper was found. So the LORD God caused the man to fall into a deep sleep; and while he was sleeping, he took one of the man's ribs and closed up the place with flesh. Then the LORD God made a woman from the rib he had taken out of the man, and he brought her to the man. The man said, "This is now bone of my bones and flesh of my flesh; she shall be called 'woman,' for she was taken out of man." For this reason a man will leave his father and mother and be united to his wife, and they will become one flesh. The man and his wife were both naked, and they felt no shame.
>
> Genesis 2:18–25

There are five essentials mentioned in this passage that make up what we believe God says forms a secure foundation on which to build a lasting marriage relationship. Four of them are specifics that come right out of the passage; the other is implied by the passage in its entirety.

A Common Desire

The common desire God gives two people is not for each other's bodies so much as it is for each other's company. It's a common desire for companionship. Look at verse 18: "The LORD God said, 'It is not good for the man to be alone. I will make a helper [who is] suitable for him.'" The word *helper* does not mean a servant. It doesn't mean hired help. We often have to remind men in particular of this. They aren't getting hired help. The word *helper* means, by definition, and literally in the Hebrew, *one who matches him, one who complements him.* This common desire is not for a housekeeper nor is it for a provider on the other side. This is for a *partner.* It is not for a roommate who splits the responsibilities but for a companion who shares a life and is willing to give of himself or herself to the other person. It is not just for a mistress or a lover who sleeps in the same bed but for a soul mate who shares his or her entire life and who encourages his or her companion to do the same.

This may surprise you, but we think that simply being in love with someone is not the best reason to get married. And we say that for two reasons. One, we are convinced that what we call being in love is often little more than being attracted to somebody for a short period of time or being infatuated with them on the basis of how they look. And as wonderful and delightful as attraction is, it is not enough to build a lasting marriage relationship on. If you don't believe us, go to Disneyland; it is filled with all kinds of attractions. That's what gets us to go there in the first place. There are many exciting things there, and we're wowed by them; but after a while even all those attractions become rather boring. Even Disney knows that, which is one of the reasons they are constantly adding new attractions to theme parks. Both Leesa and I went with family and friends to Disneyland a few times a year while growing up. However, as much as we may have enjoyed visiting Disneyland, we didn't particularly want to live there. Attractions are good and enjoyable, but we can't base our life on mere attractions.

And the second reason is, we meet with a lot of married couples who began their relationship as lovers but who don't know the first thing about being friends with each other. Really! Not the first thing! As long as they are in bed everything is fine. But they don't have a clue about how to make a relationship work the other twenty-three hours and fifty-four minutes a day. We have discovered that if they don't know how to live together as friends and companions and partners, it won't be long before they won't even *want* to have sex with each other anymore. And sadly, we see that happen time and time and time again. We marvel at the many couples who live days, months, years without enjoying sex with each other. And these are couples who at one time couldn't keep their hands off each other.

Our recommendation to you is to be friends before you are ever lovers. Leesa and I developed our friendship with one another long before we began to date. We like to think we fostered the feelings that blossomed into attraction and love for each other over water fights we had as day camp counselors together. Learn what it is to develop a companionship kind of relationship. Don't rush into falling in love, because what you are going to find is that sex creates an instant bond. And oftentimes it is only an illusion, because if all you have is this intimate relationship that lasts in bed, you are going to find that your foundation has no strength on which to build a lasting relationship. That is the danger of putting the priority of sex over companionship in a dating relationship. Under such circumstances lovers can be simply users of other people to satisfy their own desires—all under the guise of building a strong relationship.

Let us ask you a question. Did you enter into this relationship to use someone for your own wishes and whims and needs, or did you enter into this marriage relationship to share your life with someone with the goal of finding a true companion? The first essential to a secure foundation is a common desire for companionship.

A Common Appreciation

By appreciation we mean the recognition, understanding, and respect of both the similarities and the unique differences between a husband and a wife as a man and a woman.

> But for Adam no suitable helper was found. So the LORD God caused the man to fall into a deep sleep; and while he was sleeping, he took one of the man's ribs and closed up the place with flesh. Then the LORD God made a woman from the rib he had taken out of the man, and he brought her to the man. The man said, . . .
>
> Genesis 2:21–22

We may be using all the poetic license we can muster, but the Hebrew here is very emphatic:

["WOW! WOW!"]
"This is now bone of my bones and flesh of my flesh."

What Adam was saying is, "She is just like me! She is my equal. Nobody else in all creation is anything like this person." And it is noteworthy for us to remember that one hundred years ago a Bible commentator wrote that this woman was not made out of Adam's head to top him nor out of his feet to be trampled by him but out of his side to be equal with him, under his arm to be protected by him, and near his heart to be loved by him. "Wow!" he said. "She is just like me!" And if you ever forget that your partner is your equal, you are treading on thin ice as far as building a healthy home and future. Adam also said, "WOW! She is uniquely different from me. She looks different than I do. We are *not* the same!" We find it interesting that people are drawn to each other because of their differences, that opposites do attract. And there is something unique and fascinating about being attracted to somebody who is different than we are, because we know (kind of intrinsically) that the other person will round us out to some degree and complete us.

But it is also funny that as soon as we get together there is this tendency on the part of one or both of us to want to make that other person become just like us. It's understandable why we do that, because it is much easier to understand and live with somebody who thinks just like we do than someone who throws in his or her own opinions all the time. But surely we didn't enter into this relationship to gain a clone. Our desire was to gain a companion, and if we don't learn to appreciate the unique qualities that really build into that companionship, then we are hurting ourselves and our chances for any real happiness and lasting relationship in the future.

Some people in our culture today would have us believe that there are no real differences between men and women and that we should just treat each other the same. But that isn't the case. You don't have to be a rocket scientist to figure out that men and women are very, very different. The fact is that men and women are different physiologically. Do you realize that every cell in a man is different from that of a woman? Every cell in your body, guys, has an extra Y chromosome. (It is what makes you such a YUTZ in the eyes of your wife, sometimes.) Men have twice as much blood running through their bodies, and that pumps more oxygen to the muscles, making them stronger, which is exactly the way God designed them to be. Did you know men's brains are wired differently? It's been said that, before birth, a chemical is released in a baby boy's body that not only makes him distinctively male but also separates the connecting fibers between the two halves of the brain. The result is that little boys tend to become much more compartmentalized in their thinking. Either they are left-brained, which has to do with the facts, or right-brained, which has to do with the creative and the feeling kinds of things. But little boys, and men thereafter, are rarely able to think with both halves of their brain at the same time.

On the other hand, little girls tend to be much more holistic in their thinking, due to the fact this chemical event does not happen in their brains. And therein lies the reason they are able to think with both halves of their brain at the same time. That's why a woman can go to her job as a CPA and crunch numbers all day long and at the same time be wondering how her husband and children are doing.

It drives her crazy when her husband comes home and says, "I have had a tough day." The first thing she says is, "Well, did you think of me?" He says, "Uhhhh, left brain, right brain, where am I?" He doesn't understand those kinds of things; it doesn't even enter his mind, unless he makes a conscious decision to shift from one side to the other. Men are different that way. Their brains are wired differently.

Men are different emotionally, and every man reading this book right now is saying, "No kidding." But the truth of the matter is that they are. Some women live with men who express no emotion at all. They can walk through a fire and just say, "Huh?" The world could collapse, and they don't feel anything, or at least they don't express it. Oh, they're feeling it, but they have learned all through their lives that they are supposed to stuff those things and let them fester to the point where they finally have an emotional explosion. Or maybe it's just a kind of passive-aggressive thing. That is because many men were never given permission as boys to have emotions, let alone express them. And so many don't have a clue how to do it properly or effectively. They have to learn those things, whereas with women it comes rather naturally.

Men are different romantically. This is going to come as a shock to some of you guys, but romance is very important in and of itself to a woman. On the other hand, ladies, you need to understand that until a man learns otherwise, romance is often just a means to an end for him. We can guarantee you that 99.999 percent of the time that end is sex. Yes, men are different that way.

If men and women don't pursue an understanding and have an appreciation for their differences and grow as related to those differences, they are headed for some major foundational problems. Nothing chills a relationship faster or more deeply than when one partner doesn't feel appreciated for the differences that exist in a relationship and doesn't affirm the equality that should exist in a relationship.

1 Peter 3:7 says, "Husbands, . . . be considerate as you live with your wives." It is an injunction to husbands, but we can also cross it

over to wives and say, "Live with your spouse in an understanding way." "Treat them with respect," Peter says to husbands, "as the weaker partner" (and when he says weaker he doesn't mean weaker in character or weaker in intellect or weaker in ability or position, but simply in sheer physical strength). What he means is "Treat them tenderly." So the principle is this: Husbands, don't use your strengths to take advantage of your wife, but rather use your strengths to protect and care for her. Wives, don't use your mental strengths to reduce or manipulate your husband, but use your strengths to complement him and complete him. Peter is saying you should treat each other as a partner and as a joint heir and with the respect that you both deserve. To do so is to appreciate each other.

A Common Commitment

Here the key words are *leave* and *cleave*. Look at Genesis 2:24: "For this reason a man will leave his father and mother and be united [cleave] to his wife, and they will become one flesh."

Once again, God is talking about much more than merely consummating a marriage sexually. He is essentially talking about what a marriage relationship is from his perspective. It's being willing to forsake all others to be united to one person. It's leaving the previous securities of home and parents and independence to create a new security, a new home, a new priority of loyalties to one person, and a new interdependence that begins the process of a whole new way of life.

Trade-offs? You bet there are trade-offs in such a relationship, but that in part is what this commitment is all about. Recognizing those trade-offs and consciously making a choice to move in that direction is to live by your promise and wedding vows. In Thornton Wilder's play *The Skin of Our Teeth,* the character Mrs. Anterbus says to her husband, "I didn't marry you because you were perfect. I married you because you gave me a promise." At that point she takes off her ring and stares at it for a while; then she says, "That promise made up for your faults and the promise I made to you made up for mine." Two imperfect people got married, and it was the promise that made the relationship.

Whenever I (Denny) officiate at a wedding, I take some time to remind the couple that by God's design marriage is a *covenant relationship*. By *covenant* I mean a commitment or promise that is made freely, publicly, honestly, and solemnly. By the word *relationship* I mean the kind of life or the kind of behavior that is to typify that commitment and reflect that promise. This is a commitment and a promise that takes two people to ensure, not one for the other, not one over or against the other, not one hanging on to the other, but two people working together. One partner can't carry the load of this commitment all by himself or herself. It's not fair, it's not right, it's not feasible, and it's not conducive to the process of becoming one flesh. And, this idea of becoming one flesh is indeed a process.

One night as Leesa was working on a project, she sat in the study with all the lights out and worked simply by candlelight. The candles she used were some of the three hundred candles we used during our daughter's wedding. At the ceremony, the candles were a beautiful display, one that people comment on to this day. All together and freshly lit they looked amazing, so uniform and unified, serving one purpose, basically to look beautiful on Brooke and Darren's wedding day. As Leesa sat and stared at them this particular night, she realized they were still serving a purpose but looked quite different now. Even though all the candles had given several hours of light, they had burned into different patterns. They really were beautiful in their own individual way now and actually looked like separate works of art. The drips and formations had set each one apart. They wouldn't have looked that way if they had not gotten burned along the way. We came to realize as Leesa pointed out the different shapes of the candles that even though change can burn, its ultimate goal is to mold us into works of art, each beautiful in our own way.

Marriage by God's design is not a commitment we make one day and then expect it never to change. Commitment takes strength; it takes character and is guaranteed to change. As it changes it can become more and more a thing of beauty.

We could, unfortunately, introduce you to a number of people who could tell you out of their own pain and heartache that when this commitment is ignored or diminished or forgotten or forsaken, it is devastating. This only serves to prove all the more the essential nature of a secure foundation. It is crucial! Crucial! Some of you may have been fooled into believing that living together before marriage helps build that foundation. The fact is that 80 percent of the people who live together never know what it is to have a quality lasting relationship because they don't know what commitment is: 40 percent never go on in their relationship, and the other 40 percent marry but end up divorcing because they never had anything to begin with. We're not saying this to be prudes or to be judgmental. We're saying this to save you a lot of grief.

A Common Trust

Genesis 2:25 says, "The man and his wife were both naked, and they felt no shame." We are taking this idea of naked to be open and vulnerable and transparent before each other, and that Adam and Eve had no qualms about it. They felt safe in each other's presence. No masks, no covers, no dark secrets. Here's an important question for you: How safe do you feel in your partner's presence? How safe do you feel to express your insecurities and your failures and your dreams and your desires to your partner? Can you explain what you think and what you feel and what you want and what you have done without the threat of being rejected in some way that says, "Don't you dare do that again"? If the truth were told, a lot of you don't feel all that safe. Here is a follow-up question: How safe does your partner feel in *your* presence? See, it is easy to start with ourselves, but we are in a partnership here. It is not just what you think or what you feel, but what your partner thinks and feels as well.

For some of you right now, if you asked your partner that question, and they were brutally honest with you, they would say they don't feel very safe at all. One of the reasons that you may be struggling is because the issue of safety has never been developed. Is there a climate of safety in your marriage? The climate of safety we create for one another will either enhance or detract from the level of trust we experience with one another. And as trust goes, so too goes the human capacity to love. Contrary to what you might think, the opposite of love is not hate but fear. Where fear reigns trust diminishes, and a common trust is essential for a secure foundation to a lasting relationship.

A Common Conviction

There is one more essential in marriage, and that is a common conviction. It's not in any one particular verse of this passage that we've looked at, but it's implied by the whole passage. By a common conviction we mean a common faith in the Lord as the very center of the marriage relationship. He is the one who calls our marriage together, the one who directs its outcome, the one who has been given the authority to say thus and such. The shared conviction that Jesus Christ stands at the very center of this relationship, leading it, directing it, nurturing it, and replenishing it, is crucial. Psalm 127:1 says, "Unless the LORD builds the house, its builders labor in vain." Do you know what that means? Unless we're allowing God to have his say in our relationship, we're fighting a losing battle as believers. Because from God's perspective, marriage was not meant to be simply two people living together; it was meant by his design to have him be included in the process.

> Two are better than one,
>> because they have a good return for
>> their work:
> If one falls down,
>> his friend can help him up.
> But pity the man who falls
>> and has no one to help him up!
> Also, if two lie down together, they
>> will keep warm.
>> But how can one keep warm alone?
> Though one may be overpowered,
>> two can defend themselves.
> A cord of three strands is not quickly
>> broken.
>
> Ecclesiastes 4:9–12

Have you essentially invited the Lord Jesus Christ to be the third member of your marriage? He wants very much to be a part of your relationship. Like all the other essentials, this one calls for a common participation, not one partner versus the other. That is why in the New Testament, Paul says, don't be yoked together with unbelievers. He is speaking to people who are making choices about marriage, and he says when you make a choice about marriage you shouldn't neglect the faith choice. If you marry somebody who doesn't have the same convictions about the Lord as you do, you are cutting off that part of your relationship with that person. You are cutting it off! You are essentially saying, "This is a part of my life that I can never share with you."

Now some of you will say, "I'm going to win that person to the Lord, and we are going to have a glorious relationship," and that may be true. But seven out of ten times that is not true. We would venture to say that what more often takes place is that your fervor for the Lord begins to wane over the years. And this is because you begin to realize that you're not loving this person in this area, you're competing with this person. Love is not competition. So to make things go easier, what you end up doing is simply beginning to back down.

Some of you might say, "Well, I'm married to an unbeliever. Does that give me an excuse to divorce him?" No. The Scriptures are clear on that. You stay there and make the relationship an expression of Christ's love both in your life and to the other person. But if you are making decisions regarding getting married, don't neglect this issue. Don't neglect this issue of a common conviction, because the Lord wants to be a part of your relationship. He has designed it to be such. He is not simply talking about labels here, he is talking about convictions of who he is and your willingness as a couple to turn to him when you need, and desire, to find his help and his understanding.

Conclusion

These then are the essentials of a secure foundation from God's perspective to building a meaningful and lasting relationship: a common desire, a common appreciation, a common commitment, a common trust, and a common conviction. Talk about these things and pray about them together. This is where we start. This is how a secure foundation is built.

Questions to Discuss

1. On a scale of one to ten (with one being the lowest and ten being the highest), how would you rate your ability to be friends with each other? Are you just two ships that pass in the night, or are you taking the time to invest in each other to develop this companionship for a long-term basis, or have you simply fallen into the trap of just existing together and going through the motions?
2. On a scale of one to ten, how do you rate your ability to respect your differences? Do you see each other as equals, or do you see

each other as one over the other, like a parent over a child? How do you respect your differences? Do you each sense that the other is 100 percent there for you?

3. On a scale of one to ten, how would you rate your present level of commitment to each other? Is it the same as it once was? In some ways it shouldn't be; in some ways the longer you are married, and the longer you are in your relationship, the more that commitment should be growing. It is a dynamic commitment. So in one sense it should be growing, but in some of your cases it may be diminishing. If so, why?

4. On a scale of one to ten, how safe do you feel with each other? What are some of the things that you don't feel like you can share with your partner? What can you do to create a climate of safety and trust with each other?

5. What is the shape of your relationship with God on a scale of one to ten, both individually and as a couple?

For Further Reading

Stephen Arterburn, and Fred Stoeker with Mike Yorkey, *Every Woman's Desire: Every Man's Guide to Winning the Heart of a Woman* (Westminster, Md.: Waterbrook, 2001).

Gary Chapman, *The Five Love Languages* (Chicago: Northfield, 1992).

Stormie Omartian, *The Power of a Praying Husband* (Eugene, Ore.: Harvest House, 2001).

Stormie Omartian, *The Power of a Praying Wife* (Eugene, Ore.: Harvest House, 1997).

John Trent, *Love for All Seasons* (Chicago: Moody Press, 1996).

2

Creating a Safe
and Close Connection

Sharon Hart Morris

Because you both believed that the relationship between the two of you
was the most important relationship either of you have, you committed
to spend the rest of your lives together.

Anonymous

Marriage creates a strong thread that connects you and your spouse.
The strong thread that links you together is called an *attachment bond.*
An attachment bond is an emotional connection that ties you and your
spouse's hearts together. It deepens over time and through experiences.
This attachment bond is what makes closeness valuable and separation unbearable. An attachment bond is such that when your spouse
is available emotionally and physically and responds with care and
concern, your spouse is a source of comfort and security. Your spouse
becomes a secure base from which you venture out into the world and
a haven of safety to which you turn for love, acceptance, and comfort.
Being close to your spouse is soothing, and when you are separated
physically or emotionally, you search for ways to reconnect. If your
spouse is not consistently there for you or does not respond sensitively

to you, you learn ways to protest your spouse's unavailability and protect your heart from being hurt and disappointed.

The Importance of Your Marital Attachment Bond

When you marry, the relationship between you and your spouse becomes the most important attachment bond in each of your lives, probably for the rest of your lives. It is in the shelter of each other that you live and grow. All husbands and wives long for this shelter to be a safe place where they can find acceptance, love, and support. All couples long for their marriage to be a haven of safety where each is known and treasured. As you entered marriage, you and your spouse began the journey of fostering a close bond and making your marriage a safe place for each of you. In essence, you are creating a home for your hearts. And that takes time, hard work, and constant care.

The most precious part of your marriage will be the attachment bond between you and your spouse. After years of research it has been shown that the most important indicator for how long you will remain happily married is whether or not you and your spouse emotionally connect and foster a close attachment bond. Couples with a close bond trust that their partner will be there for them and will have the best interest of their relationship at heart. These spouses are able to share their hearts with their partner, knowing that their partner will listen with care and consideration and will weigh their perspective whenever making decisions. They perceive each other to be a haven of safety. Deep within their hearts they sense, *You know me and love me. I feel safe sharing who I am with you. You will be there for me if I reach for you.*

When Your Bond Doesn't Feel So Safe

Couples who are emotionally disconnected and don't trust their attachment bond to be safe and secure feel lonely, misunderstood, and unvalued in their marriage. As I have sat with couples in the counseling room over the years, I have found that the main reason couples seek counseling is because they can no longer rely on their attachment bond to be close and safe. I listen to husbands and wives with broken hearts say, "You are just not there for me. You don't understand who I am anymore." "I react the way I do because I feel you don't consider me." "I can't share my heart with you." "I go home each day and go through the motions, but inside I have put a wall around my heart." Hurting couples say they're far apart and not sure whether they're friend or foe.

When the bond between couples does not feel close, safe, or secure, couples get angry, criticize, defend, and withdraw to get their spouse's attention. And if they aren't able to restore their bond, they perceive each other as unsafe. Emotionally disconnected couples either continue to live under the same roof, protecting their hearts while going through the motions of life, or they eventually divorce. In light of this, it makes sense that the major cause for the high divorce rate is attributed to a couple's failure to emotionally connect.

When Those Close to You Don't Feel So Close

Because of your close attachment to your loved ones and your deep need for comfort and security, you will react in various ways when you feel the bond is threatened. If a loved one is perceived as emotionally unavailable, inaccessible, or unresponsive, attachment behaviors and insecurities are triggered. These attachment behaviors and responses are innate and attempt to restore closeness, security, and a sense that we are lovable.

When You Are Not There for Me

Children protest when their parents are absent or emotionally unavailable. If protesting doesn't bring closeness, children may cling or cry. Eventually these children become discouraged and sad and then detach and become self-sufficient. Children yearning for closeness but who fear rejection from their parents respond in what seem to be unusual ways. They try to get close to their parents by showing anger and aggressiveness. Or while holding their comfort blankets they may hide under a table until pursued and retrieved. Longing for closeness they protect themselves from rejection. Children whose parents are hardly ever available learn that closeness hurts because it can't be depended on to be there consistently. To protect themselves they become independent. Children who are assured of their dad and mom's love and attention are comfortable with closeness. They are able to explore their environment and return with ease to Mom and Dad for comfort and assurance.

Our first attachment bond is with our parents or with those who took loving care of us as we grew up. It is in the shelter of their relationship that we are born, develop, and grow as a person. As children, we need to experience a warm, intimate, and continuous relationship with our parents and loved ones. As we get older we develop other close relationships besides our parents. We bond with our siblings, extended family members, special friends, mentors, romantic partners, and eventually our spouse. The attachment bond is what keeps children and parents, close friends, and husbands and wives intricately connected.

What you experienced in your earlier relationships shapes who you are and becomes part of the story you bring into your marriage. Your early attachment relationships, as well as your current relationships, impact how you attach and respond to the hurts and disconnections within your marriage.

When You Sense Your Spouse Is Not There for You

The need for closeness and the reactions to being disconnected are a natural part of being human in close relationships, especially in a marital relationship. Couples also long for closeness while protecting their hearts from being hurt and devalued. Spouses cling and cry, get angry and protest, or become withdrawn and detached when actually all they long for is closeness and to be valued.

Pursue-Withdraw: A Cycle That Hurts Your Closeness

There are ways couples interact that hurt the bond of their relationship. Pursuing and withdrawing is a common way couples relate that too often leaves them far apart from each other.

Jack and Audrey are stuck in a pursue-withdraw cycle. One evening Audrey came home from work longing to share her day with Jack. But as she opened the apartment door, she found Jack flipping through the channels. She threw out a hint that she wanted to talk, which Jack missed. She felt hurt. Audrey said, "Are you going to sit there all night?" And with that she slammed the kitchen cabinet. Jack answered, "I was just about to do the dishes," and sunk deeper into the couch. Audrey answered Jack with, "Why do you always wait until the last minute?

You just don't help me out." Jack sighed, closing the door to his heart. He slowly made his way to the kitchen sink. In response to Jack's withdrawal, Audrey complained louder.

Jack and Audrey are like many couples stuck in a rigid pursue-withdraw cycle of interacting in an attempt to be seen and understood. This is where one partner pursues and, in response, the other withdraws. The more the pursuer pursues, the further the withdrawer pulls away and shuts down. In the pursue-withdraw cycle, both partners are unable to share what is going on in their heart; they are only able to share their anger, frustration, and hurt.

Audrey, longing for her husband to respond in a sensitive manner, is met with Jack's seeming disinterest. Instead of expressing her need for connection in a way that draws Jack in, Audrey angrily criticizes Jack. Jack longs to be valued and understood, but Audrey's anger feels overwhelming and hurtful to him. He often does not know what to do when she gets mad, and so in an attempt to protect his heart from feeling unworthy he pulls into his shell.

The pursuer feels the loss of his or her partner's attention, care, or concern and so searches out him or her with anger, frustration, and hurt. The pursuer feels that if he or she does not *pursue,* he or she will not be seen or understood. Wives, who are usually the pursuers, often say, "I nag because I feel he will not hear me. He's just not there emotionally. He can't shut me out like that."

The withdrawer, overwhelmed by the pursuer's emotion, feels alienated and helpless in pleasing his or her partner. And so, in protection, the withdrawer pulls away. Husbands, who are often withdrawers, say they are left feeling devalued, disrespected, and unworthy. Unable to calm and soothe their wife, they withdraw to find peace. Withdrawers frequently walk on eggshells and skirt around issues that may trigger displeasure in their spouse. Oftentimes withdrawers say that attempting to get their point across is not worth the hassle, because they feel that their spouse would not understand them anyway.

The Impact of the Cycle on Your Marriage Bond

When a spouse is busy pursuing or putting a lot of energy into withdrawing, he or she does not have the emotional space to hold his or her partner's perspective and needs. Couples begin to see each other as unavailable and inconsiderate. They say of each other, "My husband [or wife] just does not understand me. He [or she] is not there for me and no longer cares about how I feel." Sharing one's heart freely begins to feel dangerous. Couples say, "There's no way my spouse would understand me. I learned not to put my heart out there. Risking that would just mean I'd be hurt again." When husbands and wives emotionally disconnect, their relationship no longer feels safe or secure. They no longer turn toward each other for support or comfort.

Unhooking from the Cycle

How can you make the pursue-withdraw cycle not so necessary? There are two things to consider:

1. Understand the cycle between you and your spouse. Review the times when your spouse hurt you. What usually triggered the cycle? What did you do? What did your spouse do in response? Who got mad or critical and pursued, and who defended and withdrew? How did you come together and reconnect?
2. Learn how to share your heart needs and longings and listen to each other's emotions. What do you feel when you are hurt? What emotions do you express to your spouse? Anger? Frustration? What would it be like to share your softer emotions that express your hurt and longings rather than your anger and defensiveness? What would you need from your spouse to do this?

What Triggers Your Pursue-Withdraw Cycle

Something happens, and suddenly you see your spouse in a different light. You perceive your spouse to no longer be the kind, thoughtful, loving person you married but rather the person who does not care about you or value your heart. And although you might not doubt your commitment or your love, you, in the moment, dislike your spouse. We all have had a time when what our spouse did meant to us that they didn't care. And when you feel your spouse doesn't care, or is not there for you, your cycle is usually triggered. A trigger for the cycle, couples often find, is the meaning they give to their differences. Too often differences are interpreted as "You don't value me."

Mary and Joe are very different from each other. Mary is a night owl and Joe is an early bird. Joe interpreted Mary's inability to fall asleep at 9:00 P.M. as uncaring and disrespectful. Mary viewed Joe's request for her to come to bed at 9:00 P.M. as unreasonable and insensitive to her need to relax after a long day at work. Their difference in internal body clocks is not seen as that but rather as the inability of the other to be sensitive and caring. Their differences become a threat to their close attachment bond.

When differences are seen as damaging to the relationship, you and your spouse judge one another as being the enemy rather than friends. Most of the time it was the differences that drew you and your spouse together in the first place. You were outgoing and bold, and your spouse was quiet and gentle. After hurts, disappointments, and inability to talk about the complications and difficulties that arise as a result of being different, the differences in your spouse change from positive to negative.

A connection comes when you and your spouse are able to sit together and risk talking openly. Don't let the difficulties that differences bring trigger your rigid cycle of criticism, blame, defensiveness, and withdrawal. It is in this cycle that you and your spouse lose sight of each other's value.

Sharing Heart Needs and Longings

As a couple, it is important to talk about the needs, hurts, longings, and feelings of your heart in an open and honest way. In this way you and your spouse can find a path to each other instead of pursuing and withdrawing.

Instead of this openness, all too many couples choose the disconnecting path. Or they choose to communicate in ineffective ways.

Mary leaned against Tom as he sat at the desk paying the bills. She pushed against his shoulder, almost causing him to fall off the chair. "What are you doing?" he yelled. "Can't you see I am working?" "Sit there all day; I don't care," answered Mary with hurt and anger. Tom buried his face further into the checkbook. He thought to himself, *I don't believe it; here we go again. No matter what, I just can't please her.*

Mary's push against Tom was her way of saying, "Tom, please give me your attention and show me some tenderness." Tom never heard that because she only thought it. Tom had no idea of Mary's heart desire. He just took her push at face value, and it was annoying. Then when he thought about it, he felt inadequate and helpless at meeting Mary's needs. Mary was unable to articulate her longing for closeness because she feared Tom would not respond. She became frustrated. Both were left feeling disconnected.

Expressing your needs and longings to your spouse can be difficult. Some people don't know what they feel or need. Others feel that if their spouse really loved them, he or she would know what they needed without having to tell them. This expectation is very damaging to the relationship because it keeps your heart's needs and longings hidden and your pain of being alone heightened. It tempts you to up the ante and angrily pursue your spouse to keep guessing what you need. It also sets up your spouse to withdraw in frustration, because no matter what he or she does, it is just not good enough.

If you are a withdrawer, it will be important for you to share openly and honestly your feelings and needs. Risk being emotionally available to your spouse. It might be important to admit, "I can't come close to you and be there for you when you are angry and criticizing me." In this way, you can allow yourself to be there for your spouse in a more open way.

If you are a pursuer, learn to express your heart rather than just getting angry or criticizing. Reach beyond your anger and harsh words to a softer place. From that place, express your longings and fears and ask for your spouse to be there for you. Interactions then won't revolve around your anger and disappointment. You will both come together around the tender longings of your heart.

Don't be afraid to admit that sometimes you don't know what to do. Say something like, "I care for you, but I don't always know what to say or do." This invites your spouse to share what they need from you. In this way you are connecting in honesty and warmth instead of anger and defensiveness.

Emotions and Hearts

Couples don't always know what to do with each other's emotions. Husbands are taught to buck up and not feel. And wives don't always know how to express their feelings in a manner that their husbands can hear, understand, and respect. Often spouses fear that their emotions will be found unacceptable or that they will be thought of as weak. How you and your spouse deal with your emotions will be very important to your bond.

Some spouses try to make the emotion go away by saying, "Oh, get over it; it's not a big deal. What are you all steamed up about?" For some partners, their inability to know what to do with their spouse's emotions causes them to get angry. "Why are you telling me this?" "What do you expect me to do?" "Can't you see that I am busy?" Others hear the emotion but try to fix it by problem solving and providing solutions. "If you would just get more sleep you wouldn't feel so sad." "I told you what to do when you feel that way. Didn't you do it?"

So what are you supposed to do with your spouse's emotions? Try listening.

Listening to Each Other's Emotions

Listen to your spouse's emotions with an empathetic attitude. Listen not only with your logic but with your heart as well. Aim to understand your spouse's heart. To do that you often have to listen beyond the words. You don't always have to find a solution, fix what is wrong, or solve the problem. Often spouses can't just listen to their partner's heart without being defensive, reading into the conversation more than what was intended, or being hurt by what is said. Learn to say, "That must have been difficult." "Sounds like you had a rough day." "I would be disappointed if that kept happening to me too."

Both husbands and wives long to be heard, understood, and respected. Most often your spouse comes to you to share his or her heart and life. Listening is the most powerful way to show your spouse that you understand and accept him or her.

Reconnecting Your Hearts

The cycle that you and your spouse repeat may not seem injurious. You might be able to reconnect because there are lots of "sorry, that was my fault," followed by a "no, really it was my fault." But when reconnecting gets more difficult, be careful. Sweeping hurts under the rug doesn't make them go away. They go into your back pocket.

These hurts soon accumulate and move to your front pocket. They begin to redefine how safe it is to turn and find comfort and support from your spouse. "I remember when I called you and you were too busy. Now I just don't call you at work." "Whatever, I just learned not to expect that from you." "You have not understood for so long that I just don't even think of sharing this with you."

It will be important for you and your spouse to emotionally reconnect as soon as possible after being hurt and hooked into your cycle. Remember, disconnecting and not talking for days or sweeping the whole encounter under the rug and coming back together to take care of household tasks is not a reconnection of hearts, only of schedules. Unresolved hurts and issues add strain and stress to your haven of safety, and soon you and your spouse learn not to turn toward each other but rather away.

How should you connect after being hurt? Remember four things. First, God was wise when he told us not to let the sun go down on our hurts, especially anger. Turn your hearts toward each other as soon as you are able. Before the end of the day is God's preference. Second, come back together and acknowledge what happened. Understand your as well as your spouse's part of the cycle. Admit to your role in keeping the cycle going. *Remember, your bond is more valuable than your being right.* Third, share your hurts and needs rather than your anger and frustration. Remember you both value the relationship. Neither wants to hurt or be hurt. Fourth, when all is said and done, touch and talk to each other in a soft tone of voice, sharing encouraging words. This can be very powerful. The touch of your spouse is physiologically soothing and calming. It assures both of you that the bond is safe and sure.

Creating Connections

There are many ways to build the attachment bond between you and your spouse. Here are three ways that are effective (refer to the other chapters in this book on playing together, intimacy, and friendship).

First, pray together daily. Beginning and ending your day in the presence of the Lord not only turns each of your hearts toward each other, it also turns your hearts toward the safest place you will ever know: in your heavenly Father's presence. Couples who pray together stay together, because by praying together they are strengthening the bond between them in the presence of God. That's powerful.

Second, believe the best of intentions of your spouse. Your spouse is not always out to get you, even though it may seem that way at times. You long to be loved and valued, and so does your spouse. Believe that. Be there for each other as God refines and molds each of you into the image of Christ.

Third, risk doing things differently. Put down your weapons. Come out of your cave. Open up your heart and learn how to relate to your spouse in a way that draws you together.

When Your Relationship Is a Safe Place

It will be of great value that the emotional attachment bond between you and your spouse becomes close, safe, trustworthy, and predictable. If your marriage is perceived to be a haven of safety, you and your spouse will be a resource for each other and able to withstand the pressures and pains of marriage and life. But a close attachment bond does not just happen. It is over the course of time and experiences, as each of you interact and respond to each other, that your bond will be nurtured and strengthened. In this way you will experience your relationship as a safe place where your heart can safely be shared and cherished.

Questions to Discuss

1. How would you describe the attachment bonds in your child-hood family?
2. How would each of you describe the attachment bond in your marriage?
3. In what situations, or in what ways, do you sometimes experience the pursue-withdraw cycle?
4. Discuss the desire of your heart in experiencing attachment in your marriage.

For Further Reading

David and Teresa Ferguson and Chris and Holly Thurman, *The Pursuit of Intimacy* (Nashville: Thomas Nelson, 1993).

John M. Gottman and Joan DeClaire, *The Relationship Cure* (New York: Crown Publishers, 2001).

Scott Stanley, Daniel Trathen, Savanna McCain, and Milt Bryan, *A Lasting Promise: A Christian Guide to Fighting for Your Marriage* (San Francisco: Jossey-Bass Publishers, 1998).

3

The Spiritual Foundation for Marriage

Ronald and Peggy Hawkins

The Lord witnessed the vows you and your wife made to each other on your wedding day when you were young.

Malachi 2:14 (NLT)

The superintendent of construction, wearing his hard hat, looked strangely out of place in our offices. Carrying his hefty blueprints, he had come to our office to explain why he was systematically dismantling major segments of the building in which our group worked every day. Apologizing for the dust, noise, and inconvenience, he promised we would be delighted with the finished product. He went on to explain, "A lot of interior and foundational work will be required before we can go skyward with the three-story addition."

After he left, I reflected on what he had said to us, and two things stood out for me. First, his massive set of blueprints assured us that every move he made was aimed at achieving preplanned outcomes. Second, he understood that before they could go higher, it would be necessary to complete a significant amount of interior work on the foundation.

As I prepared to write this chapter, I thought about how we as Christian couples face challenges similar to those of the superintendent. We, too, have been given a set of blueprints. I believe the Bible provides us with adequate directions for putting in place the spiritual foundations necessary for going skyward with our marriages.

Building a Spiritual Foundation for Marriage

Couples today face some unique challenges as they seek to lay down solid spiritual foundations for their marriages. Our culture has become increasingly committed to a quest for individual development in every facet of life, including marriage. This radical individualism has contributed to a divorce rate that, even in Christian marriages, now exceeds 50 percent, in spite of the fact that God has provided us with the resources that are necessary for us to swim upstream and be countercultural. The good news is that we can be guided by this biblical blueprint to establish the spiritual foundation that will keep us in step with God's purposes for marriage and contribute to the production of a rewarding intimacy. Let's review the plans.

Give Attention to Salvation

Adam and Eve were created in God's image and were given dominion over all of God's creation. God provided them with all that was necessary to rule and relate well. Each possessed a sense of great value to the other, and they were wonderfully constituted by their Creator Father to make unique contributions to the fulfillment of his purposes. (See Gen. 1:26–28; 2:18–25.) But the team rebelled! Satan maintained that God was an oppressive dictator, Adam and Eve believed the lie, and devastating consequences followed their abandonment of the Creator's directives. (See Gen. 3:1–24; Rom. 5:12–21.)

Guidance from the image of God in the core of human personality was replaced by the guidance of death and darkness. (See Eph. 4:17–24.) As Adam and Eve's descendants, we are without the proper resources to begin the work of building spiritual foundations for our marriages. (See Eph. 2:1–10; John 3:1–7.) We must be transformed by God himself before we can begin to lay an adequate spiritual foundation for our marriages. The gospel, the Good News regarding the death, burial, and resurrection of the Lord Jesus, assures us that God has made available to all the opportunity to receive a salvation that enables us to begin the process of establishing a solid spiritual foundation for our marriages. (See Rom. 1:16–17; Gal. 5:1, 16–25.)

50   The Mystery of Marriage

Give Attention to the Acquisition of Wisdom

Solomon was facing the biggest challenge of his young life; his father was dead, and he felt alone and overwhelmed. Soon he would be king of Israel. He knew the challenge was large and that the people would be difficult to lead. The Lord was sensitive to his feelings and came to him in a dream saying, "Ask! What shall I give you?" Solomon replied, "I am a little child; I do not know how to go out or come in. . . . Therefore give to Your servant an understanding heart to judge Your people, that I may discern between good and evil" (1 Kings 3:5, 7, 9 NKJV). God was pleased with Solomon's request and gave to him the gift he sought, and Solomon is immortalized as one of the wisest men who ever lived on our planet. (See 1 Kings 3:5–14.)

The good news is that we can be confident that God will be as gracious with us as he was with Solomon. He will give us wisdom and understanding through his Scriptures, through Jesus, and through special acts of gifting through the Holy Spirit. (See 1 Cor. 1:30; 12:2; 2 Tim. 3:15–17; James 1:5.) He delights in giving us wisdom for the purpose of directing us and empowering us to fulfill the specifications laid out in the blueprint for marriage given in Scripture.

Give Attention to the Issue of Authority

Building an adequate spiritual foundation for our marriages is not possible without first resolving the issue of authority. Again and again in marriage we come to a fork in the road. Only when we build our lives on the foundation of the authoritative Bible do we strengthen our marriages and know the freedom that fosters spontaneity and intimacy. (See 2 Tim. 1:7; 2:15; 3:15–17.)

The apostle Paul uses the picture of the bondservant as an example of the radical obedience to the Word and Spirit that should characterize us as believers. (See Exod. 21:1–6; Rom. 6:11–23.) Bondservants forsake the appeal of personal freedom, follow the motivation of love, bear their responsibilities even if it means great pain, and commit themselves without reservation to the care of those with whom they have made a covenant. The challenge in Christian marriages is for couples to appreciate their need to know God's Word, submit to the authority of God's Word on each and every issue to which it speaks, and look to the Lord for the spiritual empowerment that will enable them to practice a style of obedience that imitates the way of the bondservant. Building a strong spiritually based marriage requires from couples a willingness to bring every thought into captivity and conform every behavior to the standard of God's Truth. (See 1 Peter 1:13.)

Give Attention to Imitating Jesus Christ and Walking in the Spirit

Strengthening the spiritual foundation in our marriages requires careful attention to walking in the Spirit and movement toward the specific goal of imitating Jesus Christ. (See Eph. 5:1–7; Gal. 5:16–26.) When the Holy Spirit invades a new believer and implants life in the core self, he or she begins a walk in the Spirit and a process commences. The powerful combination of the Word and the Spirit adds great strength to the spiritual foundation and produces a relational environment that makes marriage a source of enrichment and joy for the participants.

However, the journey of marriage is not always smooth sailing. Christian couples periodically struggle with a fatal attraction to the world and a number of things that are frightfully appealing to the flesh. We will need a great deal of patience with one another when our behaviors are not prompted by the Spirit. We are all too frequently reminded that as individuals and couples, we are works in progress. A current author, who reminds us of the challenge that is ours, says:

> Being born anew (regenerated) is a vital and necessary experience, but it is only the beginning work of grace. [The Holy Spirit's] focus is on healing the core of our being, not our whole being in one full swoop. Our personality may be altered only slightly, except for the immediate thrill or joy. Many appetites will still stay the same. Old habits may quickly return. God first renews our hearts, and then begins the slow and often painful change in our personality, habits, attitudes, beliefs and actions. We call this continuing process sanctification.[1]

In all of our struggles, however, we can still reshape our internal and external self in the image of the God who created, loves, and redeems us. We can strengthen the spiritual foundations in our marriages and our connection with the Spirit who fosters the redeeming of our marital relationships and all things human. How wonderful to know that while we as couples are working on our marriages, there is one who is equally invested in the redeeming of our entire marriage who is working from the inside out. What a powerful alliance! What amazing things we can accomplish together—things that strengthen the spiritual foundations in our marriages.

The strengthening of spiritual foundations requires that couples marshal the resources provided by the Holy Spirit and give attention to imitating Jesus Christ in some very specific ways. Specifically, we must seek to imitate him in his love, service, and submission.

Jesus loves, to the end, all who come to him and requires that all who believe in him be recognized by their commitment to fleshing out his love in their relationships. (See John 13:1; 1 John 4:7–11.) I was led recently to reflect upon my own failures to love in a manner consistent with the pattern provided by Christ. My grandson, who is seven, was seated next to me in a restaurant when he spilled the entire contents of a supersized Dr Pepper into my lap. Fortunately, my first response of anger stayed stillborn within me. As I looked into Nathan's ever-expanding eyes and saw the sheer look of terror, a deep love took hold of my inner world and engulfed the anger. In seconds, this love transformed my reactive response into one of tender assurance that all would be fine. He melted in my arms. I went from the experience in humiliation, knowing that this was the response I was capable of, to realizing that in my intimate circles, I sometimes fail to love my wife in this way and as a result the spiritual foundation of our relationship is weakened.

Another issue of great importance for strengthening the spiritual foundation of our marriages is a joint commitment to imitating Christ in our serving. (See John 13:2–17.) The environment generated through serving promotes greater trust. Servant spouses, like the bondservant, are free to make decisions that are in the best interest of their partners. Like Jesus they can rise and wash the feet of the spouse by meeting the needs that arise in the life of their mate. This freedom fosters personal spiritual growth, enhances security in the relationship, and greatly strengthens the spiritual foundation of the marriage.

Yet another way in which we are all called to imitate Christ is in our submission. It is unfortunate that the doctrine of submission has so often been pitched only to the feminine gender. Christ was a man, and he modeled submission. (See Phil. 2:5–11.) Prior to Paul's instruction that wives submit to their husbands, we read that all believers are to submit one to another in the fear of the Lord. (See Eph. 5:21.) Submission is possible because the ascended Christ has sent God the Holy Spirit to dwell in us. (See John 15:26–27; 16:12–15.) It's the Spirit's power that enables us to overrule the flesh and live with our mates in a manner that imitates Christ's love, models servanthood, and submits in a manner that enhances relationships while building on the spiritual foundation of the marriage.

Give Attention to Self-Control

Self-control is only one of the facets of the multidimensional fruit that springs from the interior of the one in whom the Spirit is doing his sanctifying work. In opposition to what Paul calls the works of the flesh, which create chaos and self-will, the Holy Spirit leads us to a calmness and to the control of the self. This results in the ability to say no to the self and to seek to understand others instead of focusing merely on being understood. We can then focus on the needs of our partner when conflict is imminent and work for a win-win outcome.

Couples who do not understand that one of the powerful fruits of the Holy Spirit is self-control fail to draw on the Holy Spirit for his power in their daily lives. They often assert that they are trying but feel powerless and give in to the push and pull of powerful stimuli. They believe that they are helpless and are merely the product of stimulus-response bonds habituated over time. We can sincerely empathize with these people. We all face powerful and multiple stimuli every day that beckon us to violate our covenant with God and our mates. However, men and women, alive in their core selves through the work of the Holy Spirit, are empowered to respond in ways that strengthen spiritual foundations and bring great enrichment to their marriages. The figure below illustrates some of the elements involved in the development of this kind of self-control.

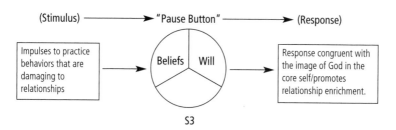

S3

S3 = Spirit's Convicting/Empowering
     Scripture's Directives
     Savior's Pattern

Christian couples can train themselves to push the pause button or create a time-out between an experience with a stimulus that could damage their marriage relationship and their actual response. The biblical process resulting in the practicing of behaviors that greatly strengthen the spiritual foundation of our marriages includes the following elements:

- We count on the Holy Spirit to be at work inside us, convicting us regarding the inappropriateness of a particular statement, thought, or behavior.
- We push the pause button or say no altogether to an impulse to act in a way that would grieve the Spirit and wound our partner.
- We will to bring our initial response against the grid provided by the Scripture logged in our minds.
- We rely on the power of the Holy Spirit to help us will into existence a response that fits with the pattern provided by the Savior.

This ability to pause and reflect on outcomes is in keeping with the prescriptions of Solomon found in Proverbs 23:1–3. In that passage, Wisdom counsels men and women to consider diligently what is before them when they are being stimulated to partake of something that promises pleasure. Wisdom exhorts that such stimuli are often highly deceptive.

Christian couples understand that establishing this level of self-control is only possible when the decision to walk in the Spirit is actively supported by a training regimen. (See 1 Cor. 9:27.) "Trying" simply will not get the job done! Christian couples must place a high value on the adoption of a training regimen that includes foundation-impacting disciplines such as:

- Scripture reading/memorization
- Prayer
- Fasting
- Meditation
- Solitude
- Worship
- Praise
- Confession

The elements in the training regimen are all significant because they are spiritually designated catalysts the Holy Spirit uses to strengthen the spiritual foundation in our lives and marriages.

Give Attention to Covenant-Keeping and the Care of the Seal

A major part of the biblical manual on marriage is found in the Song of Songs. Nearly all of the elements required for strengthening the spiritual foundations in a marriage are addressed in this poem on marital love. The woman in this biblical poem makes one supreme request of her beloved. "Set me as a seal upon your heart, as a seal upon your arm; for love is as strong as death, jealousy as cruel as the grave" (Song of Songs 8:6 NKJV). Marriage partners are called to be persons of the seal. A central element in the establishment of unshakable spiritual foundations for marriage is a commitment to absolute fidelity to one's partner.

The seal is a significant symbol in the Bible. It speaks of God's power and his pledge to and ownership of his child. (See Eph. 1:14.) Ancient kings protected important documents with a seal that spoke of their authority. The seal protects something pure and valuable, and it safeguards against the entrance of that which would contaminate. The concept of the seal is contained within the covenantal structure God proposed for marriage when he said, "Therefore a man shall leave his father and mother and be joined to his wife, and they shall become one flesh" (Gen. 2:24 NKJV). The covenant envisioned here involves delivering or entrusting something to a person with the intent of binding oneself to a particular course of action.

The covenantal seal is meant to designate the irrevocable nature of the relationship. It requires of couples something of the spirit of Hernando Cortez, who in 1519 landed his troops at Vera Cruz, Mexico. When Cortez set fire to the vessels that had brought them, there could be no retreat. The more than six thousand men were irrevocably committed to their task of conquering the new land for the mother country. That kind of no-retreat commitment in marriage is at the heart of the leaving, cleaving, and weaving pattern and is so critical to the building of spiritual foundations in marriages that it is repeated three times in the biblical record. (See Gen. 2:21; Matt. 19:4–5; Eph. 5:31.) An irrevocable commitment to covenant-keeping and a moment by moment guarding of the seal are absolute prerequisites for those who wish to place and keep their marriages on a solid spiritual foundation.

Damage to the seal compromises covenant, introduces contaminants like jealousy, and may even spell death for the relationship. The covenantal seal is at the core of a strong spiritual foundation and enables the practicing of a commitment to fidelity that causes men and women to rebel against the idea of sharing their love with any other, in fantasy or reality, but their covenantal companion. (See Prov. 5:15–20.) This commitment to exclusivity heightens the experience of intimacy for both partners. Its absence births a deadly process that is as cruel as the grave. (See Song of Songs 8:7.) The decision to entrust ourselves to another must be supported by a pattern of behavior and self-control that bears witness to the high value that the participants place on covenant-keeping. The consistent protection of the seal and practice of behaviors that validate the internal commitment to covenant foster security in the relationship and strengthen the spiritual foundation of the marriage.

Give Attention to Grace-Based Communication

Next to the protection of the covenantal seal, nothing that a couple can do offers greater potential for strengthening the spiritual foundation in their marriage than the consistent practice of grace-based communication. That is why Paul taught, "Let no unwholesome word proceed from your mouth, but only such a word as is good for edification according to the need of the moment, that it may give grace to those who hear. And do not grieve the Holy Spirit of God" (Eph. 4:29–30 NASB). It would seem that once we understand how important the Holy Spirit is for us to practice the deeds directly related to strengthening the spiritual foundation of our marriages, it would be unthinkable that any of us would knowingly grieve the Holy Spirit and cancel any portion of his available power in our lives.

Jesus admonished his disciples concerning the seriousness of our words when he said, "But I say to you that for every idle word men may speak, they will give account of it in the day of judgment. For by your words you will be justified, and by your words you will be condemned" (Matt. 12:36–37 NKJV). Idle words are careless words or words that are of no profit to the hearer. Literally they are words that communicate the attitude that one could not care less about the one addressed. Paul counsels men and women to collaborate in the creation of marriage relationships that are grace-based. Paul, like Jesus, cuts us no slack in the responsibility of our words. We are to use absolutely no cutting or corrupting words in our interaction with others. In Ephesians 4:25–32, Paul goes to great lengths to tell us what grace-based communication looks like. Note in Paul's address to the Ephesians that grace-based communication

- begins with a thorough investigation into the needs of our spouse.
- commits to listening well.
- brings into service behaviors that are meant to benefit and build up our partner.
- gets creative and withholds no resources to meet the needs of our partner. Words. Time. Touch. Nothing is to be held back that will be of benefit.
- allows for nothing that cuts, erodes, or wounds the marital relationship.
- enthusiastically engages the ministry of talk.
- is humbled by the reality that every word spoken carelessly will be brought against us in the day of judgment when we stand before Jesus.

Strengthening spiritual foundations also requires that couples understand that they are "one" in two important ways. First, because of the marriage covenant, they are one flesh. Second, because they are in Christ and in his body, they are also one; or as Paul says, "We are members of one another" (Eph. 4:25 NKJV). Paul insists that whatever impacts one member of the body or the marital team impacts the whole. Because husbands and wives are one, when one rises, the other rises as well. (See 1 Cor. 12:23–26.) If we wound our partners, put them down, cut them with our words, we also wound ourselves and bring ourselves down. If we build up our partner, we also build up ourselves. (See Eph. 4:15–24; 5:25–33.) When we engage in these simple covenants, asking God to set a watch upon our mouths that we might not sin, the Spirit is pleased, his power is unleashed in our relationships, and the spiritual foundation undergirding our marriages is deepened.

Sadly, there will be times when we will fail to fulfill this goal and we wound our partner and grieve the Spirit. In these times, our partner must possess a spirit of humility that allows us to practice repentance when grace has been violated in the relationship.

Repentance needs to be mutual if partners want to experience its full power to strengthen spiritual foundations. Both people must go through a self-examination and be ready to embrace their part of the problem and be willing to take responsibility and repent. Marriages where lasting intimacy is a reality and spiritual foundations are strong consist of husbands and wives who are always open to repentance when they identify the need for dealing with sin.

Give Attention to Friendship

The integrity of the spiritual foundations in Christian marriages is often seriously weakened because one or both partners lack an appreciation for the importance of friendship in the marital relationship. The vital role the Creator envisioned for Adam and Eve required that they form a dynamic team. Each was to draw his or her completion from the other partner. Alone, neither Adam nor Eve could experience the reward that is only within the grasp of the couple. (See Eccles. 4:8–12.) In the same way, we too can only find the reward God intended for married couples when we see ourselves as dependent/independent creations discovering rewards within the context of our friendship and our engagement together for his purposes.

Friendship figures prominently in the Bible's teaching on marriage. Husbands must love their wives as Christ loves the members of his church. (See Eph. 5:28.) Christ calls us his friends and longs to share his thoughts with us. (See John 15:15.) Christian couples are challenged to share this same level of intimacy with one another. In the Song of Songs we hear the level of desired intimacy described with the words, "This is my beloved, and this is my friend" (Song of Songs 5:16 NKJV). Elsewhere, Jehovah blasts the men of Israel because they have dealt treacherously with their wives. He states, "She is your companion and your wife by covenant" (Mal. 2:14 NKJV).

Friendship is absolutely essential if spiritual foundations are to be strengthened. Friends each possess strengths that are different from the other, but those strengths can support the other. Each person has things to offer their partner. But each person must value the differences discovered in their mate and be the joyful recipient of the other person's gifts. The sexual relationship represents a special kind of knowing in which the differences are more easily celebrated and hold great potential for strengthening the spiritual foundation of a marriage. But this is to be true of all areas of differences between husband and wife. When we can value the differences in us, it will result in a special kind of knowing that takes us to the deepest foundation of our relationship and greatly enhances our marriage.

When husbands and wives are properly related to God and experience a rich friendship with each other, life is experienced on a higher level and the spiritual foundation is strengthened. Solomon captured the ecstasy of the marital relationship when he said, "Two are better than one, because they have a good reward for their labor. For if they fall, one will lift up his companion. But woe to him who is alone when he falls, for he has no one to help him up" (Eccles. 4:9–10 NKJV). Reward is a comprehensive experience that strengthens our relationship and gives rise to spontaneous joy as we value our differences and appreciate the truth that together we represent a force greater than the sum of our individual strengths.

Conclusion

Building the spiritual foundation in marriages is one of the greatest challenges faced by Christian couples. Couples today are bombarded with opposing views on the ideal marriage. The media and the Internet afford opportunities for the indulgence of fantasies in ways that are unparalleled in history and can have a devastating impact on our spiritual foundation. Christian couples are miraculously empowered for strengthening their marriages because of the indwelling of the Holy Spirit received at salvation. Our redemption leads to our spiritual growth, which is a restoration of the divine image in the core of our personality. This empowers Christian men and women to imitate Christ and to flesh out the blueprint for marriage provided in the Bible.

Couples who understand that building a strong spiritual foundation for Christian marriage is a joint effort will elect to embrace a comprehensive training regimen and a lifestyle of accountability and self-control focused on the protection of the seal and the development of grace-based relationships. The specifications handed down by God himself are realized when couples follow the training regimen provided in the biblical blueprint and rely on the Holy Spirit who works from the inside out. They are empowered to push the pause button and implement behaviors that will greatly strengthen the spiritual foundations of their marriage.

Questions to Discuss

1. Can you think of a time when you felt overwhelmed? Did you cry out to God for wisdom? What happened? Have you ever asked God to give you, as a couple, wisdom to make your marriage all you desire it to be?
2. From Ephesians 5:15–33, write out the behaviors that are characteristic of a person filled with the Holy Spirit. Then from Colossians 3:12–25, write out the characteristics of a person whose mind is filled with the words of Christ. Now examine these lists. What does the similarity suggest to you regarding your relationship as a couple with the Word of God and the Holy Spirit?
3. Stand facing your husband or wife. Hold hands and one of you lift your hands toward the ceiling. What happens to the hands of the other? Now move your hands toward the floor. What happens to the other person? You are one! When one rises so does the other. When one is demoted, damaged, brought low, so goes the partner. Take a few moments to discuss the implications of Paul's words "We are members of one another."
4. Make a list of the ways your mate differs from you. Choose several of these differences and share with your mate why you value these differences. Why is it important to value your differences?

For Further Reading

Tim Clinton and Julie Clinton, *The Marriage You've Always Wanted: How to Grow a Stronger, More Intimate Relationship* (Greenville, Mass.: Word Publishing, 2000).

Al Janssen, *The Marriage Masterpiece: A Bold New Vision for Your Marriage* (Wheaton, Ill.: Tyndale, 2001).

Phillip C. McGraw, *Relationship Rescue* (New York: Hyperion, 2000).

Gary Smalley and John Trent, *The Language of Love* (Colorado Springs: Focus on the Family, 1995).

Part 2

Developing the Skills of Marriage

4

Love Is All You Need

Greg and Erin Smalley

There is hardly any activity, any enterprise, which is started with such
tremendous hopes and expectations and which fails so regularly as love.

Dr. Erich Fromm

What Is an Emotional or Relational Need?

Ask AAA

To give you an idea of what a relational need looks like, let me
(Greg) tell you about a time I almost drove the car into the Mississippi River.

One day my wife, Erin, and I were driving from Springfield, Missouri, to Nashville, Tennessee, to attend a conference. In the days
leading up to the trip, Erin had asked me to consult AAA about the
best way to get to Nashville. As a guy, I resented her request and felt
I could get us there as well as AAA could. I spent several hours diligently studying maps and realized unfortunately there is no straight
line from Springfield to Nashville. This was very painful for me. After
all, the only thing I actually remembered from high school math was
the "shortest distance between two points is a straight line" principle.
I couldn't let Mr. Stark, my high school geometry teacher, down.

So I continued to draft as straight a route as I could. Finally, I was finished. I had done the impossible. I had found a route that was basically a straight line. As I stood back to bask in the glory of my accomplishment, I knew that I had to share my success with "the boys." I knew that Erin would not appreciate my route like my guy friends would. As each one held up my map, it was as if they were holding directions to the Holy Grail. Their eyes moved slowly up and down the page while they uttered things like, "Wow . . . unbelievable . . . impossible . . . you da' man!" I must admit, I was impressed with myself.

When word of my accomplishment finally spread back to Erin, I was not met with praise or applause. There was no homage or even simple adoration. Nothing. To make matters worse, she begged and pleaded for me to have someone check out my route. I was deeply offended. For guys all around the world, I was not going to cave in and ask for directions. At this point, there was much more riding on our trip than simply getting there. Men everywhere were counting on me to show my wife that, as a man, I could find the way.

Several hours into the trip I was feeling great because my route was perfect. We were thirty minutes ahead of AAA' s schedule. I was king of the road. But just like that, disaster struck.

The sun was just starting to dip below the horizon. The view was incredible, Erin and I were laughing and singing, and miles back she had stopped asking me if I knew where we were. Then all of a sudden Erin said, "Did you see that sign? I swear it read 'dead end.'"

"Nice try," I joked. "You just can't admit that I was right and you were wrong."

"I'm serious," she begged. "I think this road dead ends."

"This road does not dead end," I shot back. "Don't worry. Trust me!"

Have you ever uttered something you really wished you could take back? For me, "Don't worry . . . trust me" remains one of those things I'd give anything to have back.

We continued to drive for about an hour while neither of us spoke a word, waiting for the truth to be revealed. The surrounding area began to be less populated until it became cornfields as far as the eye could see. And then it happened.

Dead end!

I barely stopped the truck in time to avoid crashing into the rather large "dead end" sign. "That's impossible!" I shouted in disbelief. "This wasn't on the map!"

The worst part was that Erin didn't have to say anything. She just sat there with that look of disdain, shaking her head from side to side. Next, I did what any man would do in this situation. I got out of the truck to survey the area.

As I gazed down at the mighty Mississippi River, I could actually see my road form again on the other side. "It's not my fault that the map didn't show that a bridge wasn't here!" I shouted back at the truck. Then I began to wonder what would happen if I drove around the barrier and . . .

Erin's voice interrupted my thoughts. "Don't you even think about it!" she snarled. "Take us back the way we came!"

As I reached to study the map, Erin quickly jerked it out of my hands. Sadly, I didn't even try to get it back. I was defeated. Sitting there watching my wife attempt to determine our location, I began to notice how scary fields of corn look at night in the middle of nowhere. It didn't help that buzzards had begun circling overhead, squawking excitedly. I started to remember a movie about murderous children who lived in cornfields. The worst part was that I couldn't recall whether the movie was based on a true story or not. The bottom line was that we needed to leave. Now!

Driving back, Erin and I didn't speak for quite some time. When she finally started to say something, I was certain she was going to give me a piece of her mind. And I deserved it no doubt. But she didn't yell or tease me. What she did was actually the same thing you can do to begin to unlock the most important relational needs of your future spouse.

Erin spoke in a calm voice and said, "I believe we can learn a great deal about each other's relational needs by answering the statement: 'I feel loved when you . . .'"

I gulped and nodded, grateful to have escaped what could have been well-deserved wrath.

"Well, I feel loved when you ask AAA about our trip route."

Touché.

Relational Needs versus Expectations

Relational needs require constant attention! In many ways a relational need is just another name for an expectation. We all enter into marriage with many expectations. Some we are consciously aware of. Many others, we are not. Expectations are always there, however, in the background of our daily experiences. Whether we are attuned to them or whether we are oblivious to them—which too often is the case—our expectations come into play in a multitude of subtle ways. One explanation for the current high divorce rate and the prevalence of marital dissatisfaction is that Americans have high and unrealistic expectations of marriage, expecting a spouse to simultaneously be a friend, a confidant, a fulfilling sex partner, a counselor, and a parent.[1]

I'm not talking about expectations that result from someone telling you that they are going to do something and then you trust and rely on their promise. That is an appropriate expectation. I'm referring to expectations we bring into the relationship based on our own set of relational ideals. The focus here is on the way we think things are supposed to be in our relationship.

Take Lisa, for example: Her birthday came and went. Lisa's husband, Steve, had seemingly forgotten to buy her anything for her birthday. That night while in bed, she decided to bring up the incident and how it wasn't what she'd expected.

"Well, for your last birthday," Steve said, "I bought you a very nice hockey stick, and you never use it. So, I decided not to buy you anything else until you do."

Lisa, understandably a little upset, held back her tears and sunk into the pillows.

So the months pass, and finally it's Steve's birthday. He gets dressed up, and he and Lisa go out for a beautiful meal. After the meal, Lisa presents him his birthday gift, and she gives him a little peck on the cheek and a big smile. Intrigued, Steve enthusiastically unwraps the gift to find a certificate for a burial plot.

As Lisa and Steve experienced, expectations are the ways we think things are supposed to be (or not to be) in our relationship. They are the things we think we want in our relationship, the things that we anticipate happening, what we believe and assume will happen, what we hope and wish will take place, and the standards that must be maintained to be satisfied relationally.

On the other hand, relational needs differ from expectations in that they reveal the specific things we want to happen in the relationship that will cause us to feel cared for or loved. Relational needs can be expectations if we think they are things that are *supposed* to happen in the relationship. But in this chapter we're focusing on caring or loving behaviors that your mate does that result in relational satisfaction. These positive behaviors, if left unfulfilled or if they are misunderstood, can send your relationship hurling toward disappointment and frustration, perhaps even toward the heartbreak of divorce. Dr. Stephen Covey says that every major conflict between couples is the result of someone's needs not being met. Furthermore, Dr. Willard Harley Jr., the author of an excellent book called *His Needs, Her Needs,* says that all affairs are the result of one mate not getting his or her emotional needs met and getting them met through someone else. It's crucial for the health and satisfaction of our marriages that we understand what the top relationship needs are and how to meet them. Although I'm going to tell you how more than ten thousand people ranked a list of relational needs, at the end of the chapter you can take a test to reveal your own list of needs.

Human Needs "Battery"

Imagine a ten-cell battery, each cell wired to one of your mate's top basic needs. Now, consider each of these needs as individual power cells in your mate's relational battery. When the battery cells are drained by everyday living, working, children, friends, and just life in general, humans need their relational batteries recharged, just like your car battery needs charging after too much neglect or overuse.

My counseling office is filled with troubled people who never understood or never fulfilled their spouse's needs. My survey of relational needs, which has included more than ten thousand couples, led to an interesting conclusion: The list of common top needs for couples, when unmet, is the same list nationally known researchers state as the most common reasons why couples argue.

What does this mean? When needs are not being met, look out! Your marriage is at stake. Your mate will become overly defensive, argumentative, jealous, belligerent, withdrawn, or degrading. When our deepest relational needs are not met, we tend to be more irritated, discouraged, edgy, hypersensitive, and reactionary to average events that occur in a typical marriage.

Furthermore, the need for companionship in a long-lasting relationship is so strong that men and women will go to any length to satisfy it. But if marriage isn't meeting their needs, they may go outside the marriage and into an emotional or sexual affair. Or they will get these needs fulfilled at work, play, through relatives, friends, children, or in the community.

To understand the current state of your mate's battery, you must examine his or her feelings. Feelings are a gauge of whether or not needs are being met. Some of the feelings that will indicate a low battery include hurt, frustration, and fear. Conversely, indications of a fully charged battery include joy, happiness, and ecstasy.

Benefits of Knowing and Meeting Relational Needs

Why focus on relational needs? Why are they important to the health of our relationship? To answer this question, let me show you how couples from Greensboro, North Carolina, and Boise, Idaho, answered this question: What is the benefit of sharing relational needs? Here's what they said in order of importance:

- *Increases positive communication.* Talking about relational needs fosters healthy communication because it fulfills the need to share wants and desires with someone. The key here is to focus on understanding and validation. If one mate starts to degrade or dishonor the other's important needs, communication will ultimately cease. Guard the sharing of needs as a priceless treasure. Do not let anyone or anything harm it. Sharing relational needs strengthens the relationship because you did something that your mate perceives as important and positive.

- *Increases understanding.* When your mate shares a relational need, he or she reveals a deep part about himself or herself. You begin to deeply understand what he or she needs in order to feel cared for and loved. Understanding is knowledge and knowledge is powerful.

- *Promotes action in the relationship.* Once you know what your mate needs, you can act on that knowledge.

- *Fosters trust, security, and safety in the relationship.* As you gain the right knowledge and take action to meet your mate's needs, this promotes security and trust in the relationship.
- *Promotes conflict resolution.* Conflict in a marriage is inevitable. But if relational needs are getting met, the conflict usually is not as intense or gets resolved faster.
- *Increases honor in the relationship.* The essence of honor is making someone feel like his or her needs and wants are important and valuable.

Before I jump into the top ten relational needs, I must provide the proper foundation.

A Foundation: Finding Fulfillment in Life through Christ

Nearly all of us want to live a full and complete life. Unfortunately, most of us forget the one place where we must first look if our needs are ever to be met. Galatians 1:10 says, "Am I now trying to win the approval of men, or of God? Or am I trying to please men? If I were still trying to please men, I would not be a servant of Christ."

God desires to be the first stop on the way to understanding our relational needs and having them met. Our relationship with Christ, the way he desires to meet our most important needs, reminds me of a story.

A young man was getting ready to graduate from college. For many months he had admired a beautiful sports car in a dealer's showroom, and knowing his father could well afford it, he told him that was all he wanted.

Finally, on the morning of his graduation, his father called him into his private study. His father told him how proud he was to have such a fine son and told him how much he loved him. He handed his son a beautifully wrapped gift box.

Curious, and somewhat disappointed, the young man opened the box and found a lovely, leather-bound Bible with his name embossed in gold. Angry and disappointed, he raised his voice to his father and said, "With all your money, you give me a Bible?" and stormed out of the house.

Many years passed and the young man was successful in business. He had a beautiful home and a wonderful family, but he realized his father was very old and thought perhaps he should go to see him. He had not seen him since that graduation day. Before he could make arrangements, he received a telegram telling him his father had died and had willed all of his possessions to his son. He needed to come home immediately to take care of things.

When he arrived at his father's house, sudden sadness and regret filled his heart. He began to search through his father's important papers and found the still-new Bible, just as he had left it years ago.

With tears, he opened it and began to turn the pages. His father had carefully underlined a verse, Matthew 7:11 (NASB), "And if you then, being evil, know how to give good gifts to your children, how much more shall your Father who is in heaven give what is good to those who ask Him!"

As he read those words, a car key dropped from the back of the Bible. It had a tag with the dealer's name, the same dealer who had the sports car he had desired. On the tag was the date of his graduation and the words "Paid in full."

Chugging Along on Half Power

We have been paid in full. God paid our price through the death of his Son Jesus Christ. As a result, God wants to be the first and foremost one to meet our relational needs. But how many times do we look to people and things to fill that hole in our hearts all the while missing his blessings because they are not packaged as we expected?

Remember the battery analogy earlier? Too many times we go through life seeking fulfillment from a 110-power source when our batteries are designed for 220-power. Imagine for a moment that all of us have a battery built inside that needs daily charging to keep us alive and feeling completely satisfied. Like many others, I believed that if I could use a 110 electrical cord to actually plug into people or things and could stay plugged in long enough, I would be fully charged and fulfilled.

Seeking the "220" Source of Life

Here's a way for you to remember a Bible verse forever. If you desire to live a life filled with 220-power, memorize this Scripture verse, which provides the real source for lasting fulfillment:

> I have been crucified with Christ; and it is no longer I who live, but Christ lives in me; and the life which I now live in the flesh I live by faith in the Son of God, who loved me, and delivered Himself up for me.
>
> Galatians 2:20 (NASB)

Therefore, the 220-power principle helps us allow Christ to charge our inner batteries because God designed our internal batteries to be wired to the 220 current, not the 110 (people and things).

The point is this: Our mate cannot fulfill our needs. Instead, God will use our mate to help him meet our needs. Therefore, we must make our needs or requests known to Christ first (see Phil. 4:6).

Love Is All We Need

Listen, Offer yourself, Value and honor, and Embrace. This is the best description of true love I've been able to find, and it plays strongly into the idea of relational needs.

One thing is certain: Before you can begin meeting your mate's deepest needs, you have to know what they are. The first law of fulfilling needs is to realize that everyone's are different, based on personalities, backgrounds, and expectations. So you must first learn to recognize your mate's individual needs, as well as your own. Based on my research with ten thousand couples, here are the top ten relational needs. For purpose of understanding, I've formed them into a word you'll all be able to remember: *LOVE.*

L = Listen

Listening means more than nodding at your spouse while keeping one eye on an e-mail letter or the latest sports score. Active listening means being devoted not only to hearing your spouse but also to understanding him or her. Within this category I found the following needs:

1. Be honest and trustworthy. In other words . . .
   - Be open.
   - Be vulnerable.
   - Share details of your life, feelings, needs, opinions, and concerns as they come up.
   - Half-truths or white lies aren't acceptable.
   - Give honest opinions, not what you think your spouse wants to hear.
   - Be genuine, a person of integrity.
   - Never give reason to doubt; avoid questionable situations.
   - Be faithful physically and emotionally.
2. Honor and value opinions, thoughts, and beliefs. In other words . . .
   - Listen honestly and without condemnation.
   - Listen with your body through attentive eye contact and body language.
   - Take your spouse seriously and don't mock him as he shares with you.
   - Challenge with respect.
   - Accept the difference between your opinion and that of your spouse.
   - Be a cheerleader and support your spouse.
   - Don't disagree too often in public.
   - Affirm without interruption.
   - Solicit your spouse's opinion.
   - Prayerfully consider things together.
3. Resolve differences, conflicts, and arguments through LOVE (Listen, Offer yourself, Value and honor, and Embrace). In other words . . .
   - Plan how to work out conflicts.
   - Come to a resolution together.
   - Work through problems and find a compromise.
   - Be concerned with your spouse's opinion—not just your own—when conflict arises.
   - Express deeper feelings and concerns.

- Develop rules that include no put-downs, no yelling, no accusing, no defensive reactions, no going to bed angry, no comparing, no allowing anger to build.

O = Offer Yourself

Offering yourself means many things, but ultimately it goes to the heart of love: Consider your spouse's needs more important than your own. In this way you will offer yourself to your marriage. You will be more concerned about meeting your spouse's needs than whether or not yours are being met. This aspect of love includes these relational needs:

4. Feel secure that you'll stay together. In other words . . .
    - Be unconditionally committed; no matter how you feel or what you do, you are committed always to be together.
    - Make plans for the future together.
    - Believe that divorce is not an option and choose never to talk about it.
    - Take action in meeting your spouse's needs.
    - Make your marriage the most important earthly relationship.
    - Express your love through hugs and surprises or whatever best meets your spouse's needs.
    - Be proactive in your relationship (seek counseling, read marriage books, attend marriage seminars).
    - Be available to your spouse.
5. Plan ahead on how to raise your children. In other words . . .
    - Offer yourself and your viewpoints to forming a plan on childrearing.
    - Decide not to disagree about childrearing in front of the children.
    - Attend parenting seminars or classes, or read parenting books together.
    - Be united in making decisions about the kids.
    - Avoid a nice-parent, mean-parent syndrome.
    - Discuss discipline and rules.

- Pray together about the direction of your future children and continue this forever.
- Help each other be consistent parents.

V = Value and Honor

One of the greatest sets of relational needs involves feeling validated and honored. This will only happen when you take time to actually verbalize the reasons you value and honor your spouse. At the same time, you must act on these feelings. Let's look at some of the value-related needs the respondents shared.

6. Feel accepted for who you are. In other words . . .
   - Provide validation that your spouse's thoughts and opinions are valued.
   - Do not rely on your spouse's permission to be yourself.
   - Have no judgmental attitudes.
   - Be encouraging and offer praise.
   - Avoid excessive criticism.
   - Tell your spouse often of your love for him or her.
   - Show PDA (public display of affection).
   - Accept your spouse's good and bad characteristics.
   - Show interest in your spouse's interests.
   - Spend time with your spouse—get to know him or her.
   - Make your spouse a priority after God.
7. Be included in most decisions that affect the marriage. In other words . . .
   - Develop a sense of togetherness and belonging.
   - Discuss important issues, purchases, or decisions in advance.
   - Make decisions that are the best for both of you.
   - Hold family meetings.
   - Work to be more inclusive with each other.
   - Don't make assumptions about your spouse's thoughts or choices.
8. Feel accepted for what you do. In other words . . .

- Recognize and appreciate accomplishments or efforts.
- Acknowledge the importance of your spouse's work.
- Recognize that your spouse's work is part of who he or she is.
- Offer words of affirmation toward your spouse's work or hobbies.
- Appreciate what your spouse does.
- Include your spouse in your work and other activities.
- Take interest in your spouse's work and activities.

E = Embrace

To maintain the oneness of marriage it is crucial that you connect with each other again and again. High on the list of relational needs is the need for physical touch. However, embracing also means to stay close to your spouse emotionally and spiritually.

9. Feel connected through physical touch and spending time together. In other words . . .
   - Look for ways to add touch to your relationship.
   - Hold hands more often.
   - Give your spouse a hug for no reason except that you love him or her.
   - Consider physical intimacy a blessing and look for ways to enjoy this time together.
   - Enjoy the physical nearness of spending time together.
   - Set aside time for each other on a regular basis.
   - Spend time doing your spouse's activity of choice—with no complaints.
   - Share activities you both enjoy.
   - Realize that time together must be mutually fulfilling to cause a feeling of connectedness.
   - Look for ways to make any moment together one of quality.
10. Maintain a mutually vibrant spiritual relationship. In other words . . .

- Pray together. Research has shown that couples who pray together every day have a divorce rate that is less than a tenth of one percent (1 out of 1,152)![2]
- Study the Word individually and together.
- Attend church together faithfully.
- Get involved in church activities.
- Have spiritual accountability with each other.
- Maintain a Christ-centered relationship by seeking God's will, living by biblical principles, and making God a top priority.
- Discuss spiritual growth or ask spiritually challenging questions.
- Read spiritual books and participate in the other's spiritual development.

Drawing Out Your Mate's Most Important Relationship Needs

Because emotional safety within a relationship is so important, I asked couples at our seminar: "On a scale of zero to ten (ten being completely secure), how secure do you feel in your relationship to share those needs?" On average, people rated their degree of safety in the relationship at a seven. Keep in mind that because the seminar participants are people who seek enrichment in their marriage, they generally are more satisfied with their relationship than the average population.

The following techniques are what the respondents cited as the most effective ways to draw out their spouse's needs:

- *Validate.* Your spouse wants to feel like you hear him or her and understand what he or she is saying. This can be accomplished by repeating back what you hear your spouse saying. Remember the meaning of LOVE? Apply it to your marriage, and your spouse will feel safe enough to share his or her needs.
- *Ask.* Although it's your spouse's responsibility to share his or her needs, realize that there will be times when you must take the initiative.

- *Focus on your spouse's needs.* When your spouse shares his or her needs, provide body feedback so he or she knows you are listening.
- *Create a positive environment.* People share their deepest needs when they are free from distractions, both physically and emotionally.
- *Reciprocate.* As you share your needs, your spouse will be more likely to share his or hers.
- *Honor.* Make your spouse feel like his or her needs are valuable.
- *Provide security.* Your mate needs to trust that the information he or she shares is going to be protected not only from your ridicule but from others as well.
- *Follow through.* Your mate must trust that once he or she opens up and shares relational needs, they will be acted on. Once relational needs are shared, it's discouraging if nothing changes in the relationship.

Back to the battery analogy. The human needs "battery" requires constant recharging. How do you do it? First, you have to discover what your mate's needs are. The examples we've given are considered among the common needs of couples, but every person has unique relational needs. Now we want you to develop the skill of finding out which needs are most important to your mate.

Your spouse's relational batteries will be recharged by attending to his or her needs. According to Dr. John Gottman, this can take place in only about twenty minutes a day! Gottman discovered through his research that the difference between a couple who divorces and one that stays together, but is unhappy, is ten minutes a day of turning toward each other. By this, he means that a couple must turn toward each other every day through positive words or affirmative interactions.

Furthermore, Gottman found that couples who stay together and are *happy* turn toward each other ten minutes more each day than unhappily married couples. From these discoveries we can surmise that a total of twenty minutes a day of turning toward each other in substantial ways can make the difference between divorce and staying together in a happy satisfying relationship.

Just twenty minutes a day!

Now It's Your Turn

Creating Your Own Top Ten List

Because every couple is different, it's important to create your own hierarchy of needs by reviewing the list of needs and then answering the following questions.

1. On a separate sheet of paper, both of you answer the statement: *I feel loved or cared for when you . . .*
Be sure you record all the responses, because this information is a gold mine of relational material.
2. To understand which of the following needs are the most important in your life, rank each one from zero to ten (ten being the most important). If there are any additional needs that are not on the list, write them after "Other needs."

____ Feel connected through talking
____ Feel connected through sharing recreation/fun times together
____ Be touched nonsexually
____ Make love
____ Receive verbal tenderness
____ Receive physical tenderness
____ Support my desire to live by the laws of man
____ Support my desire to live by the laws of God
____ Know that we'll stay together and feel secure in love
____ Know that we'll stay together and feel secure in finances
____ Feel accepted and valued for who I am
____ Feel accepted and valued for what I do
____ Feel safe when I share who I am
____ Be included in most decisions that affect my life or marriage
____ Gain agreement and harmony in decision-making
____ Know that he or she needs me
____ Support my desire to give money away
____ Support my desire to give gifts to others
____ Support my desire to serve others
____ Receive genuine appreciation of praise and affirmation

___ Support my desire to have alone time
___ Be physically attractive
___ Be honest and trustworthy
___ Support my desire to assist the younger generation in developing and leading useful lives
___ Receive gifts
___ Receive acts of service
___ Develop with me a future plan for our marriage
___ Develop complete faith in each other
___ Become emotionally healthy
___ Maintain a mutually vibrant spiritual relationship
___ Apologize and seek forgiveness
___ Resolve differences/conflicts/arguments
___ Provide mutually satisfying communication
___ Cope with crises and stress
___ Understand my personality and gender differences
___ Demonstrate a willingness to change (flexibility)
___ Agree on how to raise our children
___ Be passionate and romantic
___ Socially connect with others
___ Maintain careful control over his or her expectations
___ Notice our positive relational history
___ Strive for mutuality and equality in our relationship
___ Share negative and positive feelings without delay
___ Accept my influence
___ Periodically update his or her knowledge of my greatest needs
___ Receive genuine appreciation for my service
___ Other needs:

3. From the above list, pick your top ten needs in order of importance (e.g., #1 would be your most important need).

1. _____
2. _____
3. _____

4. _____
5. _____
6. _____
7. _____
8. _____
9. _____
10. _____

4. For your mate to completely understand your top ten relational needs, it's necessary to explain what each need means to you. For example, if one of your top needs is "Provide mutually satisfying communication," then you will need to explain what that means. Moreover, if your mate were giving you "satisfying communication," then what would he or she be doing? Make your explanation as behaviorally specific as possible. In other words, tell your mate what specific behaviors he or she would be exhibiting if he or she were providing mutually satisfying communication. In the space below, define each top need.

1. _____
_____
_____
2. _____
_____
_____
3. _____
_____
_____
4. _____
_____
_____
5. _____
_____
_____
6. _____
_____
_____

7. _____
   _____
   _____

8. _____
   _____
   _____

9. _____
   _____
   _____

10. _____
   _____
   _____

For Further Reading

Willard F. Harley, Jr., *Love Busters* (Grand Rapids: Revell, 2002).
Gary and Barbara Rosberg, *The Five Love Needs of Men and Women* (Wheaton, Ill.: Tyndale, 2001).
Gary Smalley, *Making Love Last Forever* (Greenville, Mass.: Word Publishing, 1997).
Gary Smalley, *Secrets of Lasting Love* (New York: Simon & Schuster, 2001).

5

Three Steps to Growing an Intimate Marriage

Gary and Carrie Oliver

Human love can be glorious images of Divine love.
No less than that: but also no more.

C. S. Lewis, *The Four Loves*

In Genesis we are told that God created man and woman to be in relationship with him and with each other. Some people are amazed when they come to the part that says they were "naked and unashamed." Why the amazement? In today's world it is amazing that two people can be so completely comfortable with each other that they are vulnerable, not just sexually, but with their entire selves. We are amazed when just verses later we read after both have eaten of the forbidden fruit that the man and woman covered themselves to hide from each other and from God.

Naked and Unashamed

Hiding is what most of us know how to do. The naked and ashamed part is what causes us to don our masks that help us hide, pretend, deny, conceal, and protect. Putting on these masks is a way of hiding from each other, God, and ourselves. Brennan Manning in his book *Abba's Child* calls this type of behavior putting on the imposter self. This imposter self prevents us from communicating to another person who we really are and keeps us from investing in seeing inside of someone else.

Intimacy is an illusive concept to many of us, and yet many of us are missing exactly what God designed us for—intimacy with him first and then with each other, to know and be known. God created us in his image. This means that, like him, we can experience intimacy. On the human level that means we have the ability to be naked and unashamed with our mind, our will, and our emotions. A marriage has little chance of surviving if a couple does not grasp the importance of cultivating and growing intimacy. One of the most important tasks in the first few years of marriage is to understand what intimacy is and to learn some of the practical things we can do to help intimacy thrive.

Cultivate Intimacy by Embracing Your God-Given Differences

What is intimacy? It seems as if everybody talks about it, and everybody wants it, but few know what it looks like, how to define it, or how to get it. How do we define intimacy? Simply put, intimacy means "into-me-see." What does intimacy require? The first step to cultivating intimacy is to realize that the only way we can truly know another person or be able to penetrate walls is to see them through the eyes of God. Okay, that is easier said than done. But with God's help it can be done.

When we experience hopelessness in marriage, it is often because we have lost our perspective and we have become unable to see our spouse as God sees him or her. When our perspective becomes distorted, the barriers to intimacy are more likely to grow. We know that when sin entered into the world, one of the first things man and woman did was construct barriers. Barriers are structures we build to prevent someone from seeing in.

You don't have to be married very long to experience the ability to build walls that keep others out, especially the one with whom we desire the deepest levels of intimacy. Some of us experienced that ability even in the first week of marriage. In our work with couples and from our own marriage experience, we've discovered there are things couples can do that build emotional, psychological, and spiritual barriers to the intimacy they hunger for. One of the main barriers to intimacy is our unwillingness to truly accept and then to understand our spouse's differences.

Understand Their World

When I (Carrie) married I knew that males and females had a different anatomy. Gary was grateful that I possessed this knowledge. However, I knew little about the extent of differences between these two genders and the impact those differences would have on my marriage. Gender differences are only the beginning. We can be different in our personality type, cultural background, ethnicity, birth order, denomination, etc. How many differences we have may not be as important as what we do with our differences.

The first step to making your differences work for you is to become a student of your partner. Who is this person that at one time you thought you knew so well? Ask yourself, *Do I spend more time studying and trying to understand my partner or more time contemplating how they should be studying and trying to understand and please and agree with me?* Cultivating intimacy through understanding differences requires a concerted effort to first understand how your spouse approaches and lives in their world and then to join them there and finally to embrace who they are.

Join Their World

We have many examples from our marriage. Like most men Gary typically would not seek to engage in long periods of chat time. He enjoys planning, problem solving, vision casting, but just plain chatting is not his thing. Because he watched me and learned that women enjoy this type of behavior, he began experimenting with chatting, particularly in the mornings over coffee before work. From this small effort to meet me in my world our intimacy grew. I began to learn that many men enjoy connection while engaged in activity and not necessarily talking while doing the activity. I began to join Gary in his activities. He likes to go to movies. I often thought that men designed movies so they would have two hours during which they would not have to talk to their wives. Gary actually feels connected to me while watching a movie or simply when I sit next to him in the room while he is reading. I tried scuba diving, an activity that Gary enjoys. This is a stretch for me but something I wanted to do to join him in his world. Joining our spouse in his or her world speaks love, acceptance, and appreciation for who God designed that person to be.

From our personal and clinical experience, we can tell you that it's easy for couples to get caught up in demanding that their individual needs be met, pouting because they aren't being met, or demeaning each other for how different they are. We all know how painful it is when our spouse misses our needs or doesn't understand who we really are. It's even more painful when they don't seem to want to know. Nursing that pain becomes the mortar between the bricks of the wall that will be built if we do not choose to understand and value our differences.

Embrace Who They Are

Cultivating intimacy requires that we think through the many dimensions of who our spouse is and then ask God to help us become aware of opportunities to affirm them in who they are and to relate to them in ways that are meaningful to them. The first step is to begin to see them through God's eyes. Looking at our spouse through God's eyes may mean we release some of the negative facts about them and maintain a positive focus. Intimacy is the process of two people coming together; it is not two people becoming the same. But oh, how we push, cajole, connive, and argue with our spouse to get them to become like us. Meaningful change begins with us choosing to change ourselves since we rarely have control over whether our spouse will change. Sometimes it is a very intimate moment when we can take our eyes off of ourselves and put them on the one we chose to marry and to love and to meet them in their world.

Cultivate Intimacy by Practicing Passionate Love

What do you think of when you hear the word *intimacy?* Perhaps you think of the word *passion.* Talking about passionate love may include sexual intimacy but does not necessarily begin or end there. Passion is a powerful emotion that includes love, joy, enthusiasm, dedication, intensity, and devotion. What are you passionate about? Are you passionate about your relationship with your spouse? Almost every marriage that ends in divorce had some level of passion in the beginning. Marriages that last have learned to cultivate a passionate love throughout the lifetime of the marriage.

In *Desiring God* John Piper talks about passionate love. He says, "Passionate love is the overflow of joy in God that spills over unto others in our life." Once again we must begin with God. If our joy in the Lord is passionless then chances are we will not experience the level of passionate love that God desires us to develop with our spouse. Passionate love is unconditional love. This love loves when our spouse is cranky, sad, angry, anxious, depressed, sick, and even when they hurt us. I (Carrie) began to notice as I had children that I could love them when they were doing all of these things, but why did I have such trouble when it came to Gary? I was not really loving unconditionally. I kept score. I had high expectations of him; but I didn't want him to have expectations of me, and basically I was quite selfish! We tend to love passionately when we are dating because we are more accepting, and then we get married and things change.

Unconditional Love

In John 17 we see a very intimate conversation between a Father and a Son. The point of this passage culminates with Christ talking of the love that God put in him and his desire that this same type of love would be in his beloved. Some of the most profound opportunities for intimacy between you and your spouse may not be when the birds are singing and the flowers are blooming and the rainbow is bright but rather when your spouse comes home tired, depressed, somewhat joyless, or cranky. At that point unconditional love helps you release rights and seeks to encourage, embrace, and comfort. There is nothing like the feeling of joy when we choose to love unconditionally, to give, to serve. We become alive. What does our spouse experience? Complete safety.

Intimacy is cultivated when we can see beyond the behaviors and go directly to the heart of our spouse and seek to touch them there. Passionate love enables us to do just that. The crazy thing about all of this is that the more we love in this manner the more likely we are to be loved back in the way we desire. When we are passionate about loving unconditionally, we may even be surprised when our spouse accepts us and meets us at the deepest part of our heart. We're surprised because our eyes were not focused on getting what we wanted. We're not saying we shouldn't express our needs. Part of intimacy is allowing another to know who we are and what we need. Intimacy involves having a healthy self-awareness so that we can allow our spouse to see us for who we are.

Forgiveness

Passionate love involves forgiving. Understanding and practicing the process of forgiveness is essential if we want deeper levels of intimacy. The longer we are married the easier it is to accumulate fairly long scorecards of wrongs that our spouse has committed against us. We may have even tried to work through those wrongs and think forgiveness has taken place. But just as soon as we think that is true, up crops an issue, and we will pull up one of those wrongdoings of our spouse from our scorecard and off and running we will go. We all know the outcome of this. Everybody loses. When we have a commitment to love passionately, we begin to experience forgiveness in greater, fuller, and more thorough ways. The process of forgiveness is very intimate. To fully forgive or to be forgiven creates the atmosphere for passionate intimacy.

During our twenty-one-year marriage, we've learned nine words that have helped us tear down the walls, increase the trust, and build bridges into each other's heart. These nine words are "I was wrong. I am sorry. Please forgive me." Early in our marriage it was easy for me (Carrie) to say I was sorry. I liked harmony and saying I was sorry was an easy way to achieve harmony. However, asking for forgiveness is very different from being sorry. When we admit our wrong and desire forgiveness, we have a new resolve to turn from whatever the hurtful behavior is. That is one side of the coin.

If you are being asked to forgive, you must truly forgive, release your hurt, and not use what you have forgiven as leverage or ammunition in the future. This should be a time that you recall in the future of when your spouse was tenderhearted enough to recognize his or her sin, to confess it to you, and to experience the freedom that comes from a wounded heart releasing pain. This is intimacy. This makes for a passionate relationship. Forgiveness is released by passionate love and allows us to experience each other in deep ways. Passionate, forgiving love is unconditional love that shortens the distance and weaves the cords that create the safety net that allows us to be intimate with each other.

Cultivate Intimacy through Prayer

You've read enough of this chapter to know that intimacy encompasses the totality of who God has made us to be. As we experience intimacy within our relationship, it touches other realms. As we cultivate a spiritual connection with God first and then with each other, we are touched in our sexual intimacy, our communication intimacy, our friendship intimacy, and so on. The spiritual connection is vital for deeper levels of intimacy, and prayer is the lifeline to knowing God and a way for couples to know each other that other realms of the relationship cannot provide.

Recent research has shown that when couples pray together regularly this may actually reduce their risk of divorce. Why are we so amazed by this? God says that where two or more are gathered he is in their midst. Imagine, every time we pray together as husband and wife, God is in our midst. This is our God with his strength, his power, his forgiveness, his grace, mercy, tenderness, kindness, and unconditional love. Why wouldn't we do this more often?

We have heard many reasons couples don't pray: "We are too busy and can't find the time." "We have different schedules." "The kids interrupt us." "I'm not as spiritual as my spouse so I don't want to pray out loud." "We've never done it before." "We're not sure what to say," or "We are bored with prayer." Many Christians are living lives that don't particularly look much different than those of nonbelievers. They are busy, they are tired, hurried, anxious, depressed, and sometimes bored. The vitality and joy of prayer has been lost.

Cultivating intimacy through prayer may require that there be an individual rededication to the Lord, a renewal of the heart that may be tired and shriveled. Ask God to renew your heart, to renew a right spirit within you, and then to grow that relationship with him. When two people bring their joy and love of God together in prayer as a couple, powerful things happen. First, prayer together can produce increased perspective of each other's hearts. When I (Gary) hear my wife talk to God, I hear parts of her that I do not hear otherwise. She may even talk to God differently than she talks to me, or the kids, or friends, and that is a part of her I love to know. I see her in new and fresh ways.

Second, prayer produces increased power for a relationship. As we pray together, God is in the midst of two people, and his strength and power is released. A marriage relationship exists by the strength of God. As we pray we thank God for his provision, and we ask him for what we need. His promises apply to every aspect of the marriage relationship. Philippians 1:6 says that it is God who began the good work of your marriage, and it is he who will perfect it. Philippians 2:13 points out that it is God who is at work in you as a couple for his own good pleasure. Finally, praying with your spouse increases the passion for God, thus increasing the passion for one another. Prayer provides the avenue for increased perspective, increased power, and increased passion, resulting in greater degrees of intimacy with God and thus with each other.

Couples in their first few years of marriage actually have a unique opportunity to set the pattern for praying together regularly. Prayer does not have to last long hours, nor does it require extensive prayer lists. Prayer can involve praising God together, worshiping, praying the psalms together. Prayer can be sharing simple requests for the needs of the day. Prayer provides a safe place for forgiveness of sins. Prayer provides a very intimate moment when we hear our spouse ask for forgiveness for a sin and watch the heart soften when forgiveness is felt from our loving God. Begin now to pray together. Take a few moments each day to turn to God with your spouse and share an intimate moment with an intimate God. Prayer can truly deepen the love and safety of the marriage relationship.

Conclusion

Growing an intimate marriage is an exciting, fulfilling, and sometimes overwhelming experience. Cultivating intimacy—"into-me-see," the ability to know and be known—is no easy task and many couples miss it altogether. We see numerous couples on the verge of divorce and hear them express the lonely words: "He or she has absolutely no idea who I am." Start now to risk being vulnerable, to begin to take off the mask, to renounce living the imposter life. Embrace your spouse as being different from you and study them in order to know them. Pretend that you will eventually have to take a final exam that requires you to know everything about who your mate is. You will be graded! Practice passionate unconditional love and begin to pray daily with your spouse. Your marriage will grow into a vibrant reflection of what God intended for marriage.

Questions to Discuss

1. What are topics or feelings that you find uncomfortable talking about with your mate? What are you most likely to do when you feel uncomfortable? What could you do differently to allow your spouse to join you in these things?
2. What are three qualities you like about your spouse that are different from you? What are three things that are not particularly endearing things about your spouse? How could you begin to accept your spouse and these differences and perhaps even affirm your spouse?
3. What are three ways you could express passionate love to your spouse that you are not already doing?
4. If you agree that praying together helps cultivate intimacy, how can you begin to implement this in your life? If you are already praying together, how could you deepen this, thus deepening your level of intimacy?

For Further Reading

Richard J. Foster, *Prayer: Finding the Heart's True Home* (Scranton, Pa.: HarperCollins, 1992).

Brennan Manning, *Abba's Child: The Cry of the Heart for Intimate Belonging* (Colorado Springs: NavPress, 1994).

Gary Smalley, *Secrets to Lasting Love: Uncovering the Keys to Life-long Intimacy* (New York: Simon & Schuster, 2001).

H. Norman Wright and Gary J. Oliver, *How to Bring Out the Best in Your Spouse* (Ann Arbor, Mich.: Servant, 1997).

6

Communication: Key to Your Marriage

Roger and Becky Tirabassi

The fights are the best part of married life. The rest is merely so-so.

Thornton Wilder, *The Merchant of Yonkers*

As a professional counselor I (Roger) see hundreds of couples a year that are trying to better their relationships. The first skill I emphasize is effective communication. No matter what problems couples encounter, effective communication will be necessary to successfully deal with them.

Though most people realize the importance of communication, I am amazed at how many couples don't practice good communication skills. There are many reasons couples fail at effective communication. One of the main causes of poor communication comes from both our childhood and what we continue to observe as adults through the media. The problem with years and years of observing and experiencing ineffective and poor communication is that we develop a pattern of communicating that not only feels natural but also takes a determined effort to change.

Two Systems for Effective Communication

Here are two systems that you can use for enhancing your communication as a couple in a way that will improve your relationship. You will have to study them, adopt them, and use them in your everyday conversations if you hope to experience a lasting change. I also encourage you to be diligent and patient with yourself and your spouse while you develop these communication skills.

I am convinced that all the knowledge you can gain to improve your communication skills will not only help you have a more intimate marriage but will enhance all of your relationships. My undergraduate degree was in speech communications, my first master's degree focused almost totally on active listening, and my doctoral dissertation focused on training volunteers to develop effective communication skills. Throughout my studies, almost every book I read on marriage emphasized the need for effective communication as a key to happiness. Effective communication is one of the most powerful ways we bond with another human being. But when communication skills are lacking, we simply don't feel connected with others.

A husband and wife came to me for counseling. The husband struggled with feeling connected to his wife. He shared many times that something was missing in their relationship, but he was unable to put his finger on the exact issue. As we inventoried their lives, we found that they both had serious deficits in their ability to communicate their thoughts and feelings in a way in which the other could relate. They became aware of this and learned a new system of communicating. It was not long before they both reported that there was a depth of connection that they had not experienced in the past.

We Begin with Awareness

Let's look at how they achieved their growth. First, we covered the importance of the "awareness step" in developing successful communication skills. One way I achieve this with my clients is sharing "The 14 Rules for Effective Communication."[1] I consider these rules as suggestions for improving all relationships. By taking the time to study them, you will not only come to see that following them will assist you in keeping your relationship safe but will also help you become aware of how your current communications could be hurting your relationship.

The 14 Rules for Effective Communication

RULE 1: ELIMINATE THE USE OF THE WORDS *NEVER* AND *ALWAYS*.

This rule is designed to minimize defensive reactions in your communication. When anyone hears that "they never," or "they always," they tend to get defensive. When they get defensive, they no longer are able to listen in an effective manner or respond with thoughts or feelings. By staying away from words or phrases that contain *never, always, nothing,* and *all,* we won't hook into our partner's defensive feelings. Let's look at an example:

Becky: Roger, you came home late again today. Don't you know how much that hurts me?
Roger: Yes, I do, but I can't help it. I have things I have to accomplish in order to do my job effectively. I'm not doing it on purpose.
Becky: You *always* come home late, and you *always* have that excuse.
Roger: I don't *always* come home late. I come home on time a lot of the time.

This conversation moved in a downward spiral when Becky used the "always" statement. Roger became defensive. From then on, their communication was headed for trouble. In a habitual, but unhealthy, way of communicating, Roger and Becky began to argue about whether or not Roger is always late. Unfortunately, Becky's hurt feelings over Roger's tardiness weren't identified or discussed.

Learn to use the word *often* instead of *always,* and *seldom* instead of *never.* Below are examples that will show you (1) the old way and (2) the new way that will reduce the probability of a defensive reaction from your partner:

1. *Nothing* I do ever seems to please you.
2. *Seldom* do I seem to please you.

1. This happens *all* the time.
2. This seems to happen *often.*

1. You watch *every* football game on television.
2. You watch a *lot* of football on television.

1. You *never* help me around the house.
2. You *seldom* help me around the house.

This rule by itself will not eliminate the defensive reaction of your partner. But if you use it in conjunction with the thirteen remaining rules, you will have a much better chance of experiencing less defensiveness in your relationships.

RULE 2: TRY NOT TO BLAME OR SHAME.

When we communicate in ways that indicate blame or shame to our partner, once again we set up our partner for a defensive reaction. When a defensive reaction occurs, we don't feel as if we have been heard or understood. In addition to not feeling heard, we usually enter into an argument or a verbal attack. We are no longer able to discuss our hurt or frustration. We are seldom able to move into a conflict resolution process that gives us a win-win outcome. Most couples end up arguing about some other issue that I characterize as "chasing rabbits." Here are a few examples to illustrate the point:

> Becky: If it weren't for your decision to move to this house, we wouldn't be in this difficult financial situation.
> Roger: Oh, now it's my fault. Yeah, I'm always the one to blame. Why don't you blame me for every one of our problems?

Roger and Becky will argue about who is to blame rather than deal with the current financial crisis and develop a plan to rectify it.

> Becky: We can't seem to get through our conflict about who should take the kids to school. Do you think we can discuss this without fighting?
> Roger: You started the whole fight.
> Becky: I started the fight? I didn't start the fight. You started it when you raised your voice.
> Roger: I wouldn't have raised my voice if you hadn't ignored me.

When Roger used the phrase, "You started the whole fight," he was blaming Becky. Her defensive reaction kept them from dealing with the original conflict. Thus, they were off "chasing rabbits."

Rule 3: Don't name call, label, or belittle.

Couples usually digress to the use of demeaning words once they have become frustrated, hurt, or angry. Belittling and labeling words, such as *stupid, insensitive, selfish, moron, idiot, lazy, hard-headed,* and *stubborn* are usually said to get back at our partner for hurting us. These words will cause the relationship to descend to a lower level and will seldom lead to getting back on track with the original problem.

Rule 4: Use "I feel" statements rather than "You" statements.

While almost everyone has heard of this rule, I still see it broken more than any other rule. "You" statements hook into the defensive reactions in others. Once again, instead of helping us communicate more effectively, they end up hindering our progress. When we change the "You" statement to an "I feel" statement, we have a much better chance of improving our relationships.

The following examples demonstrate (1) the type of reactions we are most likely to generate by using the "You" statement and (2) the correct form of sharing using the "I feel" statement.

(1) Roger: You make me feel so frustrated when you keep bringing up the past.
Becky: Oh, so it's all my fault.
(2) Roger: I feel frustrated when you continue to bring up the past.
Becky: I don't want to frustrate you. I am trying to resolve conflict.

Rule 5: Say you are hurt, frustrated, or irritated rather than angry.

The feeling of anger itself isn't wrong. But often the way we express our anger hooks into our partner's defense mechanisms. Anger follows an initial or root feeling like hurt, frustration, irritation, or jealousy and often covers up that feeling. Truly the best communication identifies those root feelings and does so in a way that helps our partner respond with empathy rather than defensiveness. Mary Donovan and William Ryan write:

The most common messages behind a stance of "I am angry" are "I am hurting," "I am depleted and in need of love and affection," and "I feel unappreciated and unloved." When anger is expressed in lieu of these underlying feelings, it has precisely the opposite of the desired effect.[2]

I have seen couples avoid patterns of triggering and escalating by talking about their *hurt* rather than their *anger*. I remember one day when my wife, Becky, and I got involved in an escalating argument. We were both defending ourselves and blaming each other for our current states of frustration. It seemed the more we talked, the worse it got. Eventually, we stopped listening to each other, began interrupting one another, and quickly broke most of the rules for effective communication. Suddenly Becky stopped and said, "I am hurting." Her words had an immediate effect on my attitude and response. I was quickly able to listen and respond to her in a positive way. Our conversation took a whole new direction, and we were able to resolve our conflict.

The following examples illustrate the use of this rule:

> Roger: Becky, I am so angry at you. I hate it when you tell me to clean up the crumbs off the counter before I am even finished making my toast.
> Becky: Well, I am angry at you for making such a mess—and don't talk to me in that tone.

Here is a better way for Roger to express his feelings:

> Roger: Becky, I feel frustrated when you tell me to clean up the crumbs off the counter before I am even finished making my toast.
> Becky: I don't want you to feel like a child. But I get frustrated when the kitchen gets messy.

Because Roger described his frustration rather than his anger, he was able to speak in a better tone. This gave Becky the strength not to react with anger. They both shared their root feelings instead of their secondary feelings of anger.

RULE 6: DON'T WITHDRAW, ISOLATE, OR AVOID.

When we withdraw or avoid our partner, we create an even greater problem by causing our partner to feel ignored, cut off, or abandoned. Our partner will feel as if we are trying to punish them. This often escalates and the relationship is at greater risk. It is true that a cooling-off period can help us gain perspective and help us get our emotions back under control, but it needs to be done in such a way that the other person doesn't feel as if it is withdrawal, isolation, or avoidance.

RULE 7: TAKE A TIME-OUT IF YOU BECOME ANGRY TO THE POINT OF NOT BEING IN CONTROL.

I instruct my clients to ask for a time-out to get their emotions under control. I ask them to keep their time-outs to no more than an hour. I also ask the person who took the time-out to initiate coming back together. It is always better to take a time-out if emotions are heightened to a point of physical or verbal abuse. If this is a pattern in your relationship, you must seek professional help.

RULE 8: LISTEN COMPLETELY AND TAKE PAINSTAKING STEPS TO HEAR EVERYTHING.

The key to successful communication is the ability to listen. Listening is so much more than hearing. It is becoming aware of the content and feelings the other is experiencing. It is best to repeat back to the person what he or she shared, being sure to ask, " Did I hear you correctly?" and "Did I accurately reflect your feelings?" Be aware that listening can be painful. It takes concentration, selflessness, and humility to be a great listener. But I am convinced, if you put forth the effort, it will be rewarded with a degree of intimacy that cannot be experienced without this type of communication.

RULE 9: DON'T DEMAND; RATHER, ASK.

During the early days of courtship, we are usually very courteous and kind. After the honeymoon, things can change quickly. It is amazing how lackadaisical we can become with our partner. Instead of asking, we demand. We forget to say, "Would you be willing to . . . ?" Or "Would you please pass me the salt?" Instead we say something like, "Salt." Many of us were *told* as children what to do and when to do it. Demands usually create defensive reactions in anyone. John Powell said, "The genius of communication is the ability to be both totally honest and totally kind at the same time."

RULE 10: DON'T USE THREATS.

Many times we are unaware that we use threats. When we feel hopeless, backed into a corner, or intensely frustrated, we resort to using phrases such as "If you don't stop that, I . . ." Threats cause our partner to become not only defensive but even aggressive. Try very hard not to use threats. Take a time-out, bite your tongue, but stay away from using them.

Rule 11: Don't interrupt.

Many of us have a very difficult time observing this rule. We seldom think to repeat what the person said before we share our thoughts and feelings. When we interrupt someone, it causes him or her to feel as if we don't care, aren't listening, or we only want to speak our mind. If we are prone to interrupting, we will need to work very diligently always to repeat what our partner said before we share. We might need to be reminded that we will get a chance but must wait until the other person has finished sharing his or her thoughts and feelings.

Rule 12: Stay affirming.

It is always best to begin a conversation by sharing some form of positive affirmation with your partner. Most of us are prone to take a defensive position when our partners tell us that our behavior is hurting them in some way. If we affirm our partner, we help prepare them to hear our hurts. I suggest that you even affirm your partner for being willing to talk about your conflicts. For example, "Thank you so much for being willing to listen. Thank you for being willing to share your thoughts and feelings with me." Keep affirmation a regular part of all your conversations.

Rule 13: Don't use the "D" word—divorce.

When we get totally frustrated and feel helpless and hopeless, we are more prone to say things that can be tremendously harmful to our relationship.

Using the word *divorce* can pierce a person's heart. The word has such adverse effects, and it must be avoided at all costs. It can deeply wound and cause the other person to feel ultimate rejection and hopelessness.

Many of you who are reading this have already broken this rule. If you have, you need to do two things. First, go to your partner and apologize. Let him or her know you were frustrated and out of control when you used the word *divorce*. Second, you must let them know you will never use it again. If you have used the word and feel justified, you need to seek professional help. If there is physical abuse, infidelity, or alcohol or drug abuse in your relationship, you must get professional assistance. You cannot achieve emotional intimacy or have a successful marriage in these circumstances.

RULE 14: DON'T TELL THE OTHER PERSON, "YOU BROKE A RULE."

The fourteen rules are designed to help you achieve better communication in your marriage. They can also be used in a way that causes more harm. If you use them to shame or criticize your partner, you have missed their purpose. Rule 14 can keep you from criticizing your partner when he or she breaks a rule. If you tell your partner he or she broke a rule, you end up breaking one yourself! If your partner breaks a rule, it is permissible to say something like, "It hurt me when you interrupted me," or "I was feeling defensive when you said I always come home late."

Listening

In addition to "The 14 Rules for Effective Communication," I also use a model that has been used in some form or another by most counselors for the past thirty years. It has, in fact, been used by so many theorists that it is difficult to give credit to one person. In the 1970s Thomas Gordon, author of *Parent Effectiveness Training,* coined the phrase "active listening." Currently, Harville Hendrix, John Gottman, and E. L. Worthington describe similar principles in their systems. Becky and I call it "Intentional Listening." But more than two thousand years ago Solomon wrote, "What a shame, what folly, to give advice before listening to the facts!" (Prov. 18:13 NLT).

While the "14 Rules" will assist you in keeping your communication safe and minimize defensiveness, the following eight steps of "Intentional Listening" will give you a system of communication that should substantially help you communicate more effectively.

Eight Steps of "Intentional Listening"

1. Decide who is going to share their thoughts and feelings first. This person is designated the *speaker.* It is often best to have the person who is speaking hold some object in his or her hand (as

if it were a microphone). A pencil or a remote control will help the listener remember that the other person is speaking.

2. The person with the object (the speaker) shares his or her thoughts and feelings. Thoughts and feelings are shared with "I" statements, not "you" statements. The person sharing must do the best he or she can to practice "The 14 Rules for Effective Communication."

3. The *listener* repeats both the thoughts and feelings shared by the speaker. It is important to listen intently for feelings and thoughts.

4. After the listener repeats the thoughts and feelings, the listener asks the speaker if he or she accurately understood what the speaker shared.

5. After the listener repeats the thoughts and feelings, he or she needs to respond with empathy and humility. When you empathize with your partner, it is best to think back to a time in your life when you had an experience that gave you a similar feeling. Avoid using an experience where the speaker caused *you* to have the same feeling. (If you use an experience in which they caused you to feel the same feeling, it will cause them to get defensive. They will feel as if you are turning the tables on them.) It is almost always best to look back for a childhood experience that caused you to have that same feeling. That should give you the empathetic response.

6. The listener then asks if there is anything else the speaker wants to share regarding the issue that they are discussing. It is important that the speaker does not use this opportunity to share thoughts or feelings about situations other than the specific one being discussed (otherwise, the speaker can overwhelm the listener and sabotage the system).

7. At this point, the roles are reversed. The person who was the speaker becomes the listener, and the object changes hands. The transition should be made by saying something like, "Thank you for listening so intently. Why don't you share your thoughts and feelings, and I'll listen to you?"

8. The speaker now shares his or her thoughts and feelings. If the speaker has just apologized for hurting or frustrating his or her partner, it would be best to say something like, "Before I share my thoughts and feelings, I want you to know I really am sorry

for hurting you, and what I am going to say is in no way meant to minimize the hurt I have caused you."

Here is an example that illustrates the "Intentional Listening" system:

Roger: I feel a bit frustrated about the way we are getting along. I was wondering if you would be willing to do some "Intentional Listening."
Becky: Sure, do you want to be the first speaker?
Roger: Sure. I'll hold the remote to help us remember who the speaker is.
Becky: That's fine.
Roger: I felt hurt when you fell asleep last night after you said we would make love. We haven't been intimate this past week because of how busy you were, so I was disappointed and frustrated after I got my hopes up.
Becky: So, you were expecting to be intimate because I shared with you that we would make love and then when I fell asleep you were frustrated and disappointed. Is that right?
Roger: Yes.
Becky: Is there anything more?
Roger: No.

Now Becky can respond to what Roger has been saying. She takes the object and becomes the speaker, and Roger becomes the listener:

Becky: I can see how that would disappoint and frustrate you. I would like to make it up to you. Would you forgive me?
Roger: Yes. Do you want to share your thoughts and feelings and I will listen to you?
Becky: First of all I don't want you to feel like I am not sorry for last night, but I would like you to understand some of my feelings.
Roger: Okay.
Becky: I really wanted to be intimate with you last night and had every intention to make love with you. I didn't realize how tired I was, so it caught me off guard. I felt bad this morning because I realized I had disappointed you.
Roger: You wanted to be intimate too but were not expecting to be so tired. You didn't realize that you would fall asleep so soon. Then you felt bad this morning for disappointing me. Is that right?
Becky: Yes.
Roger: Is there anything more?
Becky: No. But if I do that again, I don't mind if you wake me up. Could you do that?

Roger: If you won't be upset, I'll be happy to wake you up!
Becky: Okay.

The above system helped Becky and me communicate more effectively, and we know it will help you too. We do want you to realize that there are some barriers to using the system.

First, it feels artificial. We are so used to one person sharing his or her thoughts and feelings and then the other person immediately sharing his or her response that beginning attempts at using this system will feel very unnatural.

Second, it feels mechanical. Because this system keeps you from sharing your thoughts and feelings until you have repeated your partner's thoughts and feelings, it feels a bit restrictive.

The third barrier comes when it takes more time for one person to share completely and to follow with repeating and empathizing. The bottom line is that you will most likely resolve your conflicts much more quickly because you are communicating more accurately and effectively. In the end, the more you practice this system, the more natural it will feel and become, and the less time it will take.

You will improve your communication if you will follow "The 14 Rules for Effective Communication" and use "Intentional Listening," and we are confident you will achieve greater intimacy and satisfaction in your relationship.

Questions to Discuss

1. Which three of "The 14 Rules for Effective Communication" will help you most in improving your communication?
2. What are the recurring distractions that keep you from communicating effectively?
3. What was the style of communication used in your family when you were a child? How has that helped or hindered your communication effectiveness?

For Further Reading

Willard F. Harley, Jr. *His Needs, Her Needs: Building an Affair-Proof Marriage* (Grand Rapids: Revell, 1986).

Becky and Roger Tirabassi, *Let Love Change Your Life* (Nashville: Thomas Nelson, 2001).

Neil Clark Warren, *The Triumphant Marriage: 100 Extremely Successful Couples Reveal Their Secrets* (Colorado Springs: Focus on the Family, 1995).

H. Norman Wright, *Communication: Key to Your Marriage* (Ventura, Calif.: Regal Books, 2000).

H. Norman Wright, *Making Peace with Your Partner: Healing Conflicts in Marriage* (Waco, Tex.: Word Books, 1988).

7

Boundaries in Marriage

Tom and Lori Whiteman

Having an awareness of boundaries and limits helps me discover *who I am*. Until I know who I am, it will be difficult for me to have healthy relationships, whether they may be casual acquaintances, friends, close relationships or intimate relationships.

Charles L. Whitfield, M.D., *Boundaries and Relationships*

I (Tom) met with Marge soon after her husband's death. Totally devoted to her husband and family, Marge had always let her husband run things in the household. He had made all of the decisions, paid all the bills, and seemed to take care of her every need. She never really considered him to be controlling, yet the longer they were married, the more important he became and the more she disappeared into the relationship.

This seemed to work well. The marriage and the family functioned fine, though Marge's personal happiness was never a concern to either her or her husband. When her husband died, she suddenly realized that now she was on her own, and she was totally lost and alone. She didn't know how to pay the bills; she didn't know how to take care of many of the household needs; and she wasn't even sure how she liked to fix her own food. "I just made whatever my husband wanted," she told me. "I fixed the potatoes the way he liked them and only made his favorite desserts. Even when we went out, we only went to the restaurants that he chose. Now that I'm on my own, I'm not sure what I should even cook because he's not here to tell me what to do."

Peg and Harry came to me with a different kind of problem. Peg was very jealous of Harry's time and attention, and therefore was constantly questioning him about what he was doing and whom he was with. They had only been married about a year, and Harry hadn't really done anything to warrant Peg's distrust, yet Peg was constantly concerned that Harry needed monitoring.

Much of this suspicion came from Peg's upbringing. Her father and stepfather were both deceptive men, and both finally left her family to fend for themselves. These early betrayals created obvious trust issues in Peg, issues that were somewhat evident when she was dating Harry, but they seemed to intensify after their marriage.

Peg challenged Harry about his thought life, his friendships, and his motivations. She was convinced that he was not being honest with her. One incident occurred in church. Harry was listening to the sermon when suddenly he got a sharp elbow in the ribs. "I see what you're doing," Peg said angrily.

"What are you talking about?" Harry asked innocently.

"I'll talk to you *later!*" Peg whispered between clenched teeth.

The ride home revealed the root of the problem. Peg claimed to know that Harry wasn't listening to the service but instead was staring at and lusting after a particular blonde who was sitting behind the pastor in the choir loft. Harry, of course, denied it all.

Rob had a different kind of problem in his marriage. Married to Joyce for five years, he loved her very much. Their problem involved one of Rob's old girlfriends. Rob had dated Sally all through high school and college. They were truly best friends and had shared many wonderful moments. But after they became engaged, Sally cheated on Rob and it destroyed their relationship. Within a year after that breakup, Rob met and married Joyce. She might have been part of a rebound, but nonetheless Rob committed himself to Joyce and to their future relationship.

After Rob had been married to Joyce two years, Sally called to reconnect and apologize to Rob. They reconciled the previous hurts and were able to have a real heart-to-heart talk about unresolved problems from the past. Sally and Rob then continued to talk from time to time. Rob felt that Sally understood him so well that he even started calling Sally when he was having problems understanding Joyce. According to Rob, Sally was very insightful, helping him understand his wife's feelings about various things. As you might expect, however, Joyce wished Sally would stay out of their relationship. She was sincerely happy that Sally and Rob were able to resolve their past hurts, but she felt strongly that their contact should have ended at that point.

These three cases each have something in common. They are examples of a problem with boundaries. Every relationship needs to develop healthy and balanced boundaries. Without healthy boundaries in a marriage, all kinds of problems, hurts, and misunderstandings can occur. When a marriage is healthy, you can be certain that the partners have clearly defined their boundaries.

The Importance of Boundaries

Boundaries in a relationship are similar to boundaries on your property. Without a boundary of some kind, you are likely to have arguments or difficulties with your neighbors. The boundary line tells you, "This is where your property ends and mine begins." Some people will put up a fence or mark the line with a post to clarify where to cut the grass or which trees they can trim and which trees are not their responsibility. So it is with relationships. I need to know where to draw my own personal lines—what I am willing to give and where I need to say no in order to protect myself. Our sense of boundaries is formed in our childhood families, developed during our dating years, and solidified in marriage.

Boundaries can provide us with three important qualities in our marriage: freedom, protection, and clarified responsibilities. For example, my dog has an invisible fence. Its advantages are enormous. First and foremost, we can let him out of our door and forget about him. He has the freedom to wander around our yard all he wants. It makes his life more enjoyable and ours as well. On a nice day he can stay out there all day without any concern on our part.

The fence also provides our dog with protection. Without the fence we either had to leave him on a chain all day, which was too restrictive, denying his freedom, or just let him go loose, which always worried us, especially since we live only a few blocks from a major highway.

In marriage, healthy boundaries allow us freedom within the marriage to enjoy each other and ourselves. We have the freedom to pursue our dreams and ambitions, but only within the confines of an understood relationship. "I want you to enjoy your golf outing with the guys, but I also expect you to honor our marriage while you are gone." That sentence is seldom spoken in a healthy marriage because it doesn't have to be. It's understood.

Boundaries also provide protection in our marriage, assuring that the well-being of both partners will be considered. We saw the lack of this protection in the case of Marge, whose husband had died. She was at a loss because the marriage had been all about his needs and preferences; hers were never considered. As we set our personal boundaries, we need to be honest with our feelings and to speak up when we feel our spouse infringing on our personal freedoms.

I was once in a Bible study group that regularly enjoyed refreshments along with our discussion. One husband habitually told his wife, "Go get me some food!" Then, of course, he complained about what she brought him. After many weeks of this, one day when she seemed particularly harried, she amazed us all by replying, "Why don't you get *me* something this time?" We all cheered. The husband looked stunned, but he got the picture. It was stunning for him because they had probably played these roles for years, with her serving him, and they'd grown used to that arrangement. Most couples establish their boundary systems early in their relationship, and it's very difficult— sometimes traumatic—to change them later. It's especially hard to make changes when no one has ever discussed what these boundaries are.

The third advantage of boundary setting is what I call clarified responsibilities. I see an example of this with my neighbors. The boundary line between our properties lets us know how far to cut the grass and which trees we're responsible to trim. Now there are times when I might want to do something nice for my neighbor, like mowing a section of his lawn or raking part of his yard along with my own, but I'm not *responsible* to care for his property.

As I was growing up, my family always tended a little section of grass behind the garage. After twenty years a building permit required us to get a survey done of our property. I was surprised to find out that the piece of property behind the garage belonged to our neighbor. Our neighbor was even more surprised. But my father matter-of-factly admitted that yes, he knew it all along, but he still took care of that ground because the way the shrubs were planted, it was easier for us to access than our neighbor. All those years, as I helped mow and garden, I had been doing a great kindness for my neighbor without realizing it. And the neighbor had never expressed gratitude, not because he was ungrateful, but because he didn't know where the boundaries were.

I see the same thing in many marriages, especially Christian marriages. In some of these couples, the wives are always doing great kindnesses for their husbands, serving them in a Christ-like spirit. And that's wonderful, except that the husbands don't always respond with the same level of service. The wives give far more than they receive, and both husbands and wives begin to think that this is the way it should be, just because it's always been that way. They have no sense of healthy boundaries. In some cases it's the husband who's doing more serving than the wife. She expects him to do all sorts of things for her, just because he always has.

In a marriage, it is subtle but very important to clarify responsibilities early on, so both partners can decide on a fair distribution of responsibilities in the home. Of course there's nothing wrong with Christ-like service. I would hope that Christian husbands and wives would regularly step over the boundary lines in showing love to each other, just as my father did with that patch of ground. But it helps to know what you're expected to do and what you're doing out of kindness. Some things are duties, others are gifts.

Problems occur when one partner does something as a gift, but the other sees it as a duty. If I expect my wife to take care of her own car, but then I decide to be nice and fill up her tank a few times or change the oil, she might assume that her car is my responsibility. This might lead to a big argument one day when the tank is empty and the oil light is on.

"Why do you always do this?" I might complain. "You never take care of your car!"

"Me?" she responds, just as indignantly. "The car is *your* responsibility!" Instead of being grateful, she is resentful. She was seeing my gift as my duty.

I suspect that the same sort of misunderstanding was behind the wife's outburst at that Bible study. For years she had given him the gift of fetching refreshments, but now it was obvious that he saw it as her duty.

What's the answer? Talk about it. Stop assuming and get explicit about clarifying your responsibilities. Setting personal and relational boundaries is crucial to a healthy marriage, and the earlier you set them, the better.

Yeah, But . . .

But aren't we required to just give and give in a relationship? You know, give 110 percent and expect nothing in return? Isn't that the Christian model, following the example of Jesus, who poured himself out for us?

Well, yes. Scripture shows us a way of love that looks out for the best interests of others, that considers others more important than we are. And when we start talking about marital love, the language gets even stronger. In Genesis 2:24 and again in Matthew 19:5–6, we are instructed to leave our family and former lifestyle for the sake of our spouse. Paul also tells us in 1 Corinthians 7:3–4 that our bodies don't actually belong to us but to our spouse.

So how do we reconcile these clear biblical mandates with good boundaries?

God certainly calls on us to go the extra mile in our relationships, but we must also be wise in taking care of ourselves. Biblical Christianity does not, as some other religions do, try to eradicate the self. On the contrary, we are called to see ourselves as impressive creations of God—loved, called, and gifted by him. We are to care for our bodies as temples of the Holy Spirit, even as we give those bodies to our spouses. We are asked to love God with all that is within us. And Jesus gives us the clearest picture of balanced relationships in the second part of that great commandment (Matt. 22:39–40): "Love your neighbor as yourself."

There is a delicate and difficult balance that becomes the essence of what I am asking you to learn. Love your spouse and sacrifice for him or her as you also take care of and guard yourself. When both parties love the other and watch out for each other the way God intended, these principles work together wonderfully. But when the relationship is out of balance, problems arise.

Problems with Balance

Most people inherit their boundary problems from their family of
origin. We can define the boundary-setting tendencies of your original family and your current marriage on a continuum from *distant* to
enmeshed.

Distant   Balanced   Enmeshed

If you were raised in an extremely distant family, it would be one
in which members seem to care little for each other and in fact only
seem to care about themselves. There are very little together activities, with people passing in the hallways like virtual strangers. I see
this more often in families in which the marriage is stale or in a rut,
perhaps as a result of a pattern of bickering, which eventually ends
in an unspoken truce: "You live your life and I'll live mine." Each
spouse pursues his or her own careers, hobbies, and social activities.

Yet newly married couples aren't exempt. I've seen this distancing
in cases in which both parties delayed marriage until they had established their own careers. Sometimes these look more like corporate
mergers than marriages. Both spouses act as if their career is more
important than the marriage.

At the opposite extreme, in the enmeshed family, members smother
each other with love and attention. While this may look like a better
option, at an extreme level this leads to an unhealthy dependence.
Family members have a hard time doing anything on their own, and
decisions may be difficult because everything needs to be decided
together. Members might be emotionally punished for doing anything
that excludes the family: "You chose to be with your friends this weekend so I'm just not going to talk to you!" Moving out on your own or
going away to college can be particularly traumatic.

Again, a marriage can have the same dynamic. This is actually more
prevalent in the early years due to marital myths about love. Some go
into marriage thinking that love means "We enjoy doing everything
together." When such partners feel the inevitable need to be alone for
a while, they sense deep guilt.

The biblical teaching that "the two shall become one flesh" often
feeds into the enmeshment idea as well. But, in context, this certainly
doesn't mean that couples have to do everything together, just that

they have a new relationship that takes precedence over their family of origin.

But what could be wrong with enmeshment? What if two people want to knit their lives together tightly, spending all their time together and forsaking individual activities? The truth is that I've seen couples who seem to be joined at the hip, and they appear to be happy and healthy in a tightly intertwined relationship. There's no problem with that. My only concerns come when one of the partners loses himself or herself in the other, or when one feels guilty for *not* being totally enmeshed.

In a more balanced relationship, the couple enjoys sharing many moments and activities but also encourages each other in independent pursuits. For example, I counseled one husband who didn't like the idea of his wife going back to school for a graduate degree. At first he seemed to protest most about the cost, but when we explored it further, his real fear was that his wife would become too independent and self-reliant, thus making him less valuable in the relationship. His wife and I were able to convince him that her education would make their relationship more interesting and stable, and in fact it did.

Another couple faced difficulty because the husband was a frequent golfer. Creating the greatest conflict was the husband's annual trip with the guys. Usually, for one week in the winter, they all traveled to a warm climate for a week of golfing and guy-type festivities. While the wife wanted her husband to enjoy a time with the guys, she couldn't stop the resentment that she felt over being stuck with the kids and about the money that was spent on *his* hobby.

They resolved the conflict with a compromise: The wife would take a similar trip with her female friends to a place of their choosing with a budget similar to what he was spending for his golf outing.

These resolutions are not about evening the score but about making sure healthy boundaries are set so that neither person in the relationship ends up giving away all of himself or herself for the sake of the other. Remember, healthy boundaries involve independent and interdependent activities. Finding a good balance is tricky business at the beginning of the marriage, especially if you did not experience a good balance growing up. But in time, and with practice, boundary decisions can become more consistent and natural.

Which Way Do You Lean?

Everyone has a tendency to get out of balance, especially when they are stressed or feeling vulnerable. The key is to recognize which way you lean during these times and to keep an eye out for unhealthy responses or behaviors. Do you become smothering or clingy when you feel threatened in your relationship, or do you distance or devalue your partner when you sense a conflict? You may not be able to control your initial response, but once you recognize what you are doing, that is the time to transform your instinctive responses into new, healthier habits.

Let's say you come from a very distant family. Perhaps you felt love in your family, but it was rarely expressed. You really were on your own as far as getting your needs met, and this served you well while you were single. You're generally fine on your own.

When you dated, you liked the initial phase of getting to know someone new. You were able to express love to your spouse-to-be and felt genuine affection and passion with your spouse early in your marriage. But then you broke through the initial phase of marriage and entered the disillusionment stage—you know, the point at which you recognize that this person you married is not the perfect person you had hoped for. At that point, you responded with an earlier learned coping strategy. You withdrew emotionally, as you did in your family-of-origin.

This worked well growing up because it kept you from getting hurt. In your marriage however, withdrawing emotionally can lead to more serious consequences. It's important to recognize the way you are responding and try to change it.

Or perhaps you came from a very close family in which everyone was constantly asking about your feelings and would not let you get away with superficial answers. They pressed involvement, concern, and at times became an intrusion into your personal life. Now let's imagine you have a spouse who is depressed about dynamics going on in the office. Your spouse comes home from work quiet and reclusive. How do you respond?

That's right. You need to know what's going on. You may assume it's *your* fault and press your spouse to list everything you do that bugs him or her. This merely pushes your spouse away. Worse, your mate might end up blaming you for the depression. Notice, you weren't the cause of the depression, but you became the cause by pressing your own agenda rather than listening and understanding when your spouse needed space and wanted to talk.

Recognizing that you tend to get out of balance is only half the problem. Now you have to change your response. Again, this can be particularly difficult when the patterns are deep-seated. I suggest you help each other to change gradually by discussing your unhealthy tendencies and giving your spouse permission to let you know every time you are doing it again. This requires an unusually good and secure relationship to pull off. Most people become very defensive and resistant to change. Therefore, a therapist or counselor may be needed to guide you through these troubled waters. Done early in marriage, before the tendencies become more deeply rooted, is important. But at any stage of marriage it is critical to break the patterns of response that prevent the setting of healthy boundaries.

Within and Without

Boundaries are needed within the marriage, whereby both partners learn to assert their rights and accept their responsibilities, but boundaries are also needed outside the marriage. You may remember the example of Rob and Joyce in the beginning of this chapter. Rob reconciled with Sally, a former girlfriend, but then confided in her about problems he was having with his wife. This was a step over the line. Not that he shouldn't have a confidant, but his former flame was the worst possible choice. Out of respect for his wife's valid fears, he should have distanced himself from Sally.

Can't married men and women have friends of the opposite sex? Well, yes and no. Certainly couples can hang out together and friendships will develop, but as people start to pair off and form deeper friendships with individuals of the opposite sex, there are many pitfalls to avoid.

Here are some guidelines for these opposite-sex relationships:

- Guard your communication. You should not be revealing things about yourself or your relationship that you would not discuss with your spouse. You also should not say anything that you would not mind your spouse overhearing.

- Watch your boundaries on your level of intimacy: physical, emotional, and verbal. In other words, avoid physical touch, crude humor, or even conversations about sexual themes in movies, books, or TV shows. By all means, do not talk about your sex life.
- Avoid running to this person when you are upset, stressed, or struggling in your relationship. These are times that should be reserved for your spouse.
- Guard your emotions. If you find yourself thinking about this other person or joyfully looking forward to your next get-together, then you need to back away physically and emotionally.
- Guard your time alone with this person. It should be limited and purposeful, not just "hanging out getting to know each other better." And if you find yourself lying or misleading your spouse about time spent with the other person, then you've already crossed a dangerous boundary.

There are many other outside boundaries that you need to monitor. The list is almost endless: alcohol, work, the Internet, even church. Discuss with your spouse and examine any activity that is pulling you away from your primary relationships at home.

Improvement Needed

If you find yourself in a boundary-challenging marriage, or if you are just starting out and want to keep your boundaries in check, here are seven guidelines to help you along the way.

1. Set boundaries early and check them often.

Marital patterns start early. A new neighbor is wise to measure the boundary lines soon after he or she moves in. So it is with marriage. I refer to the first year of marriage as the power struggle stage, because this is the time when partners set the boundaries, rules, and responsibilities. It can be difficult, but once the rules are set, the marriage can begin the process of maturing. If the boundaries are not set early, change can be even more difficult. You will need to check yourself often. Discuss with your spouse how things are going and modify your communication and your boundaries as the need arises. Putting the conversation off or avoiding the conflict will often only lead to an even greater blowup.

2. Discuss your expectations.

You really should start before you marry, but since you are probably already married, it is important to discuss your expectations for the marriage. Who will be responsible for what in the relationship? Remember to clarify the boundary so that you know what to expect from your partner and what is expected of you. This needs to be reviewed throughout the marriage, as even couples who have been married thirty years need to discuss expectations as lifestyles and circumstances change. It is also helpful to know the expectations so that you know when to say thank you to your spouse for going the extra mile. Hopefully this will happen often for both of you!

3. Speak the truth in love.

When you discuss your expectations and your boundaries, do it at a time when you can be heard. Don't do it in the middle of an argument, but when things are better, discuss rationally what went wrong and what improvements you can make for the next time. Be assertive about how you feel, but do it in a way that expresses love and commitment to the relationship.

4. Focus on YOUR responsibility.

One important rule for boundary keeping is that you focus on yourself. A personal boundary has to be "I can't control the other person, I can only work on my own behaviors, reactions, and emotions." If your spouse pushes your boundaries a little too hard, then instead of getting angry, learn to say no in a loving way. If you feel resentment or anger building, then learn to be assertive in expressing your feelings so that they can be resolved. If you are in an impossible marriage, take responsibility for finding legitimate outlets for your emotional and relational needs.

5. Act appropriately even when you don't feel like it.

When you *do* feel resentment, or not particularly loving toward your partner, it is important that you act in loving ways anyway. One technique for counseling couples is the idea of "Act, and the feelings will follow." Many couples run into trouble because they are neglecting what they know they should do because they just don't feel like it. "I don't want to say I'm sorry because I am still mad." "I don't want to go on that weekend retreat with her because I'm not feeling very romantic." "I don't want to tell him how I feel because I just don't want to get into a hassle right now." It is important that you do what is right and allow (or trust) that your feelings will follow.

6. Lean in the other direction.

We previously discussed your natural leanings. Where do you tend to get out of balance? If you are a people pleaser or a giver in the relationship, then you probably tend to say yes too much. You are taken advantage of in relationships. If this describes you, you need to lean the opposite way. In other words, practice saying no. Hold firmly to your boundaries and assert your feelings. Practice these skills until they become more natural.

On the other hand, you may lean toward being too harsh. Maybe you are the taker in the relationship. You like to be in charge, and when out of balance you are controlling and overbearing to your spouse. If this describes you, then you also need to lean in the opposite direction. You need to practice saying yes to your spouse. "Let's do it your way." Try to be more loving and giving in the marriage.

7. Discern between rights and responsibilities.

When do I have the right to say no? Has my spouse really crossed my boundary line? Or do I have the responsibility to try to go the extra mile in this case? These are important questions that become the source of inner conflict as well as family discord. When trying to sort out your proper response, it is often helpful to have third-party objectivity. A counselor or pastor may provide the help that you and your spouse need to sort through these difficult decisions.

Questions to Discuss

1. Talk with your spouse about your family background. Did you grow up with rigid boundaries or a lack of appropriate boundaries? How did it affect you growing up, and how does it affect your relationship?
2. When you get out of balance, which way do you lean? Do you mother or smother your spouse? Or do you distance and devalue your partner?
3. What other relationships, hobbies, or activities infringe on the boundaries of your relationship? Are you able to talk openly about this problem? And can you work together at holding these intruders at bay?
4. Discuss some steps you and your spouse can take to set more appropriate boundaries in your marriage. Set one goal for yourself over the next four to six weeks that will help you to improve in this area, and have your spouse hold you accountable for that goal.

For Further Reading

Henry Cloud and John Townsend, *Boundaries* (Grand Rapids: Zondervan, 1992).

Bill and Lynn Hybels, *Fit to Be Tied: Making Marrige Last a Lifetime* (Grand Rapids: Zondervan, 1997).

Thomas Whiteman and Thomas Bartlett, *The Marriage Mender: A Couple's Guide for Staying Together* (Colorado Springs: NavPress, 1996).

8

Developing
Sexual Intimacy

Christopher and Rachel McCluskey

> Your body needs to be held and to hold, to be touched and to touch. None
> of these needs is to be despised, denied, or repressed. But you have to
> keep searching for your body's deeper need, the need for genuine love.
>
> Henri J. M. Nouwen, *The Inner Voice of Love*

There is probably no single thing engaged couples look forward to
more than sexual union. From the passionate pages of the Song of
Songs to the playful flirtations of dating couples, the power of sexual
attraction is obvious and undeniable. It is an incredibly powerful force
and, like all powerful forces, it has potential for good as well as for
evil. Just as sexuality can deeply bond us in marriage, it can also harm
us more deeply than perhaps anything else.

Studies of marital conflict and divorce consistently cite sexuality as
one of the top three issues with which couples struggle. This shouldn't
surprise us, because there is no other area in which we are more vulnerable—naked physically, emotionally, and spiritually. If it is in sexual union that we are most aware of our oneness with another, it is
also here that we can feel most easily wounded, used, inadequate,

118

taken for granted, or violated. Sexual union is an outgrowth and a mirror of the intimacy (or lack thereof) in the rest of the marriage.

For all its importance, most couples come ill prepared to the marital bedroom. In some cases this is because of a lack of basic information, but increasingly, as a result of our sex-saturated culture, it is the result of receiving so much bad information. From so-called "values-free" sex education programs to the movies, television, music, fashion industry, magazines, advertising, the Internet, pornography, and teen culture, most people have developed a host of unrealistic expectations of sex. They place these expectations on themselves and their spouses and develop a running critique of how their sex life is measuring up to what they believe it should be like.

What is generally lacking is not just an awareness of techniques or skills but of what sex is for in the first place. As Jesus so often emphasized, the *spirit* of an act is more important than the act itself. As Christians, we need to look first at the *spirit* of sexual intimacy before dealing with the practical things that enhance or detract from that intimacy.

The Spirit of the Act

God is the creator of sex, and just like everything else he created, he has pronounced it good. It is true that if sex is taken outside of marriage, God has declared it a sin different from all other sins: "Run away from sexual sin! No other sin so clearly affects the body as this one does. For sexual immorality is a sin against your own body" (1 Cor. 6:18 NLT). And God repeatedly states that sexual sins can keep us from the kingdom. (See 1 Cor. 6:9, 10; Gal. 5:19–21; Eph. 5:5; Heb. 13:4; Rev. 21:8.) But within marriage, God is glorified and pleased with the one-flesh union of two whom he has joined together. He pronounces the marriage bed pure and undefiled, and he has chosen sexual union as the means by which we can participate in the generation of new life. Sex is a good and glorious thing when enjoyed within God's guidelines.

The idea of God being pleased with and even glorified by sexual intercourse feels foreign to many couples. We have seen several clients over the years who never got past the idea that sex was dirty or a necessary evil. I have worked with couples who were unwilling to consummate their marriage, or who did so only to become pregnant, because of "knowing that God could see them." Sex still felt somehow wrong.

It is critical for couples to understand that when a man and woman who love each other have pledged themselves in holy matrimony, God is *pleased* with their enjoyment of his gift of sexuality. His desire is that they delight in each other sexually and that they come together frequently. (See Song of Songs 5:1; Prov. 5:19; 1 Cor. 7:3–5.)

A Form of Communication

If you take nothing else away from this chapter, please remember this: *Sexual union is first and foremost a means of communication.* We communicate powerful messages to each other and to the Lord when we join ourselves sexually. It is an incredibly intimate form of communication, enabling us to say things that our words cannot about our spiritual oneness.

The word *intercourse* conveys this notion of communication; it is not a specifically sexual term but simply means to have an exchange or a communing between persons. Couples need to ensure that the messages of their *verbal* intercourse and *relational* intercourse line up with the messages of their *sexual* intercourse. If they are communicating love throughout the day in the ways they serve, honor, and cherish each other, then the joining of their bodies in lovemaking bears testimony to that love. If, however, they are communicating anger, hatred, criticism, neglect, or disdain, the statement of their sexual union then becomes a lie. With their bodies they are saying, "I love you so much that I want to have every part of you and to give you every part of me," but they have communicated something entirely different throughout the day.

Deeply Knowing Each Other

Obviously, millions of people have sex all the time without truly loving each other or being committed in marriage, and many seem to have wildly fantastic sex lives. The problem is that not only are they living in sin and separating themselves from the Father, they are also missing out on the fullness of God's intentions for sexual union. As couples continue to mature throughout marriage, they can learn much through their sexual relationship about truly giving and receiving love, serving, patience, commitment, surrender, transparency—in short, about intimacy.

Intimacy is the process of coming to deeply know another and to be known by him or her. This is perhaps why Scripture so often refers to sexual intercourse as "knowing" each other. (See Gen. 4:1, 17, 25; 38:26; Matt. 1:25.) Our spouses are to become the one person on the planet we know more deeply than anyone else, and sexual knowledge can be the most intimate experience of that "knowing." As couples deepen their love for each other through the years and regularly express that love through sexual union, their sex lives evolve and become richer instead of growing stale, predictable, and boring.

The wildest sexual escapades fail to satisfy if they are only about chasing orgasms. But sometimes even the awkward lovemaking of an elderly couple, shared in the passion of decades of deeply knowing each other, is soul satisfying beyond measure. Our bodies will age no matter what we do; we'll get flabby and have stretch marks and our "equipment" won't work as it once did. But a sex life based on commitment, intimacy, giving and receiving, and shared in the assurance that God has blessed and delights in our union will satisfy for a lifetime.

Practical Applications

It Takes Patience

Building on this clearer understanding of God's intentions, we can look at some of the keys to developing a passionately intimate sex life. One of the most important of these is *patience*. It takes years to develop an intimate and mature sexual relationship, just as it takes years to develop an intimate and mature marriage. Couples must get rid of the notion that sex is going to immediately blossom into a consistently wonderful experience as soon as the rings are on the fingers. In fact one of the first fights many couples have over sex is on the wedding night or sometime during the honeymoon.

We lost count long ago of the women who have reported to us that they cried on their honeymoons because intercourse hurt or because their husbands made a critical remark. They cried because they were unable to achieve orgasm, became "triggered" due to past sexual abuse, were forced into activity they didn't like, or experienced some other trauma. Several couples have told us of going to see a gynecologist on their honeymoon because they feared something must be wrong—"It sure wasn't like we thought it would be!" A more realistic perspective on the time and patience required to learn about each other's bodies and the complexity of expressing love sexually could have prevented much of this pain.

A bad start can result in couples creating a self-fulfilling prophecy. Having come with faulty expectations and then discovering that things aren't like the movies, they conclude that there must be something wrong with them—"He's like an animal!" or "She must be frigid!" Any future struggles reinforce these beliefs and before long couples can actually create their own worst fears. They begin to dread being sexual. So it becomes easier to avoid it, or to simply get it over with as quickly as possible. As soon as they begin to be sexual, they become tense, self-conscious, and critical, none of which makes for intimate and enjoyable lovemaking.

Learning to Play

A second key ingredient for a fulfilling sex life is fostering a spirit of *playfulness*. Just as Christ taught that we cannot see the kingdom of God unless we come as a little child, couples cannot experience the fullness of sexual intimacy unless they come to it in childlike wonder, curiosity, and playfulness. The grown-up parts of us don't have much place in the bedroom. Disrobing and arousing each other calls for a spirit of adventure, of teasing, risk-taking, and a bit of wild-eyed invitation to join us in playful exploration.

It Takes Time

Another key component is *time*. In our fast-paced modern culture, even newlyweds can easily allow their relations to lapse into a pattern of ten-minute "quickies" before they clunk off to sleep. If couples are emotionally connected, there is certainly nothing wrong with the occasional quickie. But just as we shouldn't make a dietary habit of fast-food restaurants, couples must guard against a sexual diet of quickies. They don't feed and nourish the relationship. The Song of Songs speaks to the importance of taking time: "My lover has gone down to his garden, to the beds of spices, to browse in the gardens and to gather lilies. I am my lover's and my lover is mine; he browses among the lilies" (Song of Songs 6:2–3).

Always Use CERTS

A couple we worked with came across an acronym that is helpful in identifying additional keys to a satisfying sex life; couples should always use *CERTS!* Each letter stands for an important piece of truly making love:

"C" is for consent. Sex should never be forced, whether through physical coercion or through threats, fear of infidelity, or guilt. Lovemaking demands mutual consent if there is to be a meeting of souls and spirits.

"E" is for equality. Both persons' pleasure and fulfillment should be of equal importance. This is not sex for the man. Although there may be times when a wife is not particularly focused on her own pleasure and is desirous of simply attending to her husband, this should never become a habit. The long-term results will be dissatisfying for both the husband and the wife. Lovemaking is about giving and receiving.

"R" is for respect. Partners must respect each other's wishes. If one or the other is not in the mood on a given day, or is feeling uncomfortable about a particular position or act, the best way to make love is to respect his or her feelings and not criticize or shame him or her. Similarly, if one is desirous of trying something new, he or she must not be made to feel that he or she is a "pervert." These differing interests need to be discussed, but the vulnerability required to talk openly calls for tremendous sensitivity and respect on both persons' parts. (Satan loves to target couples in this area.)

"T" is for trust. If trust is absent or has been badly damaged, the best a couple can do is simply "have sex" rather than truly make love until that trust is restored. The acts are the same, but the spirit is entirely different. When couples are recovering from an affair or other serious breach of trust, we discourage them from coming together sexually until a real measure of healing has been established. First Corinthians 7:5 says, "Do not deprive each other except by mutual consent and for a time, so that you can devote yourselves to prayer." This is such a time, a time for prayer and fasting and healing. *Then* a couple can come together and their lovemaking will be the beautiful statement of oneness it was meant to be.

"S" is for safety. This one should be obvious. Couples should not encourage any kind of sexual activity that is not safe. A number of acts that are joked about and encouraged in pornography are not safe and are therefore not loving and God-honoring, even within the bonds of marriage. Safety also pertains to engaging in relations after an affair, if testing has not been done to ensure that the offending spouse has not contracted HIV/AIDS or some other sexually transmitted disease. Lack of safety will introduce a spirit of fear into the bedroom that should never be present in lovemaking—"Perfect love casts out fear" (1 John 4:18 NASB).

Embracing Sensuality

Attention to the senses—*sensuality*—is another critical piece of sexual intimacy. It has been said that the most important sex organ we have is between our ears. Our mind can turn us on and turn us off regardless of what our partner may be doing. But sexual arousal is also greatly cued by our senses: sight, smell, touch, sound, and taste. All of our senses can be played upon to enhance the experience of soaking up and losing ourselves in each other.

Examine the repertoire of sensate cues that arouse you both. If candlelight, soft music, a fan blowing, silk negligees/boxers, perfumes/colognes, a hot bath, or any number of other things enhance your connection with the moment without detracting from your focus on each other, they are to be encouraged. Marital sexual union doesn't have to be relegated to "lights out, no talking, missionary position" to be God-honoring. If anything, that can be the antithesis of God's invitation to "drink your fill" and to be captivated or "intoxicated" by each other's love. (See Song of Songs 5:1; Prov. 5:19.) Discuss and incorporate things that enhance your celebration of oneness in the same way you incorporate decorations, music, foods, and various rituals to enhance the experience of holiday celebrations.

In keeping with this theme, take care of your bodies so they are pleasing and arousing for your spouse. This doesn't mean you need to be a hard body, but Scripture teaches that our bodies are not our own, for "the wife gives authority over her body to her husband, and the husband also gives authority over his body to his wife" (1 Cor. 7:4 NLT). So our bodies are a gift we present to our spouse, and we should want them to be pleased with our gift. The lovers in the Song of Solomon delight in praising every part of each other's bodies, in spite of the beloved acknowledging her imperfections. (See Song of Songs 1:5–6.) As Christians, we are called to be good stewards of all that God has entrusted to us, and that certainly includes our bodies.

Naked and Unashamed

This raises another important ingredient: learning to be "naked and unashamed" (Gen. 2:25) as Adam and Eve were. We will never experience the perfection of Eden until the new heaven and earth, but as marriages mature they can experience at least some of the intimacy and innocence Adam and Eve must have enjoyed. Work to become more comfortable talking openly with each other about your sexual preferences and dislikes. Develop your own language for cueing each other throughout the day, to help each other anticipate and make time for lovemaking.

Wrestle through any body image problems: "I'm too fat or too skinny, too short or too tall." "I'm ashamed of my physical disability or surgical scars or other impairments." The media has told us that fulfilling sex is only for beautiful people. Nothing could be further from the truth. *There is nothing so arousing and deeply satisfying as a partner giving himself or herself completely in lovemaking.* Orgasm occurs at the point of surrender, when you can no longer hold back the flood of sensations and emotions you are experiencing. Practice a reckless abandon in the giving of yourself and deal with anything that threatens to block your ability to do so. This is the lover's request in the Song of Solomon when he states, "Catch for us the foxes, the little foxes that ruin the vineyards, our vineyards that are in bloom" (Song of Songs 2:15). Chase feelings of shame and reservation out of your bedroom.

Basking in the Afterglow

One of the worst mistakes a couple can make after lovemaking is to simply roll over and turn out the light, or to jump out of bed to clean up, breaking those few precious moments of afterglow. This is arguably the most intimate time in lovemaking, because not only are you fully naked before each other and still joined in physical oneness, but your central nervous systems are no longer carrying you along. You could easily choose to disconnect from each other because your bodies are no longer screaming for release. But it is here, choosing instead to soak up an awareness of what has just been shared, that couples can most powerfully affirm their love for each other and their delight in being together.

The afterglow period need only be a few minutes—not nearly so long as the other phases of lovemaking—but the verbal affirmations, cuddling, and caressing are important for cementing an awareness of how much you love each other. Without this brief time of basking, partners can easily feel used or taken for granted. It is here that couples are best able to gauge whether they have made love or simply had sex. Spend time with each other in the afterglow.

Questions to Discuss

1. What are some of the messages about sex that you brought to your marriage, whether from your family of origin, your peers, or the culture?
2. What are the sensate things that most cue you for sexual arousal? What are the ones that most easily turn you off?
3. What could be the "little foxes" in your relationship?
4. In what ways have you already been wounded sexually, whether by your spouse or in previous relationships? How can your spouse help you heal from those wounds?

For Further Reading

Archibald D. Hart et al., *Secrets of Eve: Understanding the Mystery of Female Sexuality* (Nashville: Word, 1998).

Douglas E. Rosenau, *A Celebration of Sex* (Nashville: Thomas Nelson, 1994).

9

Money Matters

David and Janet Congo

We worship it, have love affairs with it, blame it, hate it, dream about it, live for it, curse it, pray for more of it, sacrifice our families for it, hand over control of our lives for it, and wind up in bondage to it. It is our best friend and our worst enemy.

Mary Hunt, *The Cheapskate Monthly Money Makeover*

Money matters in a marriage relationship. Money may be an inanimate object, but we attach great emotional significance to it. Money only becomes our friend if we as a couple learn to partner around the decisions related to money. One of the prerequisites for partnering in the matter of money is an understanding of the meaning of money to each of us.

Early in our marriage, we had the opportunity to build a home up in Canada. I (Dave) acted as the general contractor and actually did a great deal of the construction with my two brothers and father. As with any building project, it cost more than we expected. But I just didn't bother to tell Jan that we were exceeding our budget. I wanted to appear capable to her, and I didn't want to disappoint her. The bottom line was that I kept her out of the loop. I kept her in a position of ignorance to protect my ego. When the truth came out, she felt deceived, betrayed, and felt that I had viewed her as a child who couldn't handle the truth. My motivation had been to protect her, not to hurt her. However, because I did not operate in partnership with her and for personal reasons made decisions entirely on my own, she felt deeply hurt. Through that painful experience, we both learned some important things about the meaning of money.

Money Means Different Things to Different People

Jesus tells us, "Wherever your treasure is, there your heart and thoughts will also be" (Luke 12:34 NLT). Why is it easier to open our hearts to each other but close up our hearts when it comes to working together on our finances? Because money problems are seldom about money. On the surface, the issue appears to be financial; however, that is rarely the case. There are deeper issues related to the meaning of money. Here are some examples of those who are dealing with issues other than what they appear to be—money matters.

- Carson admitted breaking into a hot sweat the day he and his bride signed up for a joint credit card. His anxiety increased. Could he really trust her? Would she put their financial future in jeopardy by her choices?
- Julie couldn't wait to leave home. She wanted to get out where no one would tell her what to do. She believed the less accountability, the greater the freedom. Now marriage made her feel restricted.
- Rick loved being the center of attention. His approval rating system demanded that he go into major debt to buy things for his friends.
- Sue used money as an antidepressant, a mood changer; so did Joe, who equated money with status. He had to have the latest clothes, toys, and cars. A new purchase worked miracles for both of them. But the fix was temporary.
- Juan only feels secure when he has a substantial savings account, so he constantly criticizes Patricia for her spending habits. She is wise in her expenditures. But he can't see that because his fear blinds him.
- Christy was struggling with a conflict between being dependent and independent. She wanted to feel protected, provided for,

and nurtured by her husband, Ken, so she had been happy to let him handle all the finances. Yet, she was becoming increasingly uncomfortable with some of his choices. It made Ken uncomfortable to hear Christy question some of his decisions.

- Lee was happy to make the money decisions because he wanted to control his own destiny. It made him feel important, and he didn't want to repeat his parents' pattern. After retirement his parents were totally dependent on him.

There is an incredible vulnerability that comes when we give another person access to our finances. The reality is they can now hurt us very badly by taking or misusing the information we have given them.

Prior to marriage, many of us had to answer only to ourselves. A major shift occurred as we began our married life. We are now accountable to each other. How do you react when someone limits you? This is where "iron sharpens iron" (see Prov. 27:17) and the sparks begin to fly.

What I want can seem so much more reasonable than what you want. Will my contribution be valued as much as yours? What if you use "my money" to purchase something I disapprove of? Will I be able to influence you? Is the money I earn my money, your money, or our money? What if I delight in spending money on us while you spend money only on yourself?

Often money fights end up fueling insecurities rather than resolving them. When Dwayne loses his temper over Shauna's spending habits, it makes her fear that he is trying to control her, and she feels she is about to lose all of her autonomy, especially her financial autonomy. When Shauna gets infuriated at Dwayne's critical comments, it fuels his fear that she is financially impulsive and unpredictable.

It's clear that money means different things to different people. But what does money represent to you? Put a check by the meanings that apply to you, and then discuss together what you have checked.

Husband	Meaning of Money	Wife
_____	Status	_____
_____	Self-worth	_____
_____	Trust	_____
_____	Security	_____

_____	Satisfaction	_____
_____	Nurturance	_____
_____	Control over your destiny	_____
_____	Control over your mate	_____
_____	Independence	_____
_____	Dependence	_____

As you discuss the different meanings money has to you, note how much of your personal meaning about money comes from your past, from your growing-up years.

Money Handling Mimics Our Background

For many of us money is the mirror that reflects our youthful fantasies and our struggles to make these fantasies come true. Daniel's father had always appeared to him as being weak and impotent. His mother definitely ran the show. What she wanted she got. Her tyranny stretched into the financial area as well. Even though his father brought home the bacon, he had no input on how it was spent.

Daniel married Kimberly. He kept her in the dark about their finances. She knew the contribution she was expected to make financially, but beyond that she had no idea what their financial situation was like. Daniel would promise to sit down and discuss this area with her, but there never seemed to be time to do it. He would get sidetracked and never follow through. However, he would analyze and criticize every purchase Kimberly made, and she was tired of being perceived as the enemy.

Money becomes a magical screen on which we project our fears, frustration, and dreams. Each of us must search our histories for clues as to why we have the attitudes we do with regard to money.

Background Check

Discuss the following questions with your mate:

- How did your input during your wedding planning reveal your attitude about finances?

- What did you learn about money from your parents' attitude regarding finances?
- Who made your financial decisions before you were married?
- Who paid your bills?
- Where did you get your money?
- How did your parents partner around financial issues while you were growing up?
- What meaning do you think each of your parents gave to money?
- Was there an overindulger in your family? Explain who and why.
- Was there an underindulger in your family? Explain who and why.
- How were credit cards handled in your family?
- Was there a person who was capable of more earning potential, but who never chose to move out of his or her comfort zone to try? Explain.
- Has anyone in your family had a gambling addiction?
- Did you have a job growing up?
- What kinds of jobs did you have?
- Did you get an allowance?
- How did you handle the money you got?
- Were you raised on a budget?
- Were you accountable to anyone other than yourself for what you spent?
- Who in your background has positively influenced you the most in financial matters? What is it you admire about them?

Marriage Magnifies Our Personal Tendencies

Each of us enters marriage with established spending habits and expectations about our future lifestyle. Prior to marriage were you ever debt-free? If your answer is no, your natural tendency probably was to overindulge. Perhaps your philosophy was "eat, drink, and be merry!" (Luke 12:19). You thought that somehow the money would always be there. Believing yourself to be deserving, it was all too easy to use credit cards and get home equity loans and lines of credit instead of budgeting and balancing your checkbook.

If you were a responsible overindulger, you settled your debts. If you were irresponsible, you acquired immense debt, which you eventually tried to escape again by acquiring yet more debt or by filing bankruptcy. Regardless of your style, as an overindulger, you no doubt faced incredible emotional stress, reduced flexibility, and restricted freedom. Perhaps you became a workaholic.

Often overindulgers marry underindulgers who perceive themselves one step away from financial disaster at all points in time. The underindulger uses money as a guarantee that there is "enough." How much does it take to feel secure? The underindulger always feels like it will take a little bit more to feel safe and secure. So he or she becomes stingy and hoards and stockpiles all financial assets. While appearing responsible, underindulgers often deny themselves or their mate the basic necessities of life. They can't really enjoy what they have.

If one mate is an overindulger and the other is an underindulger, a dangerous pattern will be established. It becomes like a precocious child who is joined in marriage to a withholding, critical parent. Neither partner really chooses to be adult and responsible. Double standards create resentments. One mate may overindulge him or herself and underindulge the spouse. Enough is never enough for both the overindulger and the underindulger.

Responsible adult choices lie at the balance point between overindulging and underindulging. Both of you have something to contribute to your relationship. The underindulger takes care of the necessities, and the overindulger who is generous and more impulsive demonstrates that it is okay to enjoy money. Both of you will need to give a little for the good of your relationship.

What are your spending habits? Rate yourself. Place an "x" where you think you fit on the following continuum:

_____

Overindulger   Underindulger

Now rate your mate. Place an "x" where you think your spouse fits on the following continuum:

_____

Overindulger   Underindulger

Money Moves Us toward Maturity

Trustworthy money management requires self-reflection, vulnerability, and the ability to communicate nondefensively and nonjudgmentally. It requires a sharing of roles, which will only happen if both partners have an equal voice. The ability to set joint goals and to make joint decisions is foundational to maturity.

Randy stopped working to start his own business with his wife's blessing. Nancy continued working full time to support the family during the transition. Randy felt pressured by family and friends who often inquired about how his business was going. As a result, he worked longer and harder, which led to exhaustion and bitterness when he didn't see results. When a bill would arrive at the house, he would accuse Nancy of overspending.

Nancy knew he was having a difficult time and was trying to be understanding of his situation. She wanted to start a family in the next few years and worried about having to postpone that dream if Randy didn't succeed. She limited her spending and felt overburdened by having to be the sole provider. There were times that she unconsciously resented her husband and his business. In the past six months he had brought in no income. He had only drained their resources.

Randy and Nancy were having a difficult time adjusting to a new balance of power. If Randy gets honest with himself, he has to admit that he is threatened by his wife being the sole breadwinner. He feels guilty when he sees her tired and overworked. He is struggling with feelings of insecurity and inadequacy. Both his wife and her job are glaring reminders of his loss of productivity. He feels like he is losing control in his marriage. The only way he can remind her that she needs him is to pester her about how much she is spending.

Nancy resents not only the burden she feels falls on her shoulders, she is also hurt by what she sees as Randy's lack of gratitude for her contribution. She finds herself withdrawing from him. She has been counting on him to make enough in his new business so that she could stay at home and start a family. His disappointment in his business becomes her disappointment. She won't complain for fear of increasing the burden on Randy, yet she finds herself angry and irritated. The responsibility of paying all the bills rests on her shoulders and is frightening to her. She is beginning to question the wisdom of their decision about who would handle the money. She also fears becoming the dominant one in the relationship and worries that this will in some way cause her to lose her femininity.

Both Randy and Nancy can move toward maturity by acknowledging their reality, discussing that reality, and the role that money is starting to play in their lives. They will need to discuss their expectations, their frustrations, and perhaps their naiveté. Maturity might mean that Randy will seek part-time employment so he can participate in their income while pursuing his dream. It also might mean abandoning his business at this time. Randy must come to grips with the fact that his self-esteem requires him to make more money. Nancy and he might benefit from setting up a joint account that they work on together, so she could have some control of her own spending and also some knowledge of where they are financially. Working through this issue led both Randy and Nancy to a deeper understanding of themselves and growth in their maturity as a couple.

Maturity also requires an ability to set boundaries on our own wishes and wants, and it involves the ability to delay immediate gratification. It requires individual integrity and the willingness to be accountable to your mate. A fulfilling marriage will open us up emotionally, will increase our willingness to be vulnerable and to be generous. It will expand our horizons, motivate us toward maturity, and move us in the direction of greater partnership. The apostle Paul wrote these words, "Let the peace of Christ keep you in tune with each other, in step with each other. None of this going off and doing your own thing" (Col. 3:15 THE MESSAGE).

Money Can Magnify the Lord

The principles we live by create the world we live in. What we believe shapes how we feel and what we do. Our money behavior is a direct reflection of our beliefs. As Christians we have a different philosophy about money than the world in which we live. We have the opportunity to magnify the Lord by the priorities we set with regard to money.

The world's priorities	Scriptural priorities
Earn	Earn
Enjoy	Give
Repay	Save
Save	Repay
Give	Enjoy

We magnify God by acknowledging that God is the source of all good things. All that comes to us, including our finances, comes from him. He alone can meet our need for security, self-esteem, and significance. As children of God, we recognize that our net worth has nothing to do with our self-worth. In God's economy, who we are has nothing to do with what we have.

We magnify God by being responsible with our debt. Debt is never the problem; it is only symptomatic of an underlying issue such as impatience, lack of self-discipline, selfishness, or greed. Having a debt is not a sin, but not repaying it is.

We magnify God with our money by giving freely, joyfully, sacrificially, generously, and sometimes anonymously. The last year of Dave's doctoral program, we didn't have two pennies to rub together. Because of unusual circumstances, we did not qualify for either Canadian or American student loans (Dave is from Canada). We were under severe financial pressure. Once a month, we would receive a white envelope with a crisp one-hundred-dollar bill inside and a slip of paper with a Bible verse typed on it. That was our food money for the month. To this day we have no idea where that gift came from, but we were blessed by someone's anonymous generosity.

Have you ever been the recipient of someone's generosity? As a couple, have you ever had the fun of surprising someone in need with your generosity? It brings new energy to your partnership.

Money is a neutral commodity. It is not power, pleasure, freedom, happiness, or security. It can't make us happy. It can't ensure a problem-free future. In and of itself, it doesn't have power. Yet our money habits betray our character and affect the quality of our life. As Christian couples, we want to use money to move us toward maturity, to model partnership, and to magnify the Lord.

Practical Suggestions for Partnering

Work with your mate to create financial goals. What does financial success mean to you? Talk about your hopes and dreams. Write them down. What difference would it make in your life if these dreams became reality? Pray together about your goals. List what each of you contributes to the relationship financially. Together write down the following:

- How much each of you earns
- The balance in bank accounts you have
- The outstanding debt you have
- The investments you have individually and together
- The assets you have individually and together
- The trust funds you have

Discuss your financial preferences with regard to the following question: How jointly and separately do you want to operate? Here are some possibilities to discuss:

- Mates combine their earnings and have equal access to a joint account.
- One mate covers certain expenses and the other carries the rest of the expenses. Some couples suggest that if you earn one half of your mate's salary, you pay one half of the bills.
- Split the expenses down the middle. Joint accounts are kept for joint expenses and individual accounts for personal expenses. A joint savings account or money market fund account is used to save toward mutual goals.
- Have separate but not equal finances. One couple saved the husband's income and lived off the wife's income so that when they wanted to start a family, she would have the option of being a stay-at-home mother.

The bottom line is there is no perfectly right way for everyone. Together you need to discover what works best for the two of you. Don't be upset if you have differing philosophies about money. Ask yourself what you need to know about your mate to better understand his or her perspective on money. Attribute positive intentions to your mate. Remember, he or she is not the problem. You are working together as a team to solve the problem.

If you find you are feuding over finances, stop! Take a time-out and answer these questions individually before discussing them together:

- Do you see this money issue as a challenge to your values or goals?
- Is this a major offense to your comfort level?
- Are you stuck on this money issue because you haven't been honest with your mate and you are really angry about another more vital issue?

Then come back to the drawing board and together create and implement a shared spending plan that takes into account each of your concerns. It needs to address the long-term problem of debt if that applies to your situation. There needs to be a plan of record keeping and a mutually agreeable budget established.

Agree to reevaluate your shared spending plan at the end of a certain period of time. Choose a time when you are both rested and full. Remember, "The road to hell is paved with good intentions," so follow through on your plan or revise it. Manage yourself. Take care of yourself mentally, emotionally, physically, and spiritually so that you are in a good place personally rather than coming to your partnership with an attitude of deprivation.

Before purchasing anything, ask yourself these tried and true questions:

- Do I really need this?
- Do I already own something that would substitute?
- Can I find a cheaper alternative?

Then wait a week before you make your purchase. At the end of the week ask yourself these questions again, and then ask if this still seems like a wise purchase. Be passionate about the options you have ahead of you and stick to your plan. Encourage each other. Once a month celebrate your successes.

Discuss together your attitude about tithing and giving. Do you agree regarding this principle, or is this something you need to study more together and discuss? If this is an issue, read together some of the books suggested or talk with your pastor about these principles.

For Further Reading

David Bach; *Smart Couples Finish Rich* (Westminster, Md.: Broadway Books, 2002).

Ron Blue; *Master Your Money* (Nashville: Thomas Nelson, 1997).

Mark Bryan and Julia Cameron, *Money Drunk, Money Sober: 90 Days to Financial Freedom* (Westminster, Md.: Ballantine Books, 1999).

Larry Burkett, *Debt-Free Living* (Chicago: Moody Press, 2001).

George S. Clason, *The Richest Man in Babylon* (East Rutherford, N.J.: Putnam Penguin, 1997).

David and Janet Congo; *LifeMates: A Lover's Guide for a Lifetime Relationship* (Colorado Springs: Cook Communications, 2002).

Jerrold Mundis; *How to Get Out of Debt, Stay Out of Debt and Live Prosperously* (Westminster, Md.: Bantam, 1990).

10

Setting Goals and Priorities in Your Marriage

Don and Jan Harvey

A cord of three strands is not quickly broken.

Ecclesiastes 4:12b

We received lots of advice before we got married, both individually and as a couple. Most of it consisted of pat phrases and humorous stories that had obvious points about personal sacrifice or respect for one another. Unfortunately, the only serious advice came from a few close relatives telling us, "It's going to take work." Even though the phrase was rather vague, we thought we knew what it meant. After all, we were in our twenties, in love, and on our own. We'd formed our identities and we were ready! Ready to commit to a lifetime together.

The goals we actually discussed were limited to always speaking positively about each other in public and living within our budget, which was a pretty tough one at the time. Maintaining love and a couple-focused relationship seemed a pretty natural endeavor in the beginning, and the need to develop a plan to keep it that way never entered our heads. After all, wasn't that God's job? He had brought us together, and we were committed to him. Surely he would provide for us, both in giving us direction for our lives and in keeping our relationship on track. Well, as Grandmother used to say, "God feeds the little birds, but he doesn't stuff it in their mouths," and we had a lot to learn about our role in establishing priorities that would keep our relationship strong and intimate in the midst of the day-to-day stresses of life. We'd like to share with you what we wish someone had shared with us. So let's start at the beginning. And we do mean *the beginning*.

We are given the design for marriage early in Scripture. "Therefore a man shall *leave* his father and mother and be *joined* [bonded] to his wife, and they shall become one flesh" (Gen. 2:24 NKJV, italics added). It is a simple model and has only two stages—first you *leave* and then you *cleave*. But following the design is imperative to the success of any relationship. God realizes that if you do not detach from the family of your birth, there is no way you will be able to attach to your spouse. And attaching is what marriage is all about.

Like a lot of things in life, this two-stage model is not nearly as simple as it appears. It sounds as if once you get the first step accomplished—making the break from home—then the second is a breeze. It sounds as if attaching is done in one clean swoop. But this is not how things work. You are designed for intimacy, for closeness. Your marriage is to be an intimate relationship. But intimacy, joining and bonding, always requires time and only occurs through a process. Leaving home (though also a process) seems to be something that is visibly accomplished. You reach a goal. But bonding to your spouse is something you will spend the rest of your life working on. You will not get it accomplished once and for all. And the understanding of this concept of process is not something young couples generally bring to marriage.

By design, a marriage is supposed to grow. Remember, we are in process. And being in process, there is probably nothing more important in encouraging this growth to occur than for you to have goals and priorities for your relationship.

The Best of Intentions

When we married, we intended to be happy. We were eager to experience life and marriage together and let the happiness emerge. Just like you. Being marital therapists and working with thousands of couples has taught us something sobering about marriage: All couples marry *intending* to be happy. Few marry *planning* to be happy. And this difference makes a difference.

When you think about it, initially in a marriage it seems natural to have an aversion to planning. The idea of having to plan for intimacy seems to take the romance—the spontaneity—out of the relationship. Establishing a plan to prevent us from becoming distant later on seems fairly artificial to newlyweds. After all, things are great. Some of you have already decided on a partial plan, like having a date night once a week. That's a great idea, but realize when life interferes (and it will), it's easy to abandon the plan for the seemingly important need of the moment. And pretty soon, you realize you haven't had that date night in way too long. What we want you to realize is the hard truth that love for a lifetime doesn't just happen—it takes thinking through and establishing priorities. Then it takes creating a workable plan to keep your love alive, no matter what.

Why, you may ask, is it such a big deal to establish this plan early in our marriage? Current national divorce statistics show that most divorces occur for couples married less than five years and the proportion of divorces is highest for couples married three years (National Center for Health Statistics, 1995). Wow! You definitely want to take preventative action early in your marriage. You can prevent your relationship from being one of those statistics. In 2000, the Center for Marriage and Family at Creighton University conducted a national study with couples that had been married five years or less. One purpose was to ascertain what were the most significant problems newly married couples experienced. Can you guess what the number one problem was? The highest ranked problematic issue was "balancing time and relationship" (*Time, Sex, and Money,* Center for Marriage and Family, 2000). For most newly married couples who are beginning their careers and their marriages around the same time, this is a huge issue.

Do you know what came in number two? "Frequency of sexual relations." Research tells us there is a significant drop in sexual activity after year two of marriage (Christopher and Sprecher, 2000). Problem number two relates strongly back to problem number one. If you aren't experiencing enough time with your spouse, or if the time spent together is spent dealing totally with the details of life, you lose touch emotionally. Your physical intimacy diminishes along with your emotional intimacy. This ebbing away of intimacy doesn't wave any red flags of warning—it's very subtle. If you don't have a plan in place to prevent it, you've gone over the waterfall before you even realized you were drifting downstream.

To plan is to have a method for carrying out a design or for doing something. When you fail to plan, you leave the most important aspect of your marriage (your love) to the pulls and pressures of an ever-increasingly hurried lifestyle. You begin to equate activity with happiness and the urgent with the important. We have found that establishing an *intimacy plan* early in our life together was one of the wisest things we have ever done for our marriage. As one of our favorite sayings puts it, "If things aren't going according to plan, perhaps there never was one." Healthy marriages follow a road that is planned. You do not have to plan in order to fail. That can be accomplished without planning and usually is. But you *do* have to plan to succeed.

Creating the Context for Intimacy

We are created as unique individuals. We then marry and form equally unique relationships. No two of us are completely alike, so it could seem a little presumptuous for *us* to suggest goals and priorities for *your* marriage. But even though no two of us are exactly the same, people do seem to share a lot in common. So what we'd like to suggest as goals and priorities for your marriage are specific things that are applicable to all relationships.

There is no one thing you can do that will automatically and instantaneously give you an intimate relationship. If experience has taught us anything, it is this: Nothing just happens, whether good or bad. Daily behaviors establish a pattern, and patterns establish a lifestyle. Remember, intimacy is a process. However, what establishing goals and priorities for your marriage will do is this: It will *create the context* in which your intimacy can develop. It's like growing plants in a greenhouse. Though the strong north wind is ferociously blowing and the snowdrifts are getting deeper and deeper outside, the plants in the greenhouse are flourishing. In the context of the greenhouse, they are protected from the harsh winter environment. In the same way, establishing goals for your behavior in your relationship and prioritizing your marriage establishes the context in which it too can flourish.

Some Basic Goals for Your Marriage

For the sake of clarity, we are defining basic goals in a marriage as behavioral decisions. And they always represent a decision to hold your commitment to the needs of the relationship over personal comfort. So, are you ready and willing to do that? Read that sentence again. Are you both really committed to doing what's necessary for the relationship to flourish? Even if it means your personal comfort level is stretched? If you are, then that's a huge step and one that you both should verbally acknowledge together. That establishes the foundation of giving priority to each other that's needed to produce a healthy marriage. There are really three areas in which you can set behavioral goals toward developing emotional intimacy: dealing, sharing, and giving.

Choosing to Deal

Dealing is a term that describes how well you handle conflict in your relationship. There are times in your marriage when your spouse does something that prompts you to become angry. This usually centers around disappointment, hurt, or frustration with something either said or done. Though becoming angry is not something we like to have happen, it's not really of great concern to us for it is neither unusual nor sinful (see Eph. 4:26).

What is of concern, however, is how this anger is handled. Healthy communication patterns require an honest, direct, and appropriate stating of exactly how you feel. You don't keep your anger to yourself. You don't go into a rage and attack your partner. You don't deny your anger and say, "What? Me angry? Of course I'm not angry." And why should you deal with your anger instead of avoiding it? Simply because avoidance does not help anything. Nothing gets resolved and nothing changes. In fact, with a little time, everything gets much worse. (We define *resentment* as "anger with a history.") Instead of drawing closer, you end up erecting a wall between you and your spouse or even pushing him or her away.

So if nothing good comes from avoiding our anger and the healthy thing is for us to deal honestly and directly with our spouse, why don't we just do that? Because doing the healthy thing is not always the easy thing. Dealing with your spouse about your anger may create some personal discomfort. And rather than do what your relationship needs for you to do (to resolve your anger), you opt for something safer— you avoid. At least it appears safer.

We once met with a couple whose marriage had gradually grown cold and distant. This wasn't what either had wanted in the beginning, but things just seemed to get beyond their control. They came to therapy when things had gotten so bad that they considered divorce. Though there were several issues that seemed to surface, there was also a clear pattern that greatly contributed to their difficulty. Tim was avoidant. He would rather tell Susan a little lie, or leave out an important piece of information, than say something that might displease her. (Tim had not mastered the concept of "the truth, the whole truth, and nothing but the truth.") We observed Susan, and she was not "greatly to be feared." Because this was obviously more of a Tim issue than a Susan issue, we asked him what he was thinking.

> I don't like it when Susan gets upset. It really makes me uncomfortable. So I try to put it off as long as I can. I know that she'll eventually find out what I've done. But I'd rather face the music later than have to experience it now.

Tim was being shortsighted, because there was much more at stake here than *when* Susan was going to get upset with him. His line of reasoning was effectively destroying any trust that Susan had in him. She could never quite believe anything he said. Not only did Tim's avoidance destroy Susan's ability to trust, it also prevented him from dealing with the things that bothered him about her behavior. So these too went unchecked and unresolved. Gradually, they grew apart.

Establishing the goal of facing and dealing with your anger is done to protect your marriage. You don't do this because it's fun, or because it's easy. You do it because it's necessary for the survival of your marriage, and because you are more committed to your relationship with your spouse than you are to your own personal comfort level.

Choosing to Share

Sharing is also a choice. We're not talking about sharing the details of your workday, though it's important to do that. We're talking about sharing your heart. The sharing of yourself, who you are, your dreams, why you think as you do, your fears can be risky business—especially if you came from a family in which emotional sharing was not validated, or even heard. Perhaps in your family no one cared how you felt. Maybe sharing certain emotions was even perceived as being weak. We've counseled couples in which one spouse or the other didn't know the first thing about how to disclose feelings. It wasn't because they didn't want to. They'd never experienced even identifying their own feelings, much less talking to someone about them. Sharing is also often harder for the more introverted spouse. They're thinking about what they're feeling and processing those thoughts, and processing, and processing. But when they share, they've owned those feelings, and you can believe what they're saying is true. Be patient.

The point here is that sharing has to happen. It has to happen to really know the other person. It may be difficult to develop the discipline of sharing yourself and your feelings, but it has to happen for emotional closeness to develop. And emotional closeness has to be felt by the wife if a vibrant sexual relationship is to be achieved. Most women need to feel that special emotional connection and trust to be able to give themselves sexually to their husbands. We've counseled couples in which the husband would bring up the fact that his wife always wanted to have long conversations before bed or before sex. What she was trying unconsciously to do was to establish some kind of emotional connection with her husband.

Even though sharing your heart with your mate makes you vulnerable, it validates that you are still the same person he or she thinks you are. Emotional vulnerability is an extremely attractive quality. It's reassuring for a spouse to feel he or she knows you better than anyone else. The message it sends is "You are valuable to me. I can trust you." And trust is the bedrock of any healthy marriage. So, even if it's uncomfortable for you to share, commit to the goal of developing the behavior. Spend some time together with the intent of getting to know what's happening on the inside of your spouse. You can accomplish this by reading together and then talking about what the content means to you. Or go out together intending to ask each other questions that allow for deeper dialog: What do you need from me in this relationship? What are your hopes for yourself and for us? Tell me about your fears. Going deeper isn't necessarily easy—and it definitely requires that you take a risk—but it is this type of behavior that helps you reach your goal of an intimate marriage.

Choosing to Give

A final goal is to be *giving*. This looks at the balance of give-and-take that plays out in every marriage. We once counseled with a couple who came to therapy because of severe hostility. The marriage did not start out that way. In the beginning, they were in love and enjoyed spending time together. But as the years went by, a pattern emerged. Jennifer described it as an imbalance in giving: "I'm always the giver, and Jason is always the taker. It's his way or no way. And I'm fed up with it."

Sometimes we hear this accusation but it's only fight talk, a way to strike out at the other person. But as we explored their history and watched what transpired in sessions, it became apparent that Jennifer's words were accurate. Jason was selfish and he had not learned the concept of a marriage being mutual. Jennifer was willing to give, and she had done so. But she wasn't willing to be the only one giving. The more she saw Jason's unwillingness to give, the madder she got. And when she got mad enough, they came to counseling.

Mutuality is key in a marriage. We finally told Jason, "Marriage is going to cost you something." That's true for any marriage and the "something" can be a lot of different things. But for Jason it meant that not everything was going to be his way, that Jennifer had some rights as well. Sometimes they would come to a consensus (it would be *their* way); sometimes they would compromise (it would not be as either preferred it, but that was okay); sometimes they would agree on what he wanted; sometimes they would agree on what she wanted; and sometimes they would simply agree to disagree. But it needed to be more than always his way.

Marriage is going to cost you something. That means you have to intend to be giving. Look for ways to give to your mate. Learn his or her love languages. Seek to do the things that he or she truly values. By nature, that seems to be easier for some of us than it is for others. But mutuality, where both of you are willing to go the extra mile for the other, to be inconvenienced, and to sacrifice is what makes a marriage grow.

Prioritizing Your Marriage

Prioritizing your marriage refers to choosing to invest in it, giving it the time and emotional energy that it needs, even when the demands of life are pulling at you from every direction. And the demands are going to be there. These demands may take on a different look as you move through the marital life cycle—being married with no kids is a whole lot different than being married with young children. But each stage has demands, and those demands make it difficult to grow close in your marriage.

Prioritizing your marriage is largely an issue of *boundaries* and *balance,* knowing where to draw the lines in the sands of life and embracing the formula for relational health: his, hers, and *theirs.* Balancing the formula for relational health means every area gets its fair share. He does *his* thing, which will involve personal time, career, family, hobbies. She does *her* thing, which involves the same list. And they do *their* thing (the time spent investing in the relationship). Each of you needs individual time, doing what you like to do, with friends or alone, but it's yours. No marriage partner can fulfill all the emotional needs for his or her spouse, nor does he or she need to try. But the goal is to fight to keep the "theirs" time prioritized so that it actually happens, and you spend some of it in meaningful conversation.

Prioritizing your marital lifestyle is insuring that the relationship does not get second best. That means that you will have to challenge some of the pressures from the new millennium. For instance, careers in the new millennium have become the "legitimate obsession." Striving for success and being a workaholic are encouraged. Jan and I both want the same thing—to grow close and stay close. But we also both realize the ease with which interferences can crop up to prevent us from getting what we want. For instance, it would be easy for us to become overinvolved in our work. We are both therapists and have spent many years preparing for our profession. By constantly following the theme of greatest interest, we have selectively narrowed our career fields. The result is that we have successfully created work that is not work. Marital therapy is a love for us.

Being a love, therapy has the potential for creating difficulty in our marriage. It could become an obsession. It would be very easy to work at the office all day, only to come home in the evening and continue to work. We love to write, to read, to create, to research. Remember, this is *not* work. Even if not actually working in our study, we could be present in bodily form yet have our minds many miles away. This is probably more offensive than actually being physically absent from the home.

As you can see, the type of interest and dedication that may be good for our careers can paradoxically wreak havoc on our marriage. To counter this tendency requires planning. So we work hard at prioritizing our marriage. Our plan does not have to be your plan, but you do need a plan. Jan and I have a time during the week when we read together, and we pray together nightly. We know there will be a time by structured intent that we will get past the superficial to the deeper areas of our lives. We have a night when we go out on a date, when we just have fun together. We try to get away for a weekend every few months or so. This is for fun but also for reconnection. And we have things that we work on together as a team. Sure, we have separate lives as well. But in the midst of our separateness, we work very hard—by intent—to stay connected as a couple.

Establishing boundaries will not be easy. It will take effort to carve out the time for your marriage. Several years ago Jan and I realized we had drifted into a period of *couple* spiritual inactivity. We decided to make our spiritual life as a couple a priority and established Monday nights as our time to sit down uninterrupted and read, discuss, and pray together. We set up some rules so we wouldn't get off target: We wouldn't discuss daily events or children; we wouldn't say anything negative, only be encouraging; we would only discuss our thoughts and feelings about what we were reading, or each other; and we would spend at least an hour together. You know what happened, don't you? The kids tested the commitment right off. They had important problems and situations that needed our immediate attention. And the phone seemed to ring off the hook. We adjusted. With our kids we adopted the attitude that there were few true emergencies, at least nothing that could not wait for an hour. And then we unhooked the phone. We took control of our lives and established this time together as a priority. Our relationship was more important to us than the demands of the world. And this choice had a significant impact on our marriage.

Taking control of your marriage, establishing it as a priority, is accomplishable. But it is something you will have to intend to do. You will have to fight for intimacy.

Fighting for Your Marriage

We do not deal, share, and give in our marriage because these are always easy things to do. Oftentimes, it is tempting to do just the opposite, to avoid dealing with unpleasant feelings, to avoid sharing the things that are deeply personal, and to cling to what we want instead of considering what the other wants. And we do not prioritize our marriage because it is necessarily the easiest thing to do. It would often be easier to give in to the demands from the outside of our marriage instead of saying no and protecting our relationship. But we do these things, though imperfectly, because we are committed to having what God intends for us: an intimate marriage. And though God gives us the design, he will not do the work. That is our responsibility. But wow! After almost thirty years, we can tell you that the payoffs are worth *every* effort!

Questions to Discuss

1. What areas in my life seem to be out of balance?
2. What things make it difficult for me to deal with conflict and/or share my heart with my spouse?
3. If we were to more clearly prioritize our marriage, what are the things we would do? (e.g., spend twenty minutes daily sharing; establish a yearly marriage inventory getaway weekend; set aside 5 percent of our budget for "us" activities).

For Further Reading

Scott Christopher and Susan Sprecher, "Sexuality in Marriage, Dating and Other Relationships: A Decade Review." *Journal of Marriage and the Family* 62 (2000): 999–1017.

Donald R. Harvey, *Love Secured: How to Prevent a Drifting Marriage* (Grand Rapids: Baker Book House, 1994).

Donald R. Harvey, *Talk Your Way to an Intimate Marriage* (Grand Rapids: Baker Book House, 2000).

Sherod Miller, Daniel Wackman, Elam Nunnally, and Phyllis Miller, *Connecting with Self and Others* (Littleton, Colo.: Interpersonal Communication Programs, Inc., 1992).

David and Jan Stoop, *When Couples Pray Together: Creating Intimacy and Spiritual Wholeness* (Ann Arbor, Mich.: Vine Books, 2000).

Time, Sex, and Money: The First Five Years of Marriage. Center for Marriage and Family (Omaha: Creighton University Press, 2000).

11

The Importance of Playing Together

David and Claudia Arp

If a man insisted always on being serious, and never allowed himself a bit of fun and relaxation, he would go mad or become unstable without knowing it.

Herodotus, *The History of Herodotus,* Book II

Take a trip with us down memory lane. Do you remember the first time you saw your mate? The first time we ever saw each other, I (Dave) threw Claudia in the swimming pool with her clothes on. Not a great first impression, but she did know I was a fun-loving and mischievous guy.

What about the first time you went somewhere together? Your first date? On our first date we went to see the movie *A Summer Place.* The theme song from that movie still conjures up romantic feelings for both of us. We must admit, it was love at first sight.

What fun times do you remember from your dating days? Do you remember laughing until you almost cried? Or when you looked at each other and time stood still? Do you remember anticipating the next time you would be together? Claudia and I were in different colleges in different cities, and our major job from Monday through Friday was figuring out how we could get together on the weekend. Why did we work so hard to get together? Because we had fun together.

We enjoyed each other. We worked together. We played together. We wanted to be together forever. We got engaged.

Wedding Bells Are Ringing for Me and My Gal

Then came the wedding. We got married in the middle of our college experience—not waiting until graduation was actually a result of the Cuban Missile Crisis. If you've seen the movie *13 Days,* you know our story. We thought the world was going to blow up before we had a chance to live together as husband and wife, so right in the middle of college studies we got married. Now we could have fun together and play together for the rest of our lives. Right? Right.

After our brief honeymoon—we were married over the Christmas break—we found ourselves back in the rigors of school and work. I (Claudia) dropped out of school for several quarters so Dave could finish. Then it would be my turn to complete my degree. During these early days of our marriage we had little money and, with school and work, not much time to play and goof off. Life became routine and while we loved each other, at times—while the thrill wasn't gone— it was just not so intense.

We both completed our studies and with our college degrees in hand we began our family, looking forward to the joy of parenting and playing with our baby. Then we discovered parenthood is about more than enjoying the product of our passion and love. With a baby to care for and careers to build, life accelerated even more. The have-to-do's of life took over, and our marriage fun quotient got rather low. Can you identify with our experience?

We still loved each other, but marriage at this stage of our life was more work than play. Of course we have to work on our relationship each day, but it's much easier if we continue to have some fun along the way. That's what we want to talk to you about in this chapter. As you launch and build your marriage, how can you stay connected, how can you keep the play and fun element of marriage front and center? We believe it is vitally important to enjoy each other, to have fun together. It's part of the glue that over the years will hold your relationship together. So in the following pages we want to share with you three secrets for keeping playfulness alive and having fun together. The first is to date your mate.

Secret One: Develop the Dating Habit

When we ask married couples about fun dates, a typical reply is, "Do you mean dates we had before we were married?" No, that's not what we mean. We believe a key to building your friendship and having playful fun together in marriage is to continue the dating habit.

Why Mates Don't Date

"I tried to date my wife," Randy told us, "but it was just too much of a hassle. Plus, we just didn't have the time, the energy, the money, babysitters—and on those rare occasions we pulled off a date, we had no idea what to do other than dinner and a movie."

Can you relate to Randy? Is dating something you did before you were married? Have you dropped the word *dating* from your vocabulary? You may be thinking, "Well that's just how life is right now. It revolves around work and family and, hey, I'm not ashamed of that. I want to be a great parent and want to give my kids the best!" Giving your kids your best is an admirable goal. Your best, however, does not mean putting them before your marriage. One day your children will grow up and leave home, but hopefully your partner is your partner for life!

We use the word *hopefully* because divorce statistics are not encouraging. Why are so many marriages breaking up? Having worked with married couples for many years, we have our own opinion. We believe life goes out of a marriage when a couple stops working on it. To take it a step further, we have observed that when a couple stops working on their marriage, they stop having fun together, they stop playing together. We work with a lot of young couples, and we tell them, "Your work, kids, hobbies, and whatever will wait while you grab some moments to build your marriage, but your marriage won't wait until your kids grow up or you retire from your job."

Why Mates Should Date

Show us a marriage that is faltering, and we'll show you a marriage where the fun is gone. And where the fun is gone, there's a mighty good chance there is no "date their mate" with that couple. Think about it. Have you ever heard of a couple having a fun let's-get-divorced date? If being a divorce preventer doesn't motivate you to plan a date with your mate, consider the following dating benefits:

1. Dating helps you focus on your marriage. Regular focused times together, away from work, kids, phone, fax, beeper, e-mail, cats, dogs, and so on, will help you build a healthy, alive, enriched marriage. In Genesis 2:24 the first act of marriage is to "leave mother and father." Perhaps leaving parents was not that difficult for you, but what about other things that vie for your attention, things like your career, kids, hobbies, sports, television, sports on television, and so on? Are we meddling? What things are a higher priority than your relationship with your spouse? In a healthy marriage, leaving is an ongoing process. What things do you need to leave today? Remember, refocusing and making your marriage a top priority is biblical, and dating will help you refocus. Let's state it another way: God intended marriage to be a promise for life, and dating will help you keep it!

2. Dating restores your communication. Is your usual mode of communication twenty-second voice-mail messages? One husband said he knew the honeymoon was over when he called to tell his wife he'd be late for dinner and got her voice-mail message that she had left his dinner in the microwave oven.

On those occasions you are together, chances are if you're a parent, you're rarely alone. Little ears are listening and little mouths are interrupting! Planned dates, even short ones, give you a chance to talk to your spouse and to talk about something other than the kids. Regularly we have "walk-and-talk" dates. We go to a lovely park greenway close to our home, or if the weather is inclement, we go to a shopping mall that is open for walkers each morning before the stores open. Once around the mall is a mile!

We have ground rules for our "walk-and-talk" dates: One, we don't talk about our work, even though we are marriage educators. And two, we don't talk about our kids or even our adorable grandkids! We talk about us, our hopes, our dreams, our desires. It's a time when we focus on each other, and for us, it's a true communication restorer as well as great physical exercise.

3. Dating prevents boredom. If your daily routine is the same old, same old, it may well be boring, and dating will help you break out of that rut. Surprise your honey with an off-the-wall date like a "card shop" date. Honor your mate with the greatest, most expensive greeting card you can find. Pick out cards that express your sentiments.

After you read them to your partner, put them back on the rack. You've expressed your love and devotion, and with the money you saved by not buying the cards, go have two cups of coffee!

4. Dating builds your friendship. According to our national survey on long-term marriages, the number one indicator of a successful marriage is having a strong couple friendship. When asked for the best aspect of their marriage, survey respondents who answered that their relationship was the best aspect—that their spouse was their closest companion, their soul mate, and their best friend—also rated their marriages the highest in marital satisfaction.

And how do you build a deeper friendship with your partner? You spend time *alone* together. And how do you do that? Intentionally! Block out time for dates with your mate. Your friendship will flourish!

How Mates Can Date

Now that we've, hopefully, convinced you that dates are essential, here's how to make them happen. Start by carving out some time to explore dating possibilities. Make a list of potential dates. Anything goes, from learning to line dance or hang wallpaper to working out with a "get-in-shape" date. Then choose one, pick a time, and list what you must do to make it happen, such as find a sitter, save the money, or clear your overly committed schedule. Start with a date that will be easy to pull off. Some fun dates you might want to consider are

Proposal Date—Go to a public place and ask your mate to marry you all over again. Tell her what attracted you to her when you first met and describe the first time you saw her. Take a trip down memory lane.

Workout Date—Get in shape together at a health club. Or if the budget is tight, walk or jog together.

Photo Date—Go to your favorite haunt and snap away. If your camera has a timer, you both can be in the photos. Simply set the timer, run back, and smile! See how many different ways you can pose. Be extravagant and take the whole roll. For instant gratification, drop the film off for one-hour developing, and while you wait for your pictures, drink hot chocolate or cappuccino at your favorite coffee shop. To continue the date, put together your own little photo album.

Window Shopping Date—Go when the stores are closed, and it will be a cheap date. For an interesting spin, instead of dreaming about what you would like to have, pick out all the things in the window you already have.

Home Depot Date—Go to a local home improvement store and dream about remodeling projects you'd like to tackle or have done someday. Talk about the first place you called home. (We lived in a tiny basement apartment and had all early-marriage, hand-me-down furniture. Our bed slats were too short and our bed kept falling in!)

Formal Dinner in the Park Date—Pull out your best duds and dress up for a great date, order your favorite dinners as take-out, and take your mate out for an evening under the stars. Don't forget a tablecloth, candles, flowers, and a boom box with your favorite CD. You'll be the most popular spouse in the park, and the most watched!

Back Roads Date—Choose a fifty-mile radius around your home and see what you can discover. No fast food or four-lane roads allowed.

Gourmet Cooking Date—Have you ever wanted to take up gourmet cooking? Learn together on this fun date. Plan the menu, grocery shop together at an upscale market, and cook your dinner together.

I'm-Just-Too-Tired Date—Put the kids to bed early, order take-out, turn on the answering machine, pop in a video, and just relax and enjoy each other—you don't even have to talk!

What Not to Do on a Date

1. Don't talk about your kids. Chances are you already spent more of your other time together talking about them, so temporarily forget the kids.
2. Don't chat about the in-laws who are always a potential subject for a fight. Don't go there.
3. Don't go to the movies. You won't have a chance to interact!
4. Don't discuss money. For a lot of couples, this is a tense topic. Avoid it on dates!

How to Start Having Some Great Dates

You can jump-start great dates. All you have to do is find a two-hour block of time. If you choose to use our book *10 Great Dates* as a dating guide, prime the pump for your date by reading a short chapter or the chapter summary. You can tear out the perforated date in the back of the book, and you're off for your great date. Suggestions are included for where to go, what to do, and so on.

If you're a groupie or need child care, consider joining with several other couples and starting your own dating club. You might want to get your church to provide low-cost child care and start the *10 Great Dates* program. The format is simple. Drop off your kids in child care, and together with the other couples, watch a fifteen- to twenty-minute video date launch. (Video resource is available through our web site, www.marriagealive.com.) Then go out on your date. (Double dating not recommended!) When you return to pick up your kids, you can have a few minutes to enjoy the other couples or just go home. However you choose to structure your great dates, you can count on fun and new life for your marriage. Here are some suggestions for starting a *10 Great Dates* Couples' Nights Out:

10 Great Dates *Couples' Nights Out*

If you need a little peer pressure to date your mate, help to organize a *10 Great Dates* group at your church. In the process you can encourage other married couples to date. Follow these seven simple steps:

1. Promote the idea. Find several other couples who want to energize their marriage. Think of like-minded friends at church, at work, in your accountability group, or in Bible study. Talk it up and recruit your group.
2. Choose a date night and set the time schedule. Jump-start dating with one date a week for ten weeks, or schedule a date every other week. Even a date once a month can make a big difference in your relationship with your spouse.
3. Find regular child care. This may be the most daunting, but it is not impossible. Consider challenging your church to provide free or low-cost child care once a month so couples in the church can fortify their marriages. If you have to, get your individual sitter or consolidate kids at someone's home and bring in sev-

eral trusted sitters. Keep brainstorming until you find something that works for you.

4. Choosing a theme for each date will help you stay on target and resist the dinner and a movie rut.

5. Take turns facilitating your fifteen- to twenty-minute date launch. Introduce the theme for the date and encourage couples to have fun!

6. Next, leave the group and actually have your date. But you must remember to come back and pick up your kids!

7. Remember, your kids will wait while you grab some time to build your marriage, but your marriage won't wait until your kids grow up. (For more details about how to start *10 Great Dates,* visit www.marriagealive.com.)

The Big Payoff

Dating comes with a big payoff, both for you and those you love. A healthy enriched marriage provides children with a unique sense of security and love. And your children will learn how to honor, esteem, and value marriage by watching you; you are the best role model for your children's future marriage. Let them see how much you care for your spouse—let them see you date!

As others observe the value you place on your own marriage by having dates with your spouse, your example will mentor other couples. We say so easily, "Honor your vows and build a strong marriage." Isn't it time to put some flesh on these words? Remember, marriage is a promise for life, and dating will help you keep that promise. What better way to start than to say, "Honey, let's have a date!" And if your spouse asks you first, enthusiastically say, "Yes!"

Secret Two: Give the Gift of Encouragement

One important way to energize your marriage and build your friendship is to become an encourager. Psychologists tell us it takes five positive statements to offset one negative statement. Listen to your conversations for the next twenty-four hours and check out how you are doing at encouraging your partner. If you want to be best friends and playmates, you need to develop the habit of encouraging one another.

Meet Our Playful Friends, Dave and Jeanie

When we think of encouraging couples, we immediately think about our friends Dave and Jeanie Stanley. Married for over fifty years, Dave and Jeanie still have fun together and look for ways to encourage each other.

The Stanleys say the basis of the joy in their marriage is their relationship with God. They start each day with wake-up prayer as they snuggle in bed. They also like to pray together on their "walk-and-talk" dates. Daily they share the Scriptures together. They tell us that this practice provides the foundation for fun and friendship in their marriage and for the fascinating ways they have found to encourage one another. Check these out:

- They look for ways to give each other compliments. "As plants need water," they say, "we need affirmation from each other."
- They write each other love letters.
- They have their own special kisses. "Romance depends on your attitude and perspective," they told us.
- They handle conflict with a light touch. They have a ten-minute silence rule. At any time either can call for ten minutes of silence. If nonverbal communication is a problem, they also have an out-of-sight for ten minutes rule. This helps them to calm down and get things back in perspective.
- They have pet names for each other like "Lover Bunny." (They love rabbits and have four—the stuffed variety—that always travel with them.)
- At grocery store checkout counters, Dave asks Jeanie to marry him all over again! Jeanie enthusiastically says, "Yes!"
- They have shared goals that are bigger than they are.

We asked Dave and Jeanie how they kept love alive back in the early days of their marriage and when they had small children. Here's what they told us:

> From the very beginning of our marriage, we had fun together, and though parenting brought many adjustments we did look for ways to find our fun moments. Sometimes we would put our children to bed early and grab time just for us for a late dinner or a game of double solitaire. We also bypassed

television. The latter definitely benefited our children. We logged many family evenings reading together and playing games. One way we kept our own sense of fun and sanity was having fun together with our children.

Take Marriage Vitamins

Dave and Jeanie know that encouraging acts are the vitamins that keep their relationship positive and on the growing edge. Consider the following marital vitamins and take at least one each day:

- Hug each other for twenty seconds each day.
- Leave a loving message on your partner's voice mail or e-mail.
- Give your mate an unexpected little gift.
- Clean the toilet without being asked.
- Put toothpaste on your spouse's toothbrush while he or she is in the shower.
- Give your spouse a one-minute shoulder rub.
- Rent your favorite old movie from your dating days and watch it together after the kids are in bed.

Secret Three: Keep the Passion Alive

We had just finished a session in our Marriage Alive seminar on being an encourager and building a creative love life when a young mom spoke up out of sheer frustration. "With young children, a part-time job, church responsibilities, extended family, and financial struggles, I feel like our marriage is stuck in the fast lane with no way to slow down. A creative love life? My greatest sexual fantasy is eight hours of uninterrupted sleep!"

Her husband chimed in, "Well, that's not my fantasy!"

In the early years of our marriage—especially when the children started coming along—finding time for loving each other and keeping the passion alive was hard for us too. Playing together wasn't in our vocabulary. We know that the two times of greatest stress on a marriage are when you have toddlers and when you have teens. The hardest time in our sexual relationship was when we had three children ages five and under. Sticky peanut butter and jelly on doorknobs, dirty dishes in the sink, and early Fisher-Price® décor didn't exactly set the mood for a loving and playful rendezvous.

Maybe you find yourself in a similar situation. Your energy is drained, and times for loving and playing are elusive and rare. We survived those stressful years and you can too. You're okay. Your body works. Your children will grow up. And in the meantime you can do several things to nurture and add a sense of playfulness to your love life.

Find a Weekly Time

If you want to add romance and playfulness to your love life, set aside some time each week to pursue it. You may think, "But that's just not spontaneous!" The fact is that spontaneity is not the guiding principle for having a creative love life during the parenting years. If you wait for spontaneity, your love life may spontaneously self-destruct! We suggest finding an hour or two each week when you can be alone without the kids around. Maybe you will want to hire a babysitter to take your kids to the playground on Saturday mornings for a couple of hours. Or trade babysitting with friends once a week. You keep your friends' kids for a couple of hours and then they reciprocate. Voila! Time alone!

Take the Initiative

Plan for fun. Spend time thinking about loving your partner. Daydream about making love while doing the laundry, dishes, and so on. Flirt with each other. Give your mate an intimate touch or kiss when the kids aren't looking. Both take the initiative in planning a romantic time together.

Choose to Be Creative

Deepening your marital bonds may require you to make yourself vulnerable by taking the initiative and choosing to be creative. Take the initiative to plan alone times. Plan a night away to somewhere you've never been before. Do something surprising—this may help you break out of a rut. Romance is not exclusively reserved for the bedroom. Here are a few suggestions to get your creative juices flowing:

- Kiss for ten seconds every morning when you say good-bye and every evening when you say hello. (It's longer than you think. Time it!)
- Flirt with each other; even when there isn't time for sex, make sure your mate knows you want to. If you communicate your desire, it keeps the passion alive.
- While getting ready for bed, light a scented candle and turn on some romantic music on the radio or CD player.
- Pull down the covers on the bed and leave a candy mint on the pillow.
- Spend time talking about loving each other.
- Tell your mate ten reasons you'd marry him or her all over again.
- Buy a new mood music tape or CD.

Your Time to Play

We've shared three secrets with you for energizing your relationship with fun and playfulness through dating your mate, encouraging one another, and pursuing more passion. Now it's your time to play. Don't get discouraged if not everything you try works. Some things may bomb. Other things will work. When you're tired and discouraged, remember why you're doing this. Your goal is to build a loving relationship that will last throughout all the years of your marriage. Hang in there. Date your mate. Look for ways to give encouragement and love to each other. Let your children see that you love each other, that you enjoy being together, that you are best friends, soul mates, and lovers. Your children will be reassured when they experience home as a fun-loving, happy place.

Someday your children may even facilitate your own playfulness and fun. One summer when our oldest son and his wife were going away for several weeks, they offered us their home in Williamsburg, Virginia, for a getaway. We took them up on it. Imagine our surprise when we found their table romantically set for two with candles and china!

Now it is your time. We hope you'll take time to play together, to date, and to give and receive encouraging love. You'll be enhancing your marriage and passing on a godly heritage of love to your children.

Questions to Discuss

1. Think back to a time when you and your spouse had a playful experience with each other. What did you do? How might you re-create a time like that?
2. Discuss together what type of dates you would enjoy having. Set a time to begin.
3. How could your partner encourage you? What kinds of statements do you find encouraging?

For Further Reading

David and Claudia Arp, *52 Dates for You and Your Mate* (Nashville: Thomas Nelson, 1993).

David and Claudia Arp, *Marriage Moments* (Ann Arbor, Mich.: Vine Books, 1998).

David and Claudia Arp, *10 Great Dates to Energize Your Marriage* (Grand Rapids: Zondervan, 1997). (Available as a book and also as a video curriculum.)

David and Claudia Arp, Les and Leslie Parrott, and Robert and Rosemary Barnes, *Marriage Devotional Bible* (Grand Rapids: Zondervan, 2000).

For information about Marriage Alive seminars or other Marriage Alive resources visit www.marriagealive.com, e-mail mace@marriagealive.org, or call 1-888-690-6667.

12

Creating Your Own Traditions in Your Marriage

Les and Leslie Parrott

> Tradition is entirely different from habit, even from an excellent habit, since habit is by definition an unconscious acquisition and tends to become mechanical, whereas tradition results from a conscious and deliberate acceptance. . . . Tradition presupposes the reality of what endures.
>
> Igor Stravinsky, *Poetics of Music*

We've got to be honest: Your love life is at risk. Oh, sure you're crazy in love now, especially if you're newlyweds, and you can't imagine that anything will change. We pray it won't. But it wouldn't be fair if we didn't let you know the truth. If recent divorce and remarriage statistics are any indication, being married does not ensure a life of love lived happily ever after. Contrary to the fairy tales we were weaned on, romance always runs the risk of fading. No, let us rephrase that, romance always fades. As human beings, we aren't built to maintain the high levels of feverish passion and romance experienced during the days of engagement and the honeymoon. And yet that's exactly what most couples expect.

Even the more mature stories of doomed love reinforce this notion. Remember the tragic twosome Romeo and Juliet? How about Lancelot and Guinevere? Rhett and Scarlet? Each snuffed out their powerful love while the heat of passion was turned up full blast. Why? Because it couldn't last. The heat of passion was never meant to. Can you imagine Romeo and Juliet as a married couple, going off to work, paying bills, grocery shopping? It's almost incongruous; at least it takes a lot of the luster off their love story. The point is that all the romancing and wooing that led up to your marriage is not what will sustain it. Not in real life.

You can't expect your marriages to be a long-running cinematic fairy tale. Those couples who hold on to this faulty expectation end up drinking the poison of adultery or trading in partners to reinvent the fantasy, hoping that this time they'll get it right. But rest assured. There's a better way.

So in this chapter we reveal a once-in-a-lifetime opportunity you have as newlyweds to put into practice the secret for a wildly successful love life that will go the distance. It has to do with establishing your own traditions, big and small. And the sooner you do this, the better.

The Secret of Lasting Love

When they married eighteen months ago, Kim never would have dreamed she'd find herself complaining that her husband, Steve, didn't show her enough affection. "He was so attentive that he would notice if I changed the part in my hair or bought a new blouse," Kim says. But the loving words and compliments come a little less often now, and frankly, Kim misses the special attention. "He thinks I'm the one who's cooling off," she shrugs, "but I just can't get interested in sex when I feel I'm being ignored."

Kim and Steve aren't alone. The frequent expressions of affection and approval that couples give each other during the courtship and honeymoon stage can dwindle during the first years of marriage. You may love each other as much, but you tend to talk about it less. There's a peak of emotional intimacy during the early phase of a relationship and then the "I love yous" dwindle and the romance fades. The good news is that if you know the secret, you can keep romantic love alive long after the honeymoon has ended. What's the secret? It's quite simple, really: *Do everything you can in your first few years of marriage to establish habits and traditions of loving behavior.*

A habit is a recurrent, often unconscious pattern of behavior that is acquired through frequent repetition. If you repeat a behavior often enough, it becomes a pattern. Eventually, you hardly give it a thought. The behavior becomes second nature. Whether it is fastening a seat belt when you get in a car or biting your fingernails to pass the time, habits shape our actions. According to seventeenth-century English writer Jeremy Taylor, "Habits are the daughters of action." And, habits can be brought about by either positive or negative action. They can lead to behaviors that cultivate and nurture lasting love, or they can lead to behaviors that serve as love's saboteur. Most importantly, once a habit is set, it's next to impossible to break, no matter how nasty. Just ask a chain-smoker.

Why all this talk about habits? If you are in the beginning stages of your marriage, or even if you have been married many years, you are at an important developmental passage where what you do in the next few months or years will determine many of the habits you have for the rest of your marriage. It's never too late to begin. The little things you do now, without thinking, will cut a groove in your relationship that will likely last a lifetime. So we urge you to take charge of your romantic destiny. Establish patterns of loving behavior that will keep romance, passion, and intimacy alive and well in your marriage. Consider behaviors both big (how you spend your holidays) and small (how you greet each other at the end of the day). We will help you do just that in our post-honeymoon plan for cultivating lasting love.

A Post-Honeymoon Plan

To the French it was a *lune de miel,* or literally a "moon of honey." Northern Europeans understood the honeymoon to be bittersweet, because it was only one month out of many and the following moon cycles would never be able to match the first. British poets of the sixteenth and seventeenth centuries often used the word *honeymooning* to represent an expected waxing and waning of affection between partners. Likewise, folk belief held that after the honeymoon achieved its full passion, it would invariably turn lukewarm, so that the cooling passion could make room for a more settled relationship.

During the early part of this past century, the typical honeymoon lasted three to four weeks, and those in wealthy circles would take four to six months! Nowadays, people are more likely to take a one-week honeymoon or even simply a long weekend.

In the 1830s, transportation had improved enough to allow for more faraway honeymoon trips. Couples began spending their nuptial journeys visiting sites like Niagara Falls and New York City. Today the top honeymoon destinations are the Caribbean, Italy, Hawaii, and the Canadian Rockies.

Whatever its meaning, its length, or its location, the honeymoon is supposed to be, as *Merriam-Webster's Collegiate Dictionary* says, "a period of unusual harmony following the establishment of a new relationship." We hope your honeymoon was harmonious, but even more, we pray that all the days that follow will be characterized by harmony and love as well.

If it's to be, however, it won't depend on your good hopes and prayers. It will depend on you taking the initiative to follow a simple plan for keeping your love sweet, even after the honeymoon is only a memory. The plan involves taking time for little things, making dating a weekly habit, and creating holiday memories worth repeating.

Note the Little Things

Have you ever been bitten by an elephant? Probably not. Have you ever been bitten by a mosquito? Probably so. It's a silly illustration, but it makes a point: Little things often matter most, especially in marriage. Too often, we think on a grand scale about romance, creating the perfect once-a-year getaway, and neglect the little opportunities that present themselves every day in marriage.

Consider, for example, how you greet each other when returning home from work. If you begin by making a consistent effort to reconnect with a tender touch or embrace at the end of your day, you will establish one of the most important patterns couples can have for setting a positive tone for their evening together. "Well, of course we'll do that," you may be thinking. Don't be so sure. The vast majority of couples end up with what researchers call the "grocery list" connection: "Did you pick up my dry cleaning?" "I'll need the car tomorrow."

"What's for dinner?" If you start with a tender touch when you get home before you get to the nitty-gritty tasks of the day, you will create an aura of love in your home that leads to a level of fulfillment most married couples only dream about. Sure, it's a little thing, but a tender reconnection at the end of your day makes a huge difference when it becomes a habit.

Other little things to consider include common courtesies like saying *please* and *thank you*. Did you know that one of the first things to go in a new marriage is politeness? In some ways this reflects increasing levels of comfort. But if left unchecked, it can lead to rudeness. Studies have shown that when paired with a stranger, even newlyweds were more polite to him or her than they were toward each other. If you establish a pattern of politeness now, you'll likely be even more polite on your fiftieth wedding anniversary!

Make Dating a Habit

Many married couples claim they spend time together. But when you question them, you find they are spending that time running errands or meeting with other friends. There's nothing wrong with that, of course, but if you are to keep romance alive, you need to have quality time together, just the two of you, when you have no other agenda except to connect. Some married couples call it their date night. And that's not a bad title. After all, there is no rule that says dating ends when you get married. Dating becomes as important as ever after you've said your vows and settled into being a permanent couple. Whatever you call it, this time needs to be scheduled, routinely and consistently.

Every Thursday evening, for example, you need to be able to count on having a date: a leisurely dinner at your favorite restaurant, window shopping downtown, a picnic at a local park, taking in a movie and ice cream, or dressing up for a special event. Do whatever you enjoyed doing before you were married. The point of making dating a habit is to keep your marriage from falling into the doldrums of working all week and collapsing on the weekends. This toxic pattern has snuffed out the romantic flame of more couples than you can imagine. Don't let it happen to you.

In addition to scheduling a weekly time for just the two of you to be alone together, consider one overnight stay at a hotel every few months and a one-week vacation every year. By the way, once kids enter the picture, these romantic interludes become all the more essential. And if you don't establish the pattern of dating now, while you are just starting out, you are unlikely to do so when your lives become all the more hectic. But with determination and desire, you can start this pattern now. Don't hesitate. Don't wait. Set a date together before reading on.

Create Holiday Memories Worth Repeating

Ever since she can remember, Mindy would wake up on Christmas morning along with her three siblings, run downstairs, and tear into the mountain of presents under the tree. "It was a free-for-all," she says. "And it was so exciting; I can't imagine celebrating Christmas any other way."

Mindy's new husband, Kevin, could. "In my family," he told us, "we always opened our presents on Christmas Eve after a nice meal. Then we would take our time, each of us opening a present in turn." Well, you can already guess the problem Kevin and Mindy faced on their first Christmas as husband and wife. It's a fairly predictable predicament. And for this reason, it is critical that you begin to establish new traditions right from the beginning. Of course, you can bring many fun traditions from your past into your present marriage, but this should not diminish making traditions of your own.

Often there is a potential conflict when it comes to blending the traditions from both your families and also trying to create your own traditions. It is important that you make these kinds of decisions together. Nothing should be assumed. Nothing should just be automatic. And even if you've been automatically going to the home of one set of parents for a particular holiday, and "that's the way we've always done it," it doesn't mean you can't create a new tradition.

We know a couple who couldn't resolve the question of which family to spend Thanksgiving with. Both sets of parents expected them to come, and neither set of parents showed any concern about the predicament they put this couple in. So after some discussion, the couple decided they would go to neither parents' home, and instead, they would go to a rescue mission in town and help them serve Thanksgiving dinner to the homeless. Their children went along with them and found it to be the most meaningful way to celebrate Thanksgiving.

We know another couple who decided on their first holiday season together to each take the same amount of money that they mutually decided on and buy each other gifts with it on Christmas Eve. They told us how they did this partly out of necessity the first few years of their marriage. Their budget was tight and they felt they got better prices on items the day before Christmas when things had already started to go on sale. Today this couple has been married for more than a decade and lives comfortably with few financial worries. But they still carry on the tradition of shopping for each other on Christmas Eve.

We know another couple who decided early in their marriage to cultivate the gift of hospitality around the holidays. They love to entertain guests in their home. And they often reach out to the needy and neglected. On Mother's Day, for example, they always invite all the single moms from their neighborhood over to their home for Sunday brunch. And on New Year's Eve, they include foreign students who can't afford to go home for the holidays in their celebrations.

So how are you celebrating the holidays this year? What about each other's birthdays? Have you given any thought to how you will make Easter meaningful? And don't forget July Fourth or even Groundhog Day if you're looking for an excuse to have fun. There are literally countless occasions and ways to carve out your own holiday traditions as husband and wife. Traditions can center around food, activities, outings, decorations, trips, and of course gatherings with friends and family. The goal is to be intentional and make them your own. Why? Because these traditions create memories of all the fun you have enjoyed as well as help you anticipate the fun you will have in the future. Traditions keep your love alive.

It's important that as you blend your marriage together you keep some holidays for your own traditions and discuss ways to blend.

Never Neglect Your Post-Honeymoon Habits

Over the years many couples return to the place of their first wedding trip for a second, third, or fourth honeymoon. It seems many work hard to recapture the bliss of their first few days as a couple. Perhaps you'll do the same. But don't wait for an anniversary or special occasion to recreate that special time. Keep love alive, starting today, by establishing daily habits of romance, passion, and intimacy. If you do, your honeymoon will become more than a memory; it will become a way of life.

Questions to Discuss

1. Had you given much thought to creating your own traditions before reading this chapter? If so, in what ways? What kinds of traditions did you imagine?
2. The chapter explored the value and the tradition of the honeymoon. In what ways can you repeat some of the special moments you shared together on your honeymoon?
3. What are your thoughts about the tradition of small things, such as how you greet each other at the end of the day? What is one specific small tradition you would like to cultivate?
4. Holiday traditions are some of the most memorable for some couples. And some make the mistake of only trying to carry on the traditions they grew up with. What are the two of you going to do to put your own thumbprint on these special occasions?

For Further Reading

Gloria Gaither and Shirley Dobson, *Let's Make a Memory* (Dallas: Word, 1994).

Susan Abel Lieberman, *New Traditions: Redefining Celebrations for Today's Family* (New York: Noonday Press, 1991).

Susan Newman and Jennifer Harper, *Little Things Long Remembered: Making Your Children Feel Special Everyday* (New York: Crown, 1993).

Part 3

The Challenges of Marriage

13

Breaking the Cycle of Conflict

Tim and Julie Clinton

Live joyfully with the wife whom you love all the days of your vain life which He has given you under the sun.

Ecclesiastes 9:9 (NKJV)

Living joyfully together is one tough assignment, especially when it seems that almost everything in life competes for our affection. Too many couples are tired of trying to keep it all together and are pained by love gone bad. And many of them just throw in the towel and give up on love.

Yet, marriage is close to the heart of God, so close that the apostle Paul uses marriage as an analogy of Christ's love for the church and how he gave himself up for her. It's that kind of love and commitment God had in mind when he ordained marriage. The most satisfying marriages—the ones best able to fulfill the Ecclesiastes call to joy and love—come about when a husband and wife align themselves with God and his original intent for spiritual and marital intimacy.

Marriage, then, is not just two people in love; it's a three-strand cord not easily broken. When God enters the marital equation, a horizontal and temporal contract is transformed into an eternal covenant relationship with vertical and horizontal dimensions. Mundane marital existence is transformed into an adventure of love and joy, lived as a gift from a gracious God.

However, this kind of marriage is not a given and doesn't come without hard work, deep forgiveness, and incredible mutual sacrifice.

Love on the Rocks

Let's be fair. Marriage can be difficult. It brings two people together, two people with very different personalities, tastes, and desires, and puts them in such close proximity that their faults and weaknesses will be discovered. As a result, all marriages go through periods of disaffection, times when love feels distant, cold, times when you just seem to have "lost that lovin' feeling." When conflict and misunderstanding occur, what happens during these times will usually set the course for the rest of the marriage.

Unfortunately, disaffection often wins out, and couples who get to that point never know God's desire for their marriage. An estimated 50 percent of today's couples will see their marriage end in divorce, most of them within the first seven years. And those are just the raw statistics. Many of those who stay in their marriages live unhappily behind closed doors. In the quiet corners of their hearts are profound sorrow and emptiness.

Couples are seeing the marriages of their friends and family ravaged like never before. They see the love that held them together crumbling, its strength and endurance gone. Perhaps you're seeing that in your own marriage.

Chances are you or someone you love has a marriage in trouble right now. If so, you've wondered what went wrong or wondered how a union that started with such promise and with the blessing of God himself could have soured.

Losing at Love

When conflict first hits, every couple has some doubt and also wonders how they might lose at love. After all, neither of them is necessarily a hateful person, neither is particularly selfish, or at least it seemed they didn't start out that way. How can things go so wrong? We have found that most couples are unaware or underaware of what happens in these circumstances. When they begin to experience trouble, in an effort at self-preservation, they dig in their heels and lay the blame for the problems at the feet of their spouse. This is a losing strategy and is guaranteed to allow the problems to fester and grow.

Believe it or not, there is an answer for why everything goes so wrong, for losing at love is often predictable. It follows a step-by-step process and creates a repeating cycle that if left unchecked can take a couple from love's first embrace to the point where love is totally destroyed and the marriage will probably end in the pain of divorce.

But there's hope for the troubled marriage. Because the cycle is predictable, if the steps are understood, the courageous couple can work to stop the cycle, arrest the destructive spiral, and literally save their marriage. Most couples want what it takes to keep their marriage afloat, and by understanding how they got to where they are, they can reverse the process and breathe new life into their marriage.

Everyday Pressures—How Disaffection Gets Started

How does disaffection start? It actually begins with everyday life, with the six pressures we all face daily.

1. Stress

Futurist David Zach refers to our age as the time of "hyper-living." We're pulled in every direction, busy and going nowhere fast, having to do more with less time. Before long, tempers flare, stomachs ache, hearts break. Hurried decisions become bad decisions. And bad decisions make people hurt.

Marriage becomes a perpetual uphill climb. And our hurt makes us irritable, discouraged, and very difficult to live with. Some have just flat out been overwhelmed by life, wayward kids, financial pressures, loss, health problems, and demanding work schedules. Take an inventory. What stresses have been tearing at your relationship since you married?

2. Evil

Since the time of Adam and Eve, the evil one has sought to destroy this God-ordained intimate bond of marriage. He is the great confuser and the ultimate liar. He magnifies our weaknesses and fears and uses them as wedges that come between us.

The apostle Peter described the evil one as a "roaring lion, seeking whom he may devour" (1 Peter 5:8 NKJV). And, he's out to take as big a bite as he can out of your marriage. If he does, he stands to win a lot, possibly causing fatal blows to you, your spouse, and your kids.

3. False Expectations

Unrealized expectations leave us disappointed. If our expectations are unrealistic for our marriages, we're setting ourselves up for a fall. A few of the most common expectations include:

- *Marriage will complete me.* Perhaps we grew up with parents who didn't care for us like they should, or with siblings who stole the limelight, or in some other painful environment. We may expect marriage to reverse all the negatives we're carrying into it.
- *My spouse won't hurt me.* As the first expectation sees marriage as the healing agent, this one sees marriage as the ultimate safe haven. The first hurt we receive from a spouse is catastrophic.
- *Life will be easy now.* This is the happily-ever-after expectation of fairy tales. If we have this expectation, every unhappy moment in a marriage then brings disappointment and possibly fear.
- *Love will keep us together.* As the song says, "All you need is love." Well, not so, because you need more than your love. This expectation, by far, produces the greatest disappointment as it batters the very thing that is supposed to hold us together—our love. Every time we hurt one another, intentionally or unintentionally, love is perceived as increasingly less effective until, in the end, we can easily say our relationship just wasn't meant to be.

How do you combat unrealistic expectations? With realistic biblical ones. No one is perfect, including your spouse. No one person will ever fulfill all your needs, nor will you supply all your spouse's needs.

Only God can. No marriage is free from discord, and no spouse is completely unselfish.

Marriage brings together two people who have many human frailties that are at first magnified, then hopefully, in Christ, strengthened into godly traits. But it takes a lot of humility, grace, and constant work at understanding what is reasonable for you and your spouse to expect from each other.

4. Selfishness

During dating, most of our energy is exclusively focused on the other. But something strange happens after we say, "I do." The giving often becomes taking. The "island of we" becomes an "island of me." In our marriage we don't really want to hurt each other. But we do. We fail each other. We say hurtful words. You know the routine. Like the apostle Paul in Romans 7:15 (NLT), regarding his walk with the Lord, we can say, "I don't understand myself at all, for I really want to do what is right, but I don't do it. Instead, I do the very thing I hate."

Marriage was designed to be a team effort, one of loving and giving, of making a commitment to our mate. Lately, in our culture, marriage has been reduced to prenuptial agreements, occasional intimacy (or none at all), and quickie divorces. Selfishness creates an "island of me," where there is a wall around me. On the "island of we," there is a wall around us.

5. Scripts from the Past

A lot of our behavior is influenced by our past scripts, scripts that were written for us long ago. We find that we now faithfully follow them, and our scripted behavior is reinforced as we hold tightly to them. For instance, if one or both of our parents abandoned us when we were children, we will live today as if we expect those we love to abandon us in the here and now. Such scripts distort current reality and cause us to act and react in what can be very destructive ways. These scripts also impact how we give and receive love.

If this sounds true for you, look for those elements of your life that are unresolved. Look for the physical, emotional, or sexual abuse, the effects of parental divorce and/or abandonment. Look for the gross failures and the emotional loss and deal with them in sound biblical ways.

6. Speed

Relationships and intimacy take time. Time to understand, enjoy, and respond to one another—time to satisfy the other's needs and have your own needs satisfied. When we live life in the fast lane, there is precious little time for the building of intimacy. We're the microwave generation addicted to speed. Every element of our lives seems to be a tradeoff, and often we end up trading off the very steps to intimacy— the time to nurture our mates and our marriages.

Both partners in a marriage succumb to these pressures to varying degrees at various times. So we think a date night will solve our problems. What happens on date nights when things haven't been going well? One lousy night! The result is loneliness, anger, feelings of rejection, and sorrow—enough to rip the foundation out from under most couples. A natural response to this pain is to create space, a gap between you and your partner. A subtle, even unintentional severing of relational strands takes place characterized by some pretty hurtful communication patterns.

The Negative Cycle Begins

Distancing

"Why does God hate divorce, Tim, when he knows how awful a marriage can be?" a broken woman asked when telling me of her marital plight. She told me of the hateful words that cut deeply and the lack of touch and the silent treatments that would tear at her heart.

"I have prayed for my future husband since I was a little girl. Why is this happening to me—to us? I cry alone a lot, and I'm so tired of trying to make this marriage work," this desperate woman said.

It's hard to hold on when you are faced with persistent hurt and rejection.

As we've shared, just the everyday pressures like stress, evil, sin, false expectations, the speed of living—all are enough to leave one or both partners confused, empty, and expecting. But, the path of disaffection goes deeper. A negative cycle begins step-by-step, day-by-day, emotion-by-emotion, until love is destroyed.

When you are in a relationship in which there is little or no respect, no warmth or closeness, or you feel as if you are taken for granted, abandoned, or shamed, it's only natural to drift apart, to distance, and to insulate yourself from the other.

Distancing is a reasonable response to an unreasonable situation. But, it can also be a primary killer of love in marriage. Even before we know what has happened, distancing begins occurring in small ways, moments when we ignore or put down our partners, lapses of love that subtly eat away at the relationship. The early signs of this negative cycle include tuning out your partner, ignoring important comments, and a general lack of sharing about everyday life. These are strong signals of love's early demise. Such behavior often kills simple acts of thoughtfulness, such as a note placed in a lunch box or flowers sent for no particular reason.

Raising the Bar

Raising the bar is setting a love trap for your mate. It's creating a hurdle your mate must leap over to prove his or her love. For instance, "I just hope he'll bring me flowers this week." He hasn't brought home flowers in five years. Is he going to bring home flowers this week? No.

Raising the bar is a form of desperation. One or both partners want assurance that they're still loved, so they set the hurdle—in secret. As the cycle spirals, the bars become increasingly high and increasingly unlikely to be hurdled. Raising the bar is a horribly destructive act; it's a love trap and it always leads to increased failures.

Increased Failure

The instant the partner fails to leap the hurdles, one partner gets angry and the other feels guilty. For the one who was disappointed, thoughts like *You just don't care* or *You never show me you love me* abound. For the one who failed to jump the hurdle, there are thoughts such as *You're impossible. There's nothing I can do to please you. You're the problem. You're the one who needs help.* Increased failures only cause both to shut down even more.

Increased Negative Evaluation

Before long, both people become locked in the dank cellars of their own minds, and both are thinking the same thing—*Our marriage is getting worse.* And the worse it gets, the less each is willing to invest in it. They've reached a very dangerous point. If you've ever gotten to this point, you were probably consumed with how your mate was failing the marriage. Simply put, you believed your mate was wrecking your marriage.

So what do most couples do when they get to this point? They begin to vilify their mate. In their mind, the mate has intentionally hurt them. He or she is destroying their relationship on purpose. At this point, the negative thoughts and their resulting distortions begin to abound in the relationship.

And what do you do with villains? You punish them. And what do villains do to you? They hurt you. So now there's an even greater need for self-preservation.

Greater Self-Preservation

Because you're now living with a "villain," the protective walls go up quickly, and you make them as thick as possible. You begin to watch every move your spouse makes with heightened suspicion. You believe your cry for love will be rejected because your spouse can't possibly love you in return. It becomes just too dangerous to open yourself up like that. You become more exhausted, empty, and expect to live in eternal vigilance. Whatever spontaneity was left in your marriage drains away.

But the assault on joy can come from another direction too. When in distress people often default to their strengths. If they're organized, they begin to organize everything. If they're gregarious, they forget their responsibilities altogether. And when that happens, those little characteristics they found so endearing in their mates, they now hate.

This leads to more needs not being met, which leads us back to step one in the negative cycle, which is increased distancing and polarization.

Cycling Back Again

Each time we cycle through this negative cycle, disaffection grows and the secret resentment locked in our heart intensifies. The fight left in us turns to a strong desire to take flight, to just leave. As the cycle of disaffection grinds on, within it develops a response, which only feeds the negative cycle. It goes like this. When a spouse complains, and the complaint is ignored, the offended partner may begin to sulk—sulking being a way of calling attention to the pain without saying anything about it. When the sulking is ignored, then come the accusations.

People don't actually believe these accusations, at least the reasonable part of them doesn't. They are just trying to get a reaction. The spouse wants to hear, "Of course I want you to be happy." When he or she doesn't hear an affirmation like that, and it is, in fact, ignored again, then come the threats. "You want me unhappy? I'll show you unhappy. You just wait."

This growing problem of disaffection is like a death grip. But it's not just a steady walk away from love, it involves hurt, distancing, hurt again, more distancing. It's a pattern of clearly definable behaviors that spiral back on themselves, each time becoming more severe and more destructive. It's like quicksand. The more you struggle to pull yourself out of the hole and subsequently get rejected, the more easily discouraged and tired you become. Before long, you become "islands of me," where one cries for love but no one sees the pain or hears the cry for affection. That isn't to say there's no way out. It does mean, however, that battling with one another to somehow stop the marital decline only seems to make things worse.

Breaking the Cycle and Coming out of the Pain

If you detect your relationship sliding down this destructive, predictable cycle, immediately seek help from a Christian marriage counselor and extricate yourself. If you don't seek help, your natural emotional survival skills will take over. When that happens you'll continue to experience a downward spiral spiritually, emotionally, and physically—one that will eventually overwhelm your marriage and require you to work harder and harder just to stay even. And eventually, the vitality that God has put in your marriage will simply die.

Losing at love is a horrible thing to experience. It is made even more so by the possibility that it could all be avoided with a commitment to break the cycle and return to the love God wants for you and your mate. Your marriage should be filled with more joy than sorrow. God wants you to have more warmth than indifference, more love than anger.

The pathway out of pain will involve at least these four ingredients:

1. Empathy

The most significant first step in getting beyond your pain is stepping back from the marriage and honestly looking at how you lost at love in your marriage. Could it be that your spouse is hurting too? That doesn't mean he or she isn't to blame for what's happening, at least to some degree, but just maybe you both very subtly, even unintentionally, lost sight of each other. You started to drift apart and then life just got out of control. If so, why not turn to Psalm 139 and ask God to search your heart to see if there is any wicked way in you and ask him to do a new work in your life. Sure you'll need to keep in place healthy boundaries, but you can begin anew by simply asking God to help you be defined as a person of love and begin to exhibit the behaviors of love (see 1 Cor. 13). The God of Hosea knows betrayal (see Hosea 11:1–11). He knows heartbreak, and he is there for you even now. Trust his heart and remember that your marriage is to be built on a spiritual foundation.

2. Safety

For positive changes to begin to take place, each spouse needs to feel safe. Creating a place of safety is crucial to reduce the pain and to allow the feelings of love to flow again.

It takes about five positives to counteract one negative experience, even one hurtful word in marriage. You can increase the ratio of positive to negative by cutting back on the negatives. Stop the yelling, nagging, badgering. Be judicious with your words and actions. First Peter 3:8–9 (NKJV) reminds us that in our relationships we are to "be tenderhearted, be courteous; not returning evil for evil . . . but on the contrary blessing, knowing that you were called to this, that you may inherit a blessing." These are sound principles for how to treat our spouse.

3. Affection

This is not just "You know I love you, baby," but these are to be clear demonstrations of love in ways that your partner likes to be loved. Ask yourself:

1. How do I show love to my spouse?
2. How does my spouse show love to me?
3. How would I like to be loved by my spouse?

Now, have your spouse do the same thing. Compare notes and make changes in your behavior so that you are doing the things that communicate love. Just saying "I love you" is never enough. You have to be sure that your spouse knows, feels, and receives your love.

4. Forgiveness

As long as the two of you are alive, you are going to have to work through times of heartache and disappointment. The oil of forgiveness is the only way you will survive. Forgiveness involves both forgiving and asking for forgiveness. Someone might be thinking, "I can't forgive." Ephesians 4:32 (NKJV) has helped us get over that hurdle. Paul tells us to "be kind to one another, tenderhearted, forgiving one another, even as God in Christ forgave you." There is nothing that God cannot forgive through Jesus Christ. So based on the fact that God has forgiven you in Christ, there is nothing you can't forgive because you have been forgiven so much.

Forgiveness is always *my* responsibility, even as I have been wronged. It means canceling a debt. That's something I do within myself. Don't confuse forgiveness with reconciliation. That takes two people. When I choose to forgive, it frees me to love.

Conclusion

Ultimately, the marriage you've always wanted will only come as you heed Psalm 127:1 (NASB), "Unless the LORD builds the house, they labor in vain who build it." Spiritual intimacy is not about changing your spouse and demanding vulnerability. It will begin to flow as the two of you just simply seek to embrace the heart of God in your marriage.

Questions to Discuss

1. How have you handled conflict in your marriage? What concerns you most about the way you typically handle conflict?
2. What are the expectations you brought to your marriage? Are any of them similar to the false expectations described in this chapter? What good expectations did you bring to the marriage that are now being met?
3. What strategies have you used in your marriage that have successfully stopped, or broken, negative cycles?
4. Talk together about ways you can increase the affection in your marriage. What does your spouse consider to be meaningful ways to experience affection?

For Further Reading

Tim Clinton, *Before a Bad Goodbye* (Greenville, Mass.: Word Publishing, 1999).

Tim Clinton and Julie Clinton, *The Marriage You've Always Wanted* (Greenville, Mass.: Word Publishing, 2000).

David Stoop, *Real Solutions for Forgiving the Unforgivable* (Ann Arbor, Mich.: Vine Books, 2001).

14

Threats to Sexual Intimacy

Christopher and Rachel McCluskey

"And the two will become one flesh."

Mark 10:8a

God's plan for sexual intimacy is awesome beyond description. As stated in chapter 8, sexual union can communicate our love and oneness in ways that words are simply inadequate to express. But sexual conflict and violations can also do unspeakable harm. There is perhaps no other pain a husband or wife can inflict upon their partner that cuts so deeply as a strike at their sexuality.

There are several areas in which sexual intimacy can be threatened. It is beyond the scope of this chapter to address any of these in much detail, but a brief overview can alert you to the problems most commonly experienced and should encourage you to do further reading or seek help if any of these begin to rob your intimacy.

Frequency

One of the first areas of disagreement often encountered is the desired frequency of lovemaking. We have been interviewing marriage partners separately and heard one husband complain, "She hardly ever wants to have sex!" The wife complained, "All he wants to do is have sex!" Obviously these two have differing desires for frequency. There can be many reasons for low sexual desire, or for an overly active sex drive, from pain disorders and medication reactions to past sexual abuse and sexual addictions. Both partners must be very careful with the other's feelings and must continue to talk openly about their differing preferences until they arrive at an agreeable arrangement or seek help.

Many spouses, and even well-intentioned pastors and counselors, have quoted 1 Corinthians 7:5 about not withholding ourselves from each other as a means of forcing a partner into compliance. This can be a gross misuse of God's Word and an overly simplistic means of addressing an often complex issue. We urge couples to seek professional Christian counseling if they are unable to arrive at a mutually agreeable and satisfying frequency of lovemaking.

"Sex Hurts"

One of the possible reasons for low sexual desire is pain during intercourse—acute, diffuse, consistent, periodic, stabbing, burning, aching, pulling, etc. There can be many reasons for experiencing pain, but they absolutely *must* be dealt with. The mantras of the athletic world don't apply to sexual relations; you don't "play through the pain." You don't "just do it." God designed us to be pain-avoiding creatures, and if pain begins to be associated with sexual intercourse, we will quickly develop a natural and very powerful aversion to it. Most complaints of pain can be dealt with effectively once the cause is identified, so an evaluation by a Christian sex therapist, gynecologist, or urologist is always a wise step. Don't try to ignore it or tell yourself, "It's all in my head." It's not likely to go away on its own.

Triggering of Past Sexual Abuse Memories

We store memory in all five of our senses as well as in our cognitive mind. For many people who have been sexually abused, or even those who have had sexual experiences they might not consider to have been abuse per se, a triggering effect can occur when they begin to be sexual with their spouse. Although their mind tells them, "This is okay. This is good. This is not like the other things that have happened," their senses may react to the sensory cues and override their will. When this occurs, their bodies will not respond properly, and they may become angry with themselves, or worse yet their spouse may become angry, adding to their negative pairing.

Pairing of stimuli with sexual cues, whether as a turn-on or a turnoff, is a natural process and can be addressed quite effectively. Once again, though, it is not something that is likely to get better on its own. If a person is experiencing these reactions, he or she should avail himself or herself of Christian resources for sexual abuse recovery, attend a support group, or seek out a professional Christian counselor skilled in sexual abuse work. The important thing is to be proactive rather than allowing your body to continue to be reactive, sabotaging both the beauty of what God has given you as well as the healing he has waiting for you.

Difficulty with Orgasm

There are many possible reasons for experiencing difficulty with orgasm, and this is another issue couples need to discuss openly and address proactively if it is a struggle. It may be tempting to say, "It's not that important. I don't mind. I still enjoy being together," but the experience of both partners being able to achieve climax fairly regularly (though not necessarily simultaneously) is deeply bonding and well worth the embarrassment and work that may be required to attain it.

It has been said that as much as 80 percent of sex therapy is sex education. We don't know if that's true, but we can certainly attest to the impact of a little clarification and education on numerous marriages. Many people are not aware of the side effects of many drugs—even over-the-counter ones and especially birth control pills and antidepressants—that can practically kill a sex drive and impair or block orgasmic potential. Alcohol, stress, fatigue, various physical ailments and disorders, and many other things can all compromise sexual functioning, though they may not at first appear to be related.

Masturbation is another saboteur of orgasm with a partner. The quick and predictable climax a person can achieve through self-stimulation is difficult if not impossible for a partner to match. Masturbation is not specifically forbidden in Scripture, but lust is, and lust is almost always connected with masturbatory patterns. In our opinion, masturbation falls under Paul's instructions to the Corinthians: "'Everything is permissible for me'—but not everything is beneficial. 'Everything is permissible for me'—but I will not be mastered by anything" (1 Cor. 6:12). Masturbation can rarely be considered beneficial, and it has certainly mastered many an individual, robbing them of the richness of God's gift and leading them into greater sins.

If a married person is engaging in masturbation apart from their spouse, he or she can easily short-circuit his or her ability to achieve orgasm during lovemaking. This is because real life rarely measures up to fantasy. Solitary masturbation disconnects intimacy from the sexual response cycle, creating a mere shadow of what God intended and lessening the chances of deeply connecting during lovemaking. Choosing the quick satisfaction of self-stimulation over the more difficult but far more satisfying and God-honoring acts of lovemaking should always be discouraged unless it is by mutual consent and for some specific purpose.

Although there are many other reasons for difficulty achieving orgasm, there is at least one more that must be mentioned in a chapter like this. Many couples are not aware of the importance of the clitoris for orgasm in the woman. When we talk about sex, we normally speak of penis and vagina—those are the organs involved in intercourse and in procreation. But when we speak of sex for pleasure's sake and especially for orgasm, we are talking about penis and clitoris. Studies have shown that more than half of all women, and in some studies as many as two-thirds of all women, are unable to achieve orgasm without direct clitoral stimulation.

The clitoris is a small bundle of nerve endings and tissue located above the vaginal and urinary openings. Many couples are not even aware of it, or are unsure of where it is. It contains many of the same nerve endings that are distributed along the entire shaft of the penis in the man. For a woman to achieve orgasm without clitoral stimulation can be as difficult as it would be for a man with no direct stimulation of the penis. Because most women do not receive direct clitoral stimulation during the act of intercourse, manual stimulation before, during, or after is generally required to produce an orgasm. (This is one of those times when the principle of "ladies first" works nicely!)

We must remember that God created the clitoris, and it does not serve any other function than sexual pleasure and facilitation of orgasm in a woman. It says a great deal about God's interest in our pleasure, and it presents a tremendous invitation to couples to risk, explore, learn, and grow if they have not fully discovered the importance of the clitoris.

Premature Ejaculation

Many couples experience frustration when the husband is unable to withhold ejaculation for more than a few minutes during intercourse. Actually, several studies have shown that most men are unable to prevent orgasm during active thrusting for more than two to five minutes. So if couples are frustrated with premature ejaculation, it is important first to have a frame of reference for what is actually "premature." For our purposes, we will define it as experiencing orgasm considerably before couples desire it and repeatedly being unable to improve upon that pattern.

As with most other problem areas, there can be a number of reasons for truly premature ejaculation. Probably the most common is simply that the man is allowing too much sensate arousal to flood over him as he "drinks in" everything that is happening. Recalling the importance of sensual cues for arousal, the man needs to work at paying more attention to his wife and her pleasure first before turning his attention to his own enjoyment. With practice, this can become easier to do without becoming emotionally absent in bed. It's important that he remains emotionally connected with her, but not so attuned to his physical arousal.

There are also exercises that the man can do and that couples can do together to decrease premature ejaculation. Again, it would be wise to get some Christian texts specifically on sexuality if this is a problem, and it is critical for couples to talk openly and to deal with their frustration proactively. As with almost any other sexual problem, premature ejaculation can be greatly improved if couples are willing to work at it.

"You Want to Do What?"

In every talk we have ever given on sexuality, the question of oral sex is raised. "What does the Bible say about oral sex? Is it okay? Is it a perversion?" This is another topic, like masturbation, that is not specifically addressed in Scripture. Nowhere do we read that it is expressly forbidden, nor do we clearly read that it is encouraged. However, just because something is not expressly forbidden does not make it right or necessary, and just because something is not clearly affirmed and encouraged does not make it wrong or sinful. We must look to other scriptural principles to guide us.

Many read passages such as Jude 7, which refers to the sexual immorality and perversion of Sodom and Gomorrah, as including oral sex, because they consider it a perversion of God's design for sexuality. Their position is strengthened by the fact that most dictionaries define sodomy as including not only homosexual acts and bestiality but also anal and oral copulation with the opposite sex.

However, others interpret the many references to oral delights in the Song of Songs as an indication of the total body enjoyment that the couple celebrates throughout the Song. They bolster their position by the fact that the two most densely concentrated bundles of nerve endings in our bodies are in the penis or clitoris and in the tongue. Oral sex then is seen as a natural means of pleasuring each other, in keeping with God's design of our erogenous zones.

These are issues couples need to consider openly and discuss outside of the bedroom. Most individuals will have fairly strong convictions one way or the other. If both are in agreement on the issue, there is not a problem—they are free to act in accordance with their desire to abstain or to engage without further concern. (However, we do strongly caution couples engaging in oral sex against focusing primarily on that pleasure and forfeiting the greater connection and oneness of intercourse.)

If partners disagree, and especially if they feel strongly about their positions, this can become a bitter battleground, and *that must not be allowed.* It is certainly more loving to abstain from an act that is not necessary than to push for it when one's spouse is uncomfortable, feels violated by it, or believes it is wrong. The issue should remain one that either party can bring up from time to time for reconsideration, but it is impossible to envision God being pleased with such an intimate act if it is engaged in under duress.

Scripture probably speaks most directly to issues such as this in Romans 14:3–5, where Paul addresses disputable matters such as dietary restrictions and observance of sacred days:

The man who eats everything must not look down on him who does not, and the man who does not eat everything must not condemn the man who does, for God has accepted him. Who are you to judge someone else's servant? To his own master he stands or falls. And he will stand, for the Lord is able to make him stand. One man considers one day more sacred than another; another man considers every day alike. Each one should be fully convinced in his own mind.

Concerns about Pregnancy and Birth Control

Obviously, when a couple of childbearing age are engaging in sexual relations, there is always the chance of becoming pregnant unless there is a fertility problem. Even the most reliable forms of birth control are not 100 percent effective, and some are actually fairly ineffective. Pregnancy is one of God's greatest miracles and perhaps his richest blessing, but it is not always desired at a specific time, and that is okay. Couples should talk a great deal about their desires for children and would be wise to do a degree of planning unless they want to have as many children as possible. These can sometimes be difficult discussions, but they are vitally important.

Until the turn of the twentieth century, most mainline Protestant churches held the same position as Catholics on birth control; that is, that the only acceptable form is Natural Family Planning (NFP) and that no form of artificial contraception is acceptable. There are many reasons for this position, but only two will be mentioned here. The first is that couples engaging in intercourse but impairing the potential for pregnancy are seen as embracing a part of God's gift while rejecting another. They are blocking God's ability to bless them with a child and are therefore impairing his ability to fully bless their union, moving and acting within it as he so desires.

A second reason Protestants and Catholics have historically opposed artificial contraception goes back to the discussion mentioned in chapter 8 on the messages being communicated in the sexual act. If a couple is saying with their bodies, "I am giving you every part of myself, and I want to have every part of yourself," but are then placing a barrier between themselves to block their fertility, they are not actually giving and receiving every part of their beings. They are sending conflicting messages in their lovemaking.

Most every Protestant denomination now accepts various artificial means of birth control, and studies show that even many Catholics do not follow their church's teaching on this issue. There are some logical arguments to be made in favor of contraception, but the Protestant church still has a long way to go in developing a true theology that supports artificial birth control.

For those who do elect to use contraception, there are a host of other decisions to be made. All forms create greater freedom and spontaneity, but each has potential consequences. The pill causes many women to experience hormonal imbalance and decreased libido (sex drive). It can also cause the abortion of a fertilized egg. Condoms generally cause decreased sensation and occasional allergic reactions. Diaphragms, cervical caps, and spermicidal sponges carry the potential for infection and, on rare occasions, toxic shock syndrome. Intrauterine devices and the so-called "morning-after pill" cause the abortion of a fertilized egg. Vasectomy and tubal ligation are perhaps the most effective forms but are fairly permanent.

All of these concerns make this yet another issue that requires couples to talk, read, pray, and consult with physicians and/or their clergy to ensure that they feel peaceful about their decisions. As difficult as these discussions can be, each can result in a deepening intimacy for couples who are learning to really know each other.

Infertility

One of the most painful struggles many couples face is the inability to become pregnant, or to sustain a pregnancy, when children are greatly desired. Few things introduce so much tension into the bedroom and threaten to reduce lovemaking to a mere duty. The various fertility tests and treatments available can be a wonderful blessing, but they can rob any feelings of privacy, mystery, spontaneity, or passion. The pain of disappointment month after month easily becomes paired with sexual union, requiring couples to aggressively guard against emotional withdrawal and disconnection.

Unless friends and loved ones have experienced this struggle themselves, many of their attempts at encouragement will only worsen the pain. Couples struggling with infertility often withdraw from social circles because of the constant reminders of how friends have been blessed when they have not. Even simple things like seeing a car seat in an automobile or passing the nursery wing at church can be overwhelming.

As in every other area of sexual difficulty, the most important response is for couples to talk—openly, honestly, and frequently. There is a grieving process to go through, grieving the loss of something they never really had, or had only briefly. And there are options to consider, options that sometimes threaten one's beliefs and can cause division in the marriage. Couples are encouraged to seek out support groups and/or professional counseling in addition to medical advice if they are unable to conceive when trying to do so for more than twelve months.

Conclusion

We can only touch on some of the things that can threaten to spoil the richness of God's plan for marital sexuality. If it has fostered a clearer understanding of the spirit of making love and of the messages couples communicate through those acts, as well as a greater awareness of the things that can enhance and diminish that connection, then it has accomplished its purpose. There are few things in marriage that are so difficult but so important to discuss, and which can yield such sweet fruit or bitter harvest depending on how they are handled.

Questions to Discuss

1. What do you believe are the ways in which your sexual union could be most threatened?
2. What subject covered in this chapter is difficult for you as a couple to talk about? What do you think makes it difficult?
3. What is at least one area in your sexual relationship that you are determined to talk through more, read on, pray over, or seek help with, to deepen your experience of truly making love?

For Further Reading

Christopher McCluskey, *Coaching Couples into Passionate Intimacy: God's Intention for Marital Sexual Union* (videotape), Coaching for Christian Living, 2001. (Can be ordered at www.christian-living.com.)

Clifford and Joyce Penner, *The Gift of Sex* (Waco: Word, 1981).

15

Two Barriers
to Experiencing Intimacy

David and Jan Stoop

> It is not time or opportunity that is to determine intimacy; it is disposition alone.
>
> Jane Austen, *Sense and Sensibility*

When we have boundary problems in our growing-up years, they can create one of two barriers to our being able to experience the intimacy we long for in our marriage. These two barriers are two basic fears we will experience in all of our relationships, but more so in our marriage. All of us have fears. It's a normal part of being human. The two basic fears that block intimacy are the fear of abandonment and the fear of being controlled. Both profoundly affect our ability to trust and therefore our ability to experience intimacy.

The Fear of Abandonment

Sandra grew up in a home with a dad who traveled a lot in his work, and when he was away, Sandra would often count the days until his return. But when he came home, she was always disappointed because he was "just too busy with his work." Her mother was emotionally unpredictable and sometimes very critical of Sandra and her brother.

197

At other times, her mom could be warm and caring. But her mom's inconsistency was not only in her warmth, it carried over into the way she listened to her children. Sometimes she would give full attention to Sandra; other times Sandra would be talking to her mom about something important and Sandra would realize that her mom wasn't even listening. As a result, Sandra grew up with a very critical attitude toward herself, often blaming herself for not having her emotional needs met by her parents. Somehow, she believed she was at fault. She shouldn't have needed so much from them. If she could have just been a better daughter, everything would have been fine.

Now, in her marriage, Sandra longs for emotional closeness from Ray, her husband. But whatever Ray does with or for Sandra never quite satisfies the hunger inside of her. She finds herself repeating the pattern of her childhood, trying harder to be the perfect wife so that Ray will become the emotionally warm person she longs for. Then at other times, she becomes quite critical of Ray, angry at his "not caring enough." Often a huge fight would be the result, and Ray would storm out of the house and stay away for several hours.

After one fight with her husband, Sandra's anger quickly turned into panic. She had thoughts like, *I know I overreacted. How could I be so wrong? He does try. What if he doesn't come back? Where is he? What can I do?* Before Ray came back, she had baked him some of his favorite cookies, and when he did return, she apologized over and over. She lived in constant fear that she would say or do something that would cause Ray to leave and not come back. Sandra suffered from the fear of being abandoned.

The Fear of Being Controlled

As so often happens, Sandra married someone very different from her. She loved that Ray seemed so independent, solid, and secure within himself and was very responsible. But after they were married awhile, she wished at times that Ray wasn't so responsible to everyone else. He was a Sunday school teacher for fifth graders, served on the church education committee, was an usher, and put in what seemed to her like too many hours at work. She had no doubts about his loyalty and faithfulness to her; she just wished he were home more.

Ray had grown up in a home with a dad who would probably have been labeled a workaholic. Ray never recognized that in him; he just felt his dad had to work hard to support the family and thought that was very admirable of him. Because Ray's dad was at work so much, his mother turned all of her attention on Ray and his younger brother. "She was pretty involved in our lives," Ray willingly admitted. But he went on to say that her hovering over him and his brother was just her way of being a good mother. Ray's younger brother still lived at home, but Ray had left home as soon as he graduated from high school. He went to college two thousand miles away and never moved back. He didn't go back to visit very often either. When his mom and dad came to visit, it was often a tense visit, for Ray either found ways to work more to be away from the house or, if he was at home, he always felt crowded by his mom. Ray was afraid of being controlled.

The Push-Pull of These Two Fears

We are often attracted to people who are trying to work through the opposite fear from ours. Those who most fear abandonment seem drawn to relate to those who most fear being controlled by others, and the opposite is true as well. On a rational level that doesn't make sense, but fear causes us to operate on the irrational level. Ray and Sandra are an example of a couple that has opposite fears.

Of course, Ray and Sandra don't always act this way. Their primary fear doesn't operate in isolation. In truth, they each may experience both fears at times. Sometimes Sandra's fear of abandonment causes her to try very hard in her marriage, but then she might experience more closeness than she can handle, temporarily feeling controlled and engulfed, so she backs away from Ray. Eventually her fear of abandonment rises up again, and she tries harder to be close to him. In another situation, Ray may find that Sandra is very busy with her family, and he suddenly begins to feel some abandonment, and so he moves closer to Sandra, which, if he stays that close, will stir up again his fears of being controlled.

A lot of marriages represent the push-pull of these competing fears. One fear dominates in one person and the other fear dominates in the other person. Breaking this cycle is not as easy as it looks. For one thing, if I fear abandonment, I will do a lot of things for the other person to keep him or her interested in me and enjoying my companionship. Because I am such a good caretaker, the other person has it made—or so it seems. My spouse doesn't need to do much to keep the relationship going. But what we fail to take into consideration is that, usually, the other person is operating with the fear of being controlled, and all my efforts to take care of him or her feel very controlling.

In our culture, it is usually the woman who struggles with the fear of abandonment and the man who struggles with the fear of being controlled. Although we've met couples who are the opposite, for the sake of illustration, we will identify the wife as having the fear of abandonment and the husband having the fear of being controlled.

One way of understanding this is to look at a marriage relationship as a set of two circles, each circle representing one of the marital couple. Many people have an idealized image of what these two circles should look like, especially in the early stages of a marriage. They think they should look like this:

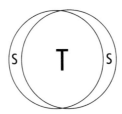

In the illustration, the "S" represents the separateness and the "T" represents the togetherness. Here we see a whole lot of togetherness and very little separateness for either person.

This is an illustration of the oneness we may think we desire to experience in our marriage. But if we try to create this kind of oneness, it soon begins to feel smothering to at least one of the two people in the marriage. And, of course, the big question is going to be, "If we are going to be one, then which one of us are we going to be—you or me?" There's too much of "us" and very little left of either "you" or "me." So after the first fight, our two circles may look like this:

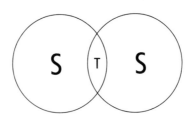

Now there is very little togetherness, or the "us," and way too much separateness, or the "me" and "you." That doesn't feel very intimate or satisfying—that's not why we got married, although some couples will settle for this over the years. They are content with a very detached, distant marriage relationship because they are both fearful of being controlled by anyone else.

Eventually, most couples work out a pattern that looks more like this:

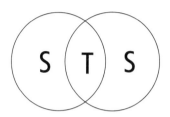

Now there is more of a balance between the "us" and the "you" and "me." We have our togetherness (T) and we still have our separate selves (S). Now let's put a box around the circles to represent the marriage unit as a closed system, or a closed economy. Let's suppose that in this economy there are two hundred coins. One hundred of these coins have a "T" stamped on them and represent the amount of energy that can be expended on togetherness. One hundred of these coins have an "S" stamped on them and represent the amount of energy that can be expended on the development of our separateness.

If you are like our typical couple, after a few years, the distribution of the coins will probably end up looking something like this:

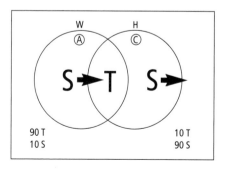

In our example, the wife has as a primary fear, the fear of abandonment (A). The husband has as a primary fear, the fear of being controlled (C). She has more togetherness coins; he has more separateness coins. Because of these primary fears, this couple will have a very stable but unsatisfying relationship. One person (in our example, the wife) spends the majority of her energy building togetherness and taking a lot of responsibility for the relationship, while the other person (in our example, the husband) spends the majority of his energy being responsible outside the marriage relationship. He is very responsible in that his energy is directed toward church activities, children-centered activities, and his job. In this arrangement, the wife becomes the pursuer, and the husband, the pursued.

In this example, because the wife fears abandonment, she will work hard to alleviate her fear of abandonment. So she places a lot of her energy and effort into working on the togetherness in their marriage. She expects them to spend time alone together on weekends and encourages her husband to leave the office at 5:30 rather than work late. She wants to spend time talking together. In addition, she plans their social calendar with other couples. But at the same time, this husband feels that all of his wife's efforts on their togetherness come across as controlling. So he puts more effort into acting responsibly on things outside the marriage. He's involved in leadership at the church; he's very responsible at his job; and he's very involved in the kids' activities, all for "the sake of the marriage." He is a good dad and a good guy.

As we said earlier, this can go either way; we're just illustrating it with the wife fearful of abandonment and the husband fearful of being controlled.

Finding More of a Balance

What needs to take place for this relationship to be more satisfying for each person? Here one or both parties needs to bravely face their fears. Fear never goes away by itself—we must always stand up and face what we fear. In this case, I'm sorry to say the burden of the work usually falls first on the one who is already doing most of the work on the relationship. The one who is fearful of abandonment (in this example, the wife) must begin to face his or her fear and chart a new course for change. But a different kind of work is required.

The person with the most togetherness coins is going to have to give up some of them. That means that he or she is going to have to stop being so responsible for nurturing the relationship—to stop being the pursuer.

For Sandra and Ray to have a more satisfying relationship, it's important to see how Sandra can change the balance. Often the person in Sandra's position—the one with the most togetherness coins—gets fed up and reacts with cold, hard anger. Usually when this happens, the other person makes some temporary adjustment, but when things cool down, everything goes back to the way it was.

For there to be real change in the way Sandra and Ray relate, Sandra will need to back off on some of the things she has done to work on their togetherness. At the same time, she will need to put more energy into her own separateness. But she needs to do this graciously and without hostility for it to be effective.

In a session with Sandra, I (Dave) helped her understand that she needed to make her change without being angry. It took awhile for her to understand how she was going to be the catalyst for change, but I coached her in how to act. First, she said to Ray, "I know I've been on your case about all of this, wanting you to be more a part of the family. I apologize for being so angry. Part of the problem is that you have your work and all those you relate to at the church, and I only have you and the kids to look after. I know I need to do something about that."

Sandra did do something about it, and Ray didn't know quite how to respond. Sandra found an art class that she had been wanting to take for several years. But it was always held on a night when Ray was either tied up at church or needed to work late. This time she signed up for it and then made arrangements for a sitter so Ray could be at the church as late as he wanted, or work as late as he wanted on that particular night of the week. She kindly told Ray of her plans and the arrangements. Ray wasn't too sure about what Sandra was proposing. He felt better when she was at home taking care of the kids. But Sandra graciously held her ground. It wasn't easy, for these changes stirred up a lot of Sandra's fears of abandonment. She really needed the reassurance of several close friends to help keep her on target.

After several weeks of Sandra's attending the art class, Ray started to get anxious. He tried to pick fights with her about the babysitting arrangement; however, she stayed in her cordial but firm position and refused to enter the battle. Next, Ray came home from work earlier on the night of her class, suggesting that, since they already had a sitter, they could have a night out together—something Sandra had longed for before. But Sandra held her ground and stayed the course—she continued with her art class. She was beginning to understand the process.

Sandra noticed over several weeks that Ray seemed more insecure and that gradually he was beginning to show signs of needing her and was taking more of an interest in the relationship. She responded to this, and it took awhile for things to shift more in the direction of balance. Gradually, they together began to work on a relationship in which each had a more equal sense of responsibility for their marriage relationship, and for their own individuality.

An interesting thing happened when Sandra faced her own fears of abandonment and started graciously acting more independent in her marriage relationship. Ray's fear of control seemed to lessen and in its place Ray became aware of his own fear of abandonment. As long as Sandra was spending all her effort on their relationship, he was secure. But once she started to work on something that was good, yet important to her individuality, he became more insecure, and his own abandonment fears rose to the surface. As Sandra became aware that Ray wasn't so secure, she became more confident in the marriage relationship, and they were able to redefine the balance of their "togetherness" coins and their "separateness" coins. Eventually, their relationship looked more like this:

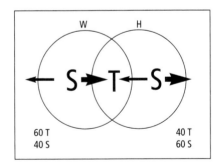

Think about your own childhood. Your sense of balance in these two basic fears is based on how well a solid, emotionally bonded relationship was built with your own mother, and then how able you were to find some separateness from her through your relationship with your father, or some other significant adult. When this process is incomplete, you will experience problems with one and/or the other of these two basic fears, which become barriers to intimacy in adulthood.

Are you afraid of being abandoned? Or are you afraid of being controlled by someone? Adults who had parents who left home, or parents who weren't home much, or a parent (or parents) who died when they were young, or who were neglected emotionally, often fear abandonment. On the other hand, adults whose parents were the overwhelming, hovering, or smothering kind often fear being controlled. Once we understand the basis for these fears that are barriers to intimacy, we can begin to face our fears and build into our marriage the right kind of behaviors that lead to intimacy.

Questions to Discuss

1. Which fear do you think is predominant in you? Which fear is predominant in your spouse?
2. The one who holds the most togetherness (T) coins in our marriage is _____.
3. The one who holds the most separateness (S) coins in our marriage is _____.
4. How even or uneven is the distribution of the coins in your marriage?
5. What are some steps you can begin to take to bring more of a balance in the distribution of the togetherness and separateness coins in your marriage?

For Further Reading

Henry Cloud, *Changes That Heal* (Grand Rapids: Zondervan, 1993).
Les Parrott, *Love's Unseen Enemy* (Grand Rapids: Zondervan, 1994).
Gary Smalley, *If Only He Knew* (Grand Rapids: Zondervan, 1988).

16

Cultivating Healthy Anger in Your Marriage

Gary and Carrie Oliver

In your anger do not sin.

Psalm 4:4a

Greg and Karen had been married for two years, and both expressed a deep love for each other and a strong commitment to their marriage. When they called for counseling, they expressed a desire to improve their communication, but it didn't take long for one of their core concerns to emerge.

It was in the middle of our first session when Greg finally opened up. "For many years I've struggled with the emotion of anger. It seems like I can go along for a while and it doesn't bother me, and then all of a sudden I lose my temper and say things I'm usually sorry for later. And I'm not the only one in my family with an anger problem. My father, who is a wonderful Christian man, has for many years had a reputation for being hot-headed. He doesn't get angry very often, but when he does, watch out."

After a brief pause Greg continued, "I didn't realize it was all that bad until Karen and I got married." He then began to relate an all-too-common story of little hurts and frustrations building into painful expressions of unhealthy anger that wounded the person he loved most. We explained to Greg and Karen that most newlyweds are surprised to discover that marriage probably generates in couples more anger than they will experience in any other relationship. When two people live together with a commitment to increasing closeness, vulnerability, and intimacy, the potential for fear, hurt, frustration, and misunderstanding is enormous. So is the potential for the emotion of anger.

After a deep and thoughtful sigh, Greg slumped down in his seat and asked, "Is there any way I can get rid of my anger?" Our response caught him by surprise. "Greg, the problem isn't the emotion of anger. The problem is that you don't understand your anger and haven't learned how to cultivate healthy anger." He immediately responded, "Healthy anger . . . you've got to be kidding me!" He continued, "I've heard anger referred to in many ways but never in the context of it being healthy." If you are like Greg and most people that we've worked with, you would have had the same response.

In our experience most people tend to view anger only as a problem, something negative, something to be avoided. Why is it that of all the various emotions anger has such a bad reputation? Why is it that so many people have a totally negative view of the emotion of anger? Is all anger bad? Is it always a sin to be angry? Is it possible for the energy of this "enemy" emotion to be constructively redirected? Can anger be used to mobilize us rather than neutralize us? In what ways can this unwelcome and potentially destructive emotion be considered a gift rather than a time bomb?

What do you think of when you hear the word *anger?* In the workshops we've led dealing with emotions, we will often ask for a word association to anger. The responses are invariably 95 percent negative. Clearly the vast majority of Christians view anger from an almost exclusively negative perspective.

In my (Gary's) more than twenty-five years in the ministry, I've spent hundreds of hours with people stymied in their effort to grow and live effectively because of their failure to acknowledge, accept, and understand the God-given emotion of anger. With the evangelical taboos on anger, many Christian couples are particularly blind to the hidden agenda of anger. Instead of naming the emotion and facing it squarely as a fact of life, they try to sit on it, shut it out, and silence it.

Anger Is a God-Given Emotion

Here are several reasons why it is important for us to understand this God-given emotion.

Anger Is a Fact of Life

One of the most fundamental aspects of being human is that we were created in God's image. This means that we are image-bearers. Even though God's image in man and woman has been damaged and distorted by sin, we are still image-bearers. Part of what it means to be made in God's image is that we, like God, have a variety of emotions and are able to experience the emotions of others. One of these emotions is anger. From Genesis 4:5 through Revelation 19:15 the Bible has a lot to say about anger. In the Old Testament alone anger is mentioned approximately 455 times with 375 of those passages referring to God's anger.

What exactly is anger? There are many words we use to describe the emotion of anger. Words like *rage, fury, wrath, resentment,* and *hostility.* Webster's defines anger as "emotional excitement induced by intense displeasure." Anger is a strong feeling of irritation or displeasure. Anger involves a physical state of readiness. When we experience anger, our mind and our body prepare us to act. Anger involves physical and emotional energy. It is up to us whether we use that energy in constructive ways or use it to abuse ourselves and/or those we love.

Anger Is a Frequently Experienced Emotion

The emotion of anger is experienced much more frequently than most people would like to admit. When we begrudge or disdain others or when we are annoyed, repulsed, irritated, frustrated, offended, or cross, we are probably experiencing some form of anger. The results of research as well as our own experience suggest that most couples experience the emotion of anger a minimum of eight to ten times a day—and that's before they have kids.

Anger Is One of the Most Powerful Emotions

The emotion of anger can provide tremendous energy to right wrongs and change things for the good. But when we allow it to control us, it can lead to negative destructive actions such as emotional, verbal, or even physical abuse and violence. In any intimate relationship there will be times when you will be hurt or wronged. When that happens it is likely you will experience anger. The next step is that our human nature wants revenge, and anger can easily distort our perspective, block our ability to love, and thus limit our ability to see things clearly. There are potentially great benefits in allowing ourselves to experience and express anger appropriately. There are also potentially devastating consequences in allowing ourselves to be controlled by our anger.

Anger Is a Secondary Emotion

Most couples don't understand that anger is a secondary emotion that is usually experienced in response to a primary emotion such as hurt, frustration, and fear. Anger can be an almost automatic response to any kind of pain. It is the emotion most of us feel shortly after we have been hurt. When your spouse corrects or talks down to you in public, it hurts, and you may respond to him or her in anger.

Anger is usually the first emotion we see. At the moment it may be the only emotion that we are aware of, yet it is rarely the only one we have experienced. Just below the surface there are almost always other, deeper emotions that need to be identified and acknowledged. Hidden deep underneath that secondary emotion of anger are the primary emotions of fear, hurt, frustration, disappointment, vulnerability, and longing for connection.

Unhealthy Anger Has Tremendous Potential for Harm

Not only is anger an uncomfortable emotional state, it is also a potentially dangerous one. Most of us have, at one time or another, been pushed so hard and become so angry that we could have or indeed have become violent. I recently came across some sobering statistics that clearly demonstrate the potential harm of anger out of control:

- Ten million children were beaten by angry parents, two-thirds under the age of three.
- Sixty percent of all homicides were committed by people who knew the victim.
- Twenty-seven percent of all policemen killed are killed breaking up domestic arguments.
- More than 70 percent of all murderers don't have a criminal record.

One psychiatrist interviewed more than one hundred inmates convicted of murder and concluded that most were not angry people. In most cases they had stuffed their emotions and allowed their anger to build and build, and they had finally expressed it in an out-of-control and violent way.

Healthy Anger Has Tremendous Potential for Good

For most people the emotion of anger is considered negative, a problem, something to be eliminated or solved. What we so often fail to see is that every problem is really an opportunity in disguise, an opportunity to learn, to grow, to mature, to be used of God to make significant changes for the good. Anger, like love, is an emotion that has tremendous potential for both good and evil. That's why it is so important for us to understand it.

In her helpful book *The Dance of Anger,* Harriet Lerner notes:

Anger is a signal and one worth listening to. Our anger may be a message that we are being hurt, that our rights are being violated, that our needs or wants are not being adequately met, or simply that something isn't right. Our anger may tell us that we are not addressing an important emotional issue in our lives, or that too much of our self—our beliefs, values, desires or ambitions—is being compromised in a relationship. Our anger may be a signal that we are doing more and giving more than we can comfortably do or give. Or our anger may warn us that others are doing too much for us, at the expense of our own competence and growth. Just as physical pain tells us to take our hand off the hot stove, the pain of our anger preserves the very integrity of our self. Our anger can motivate us to say no to the ways in which we are defined by others and yes to the dictates of our inner self.[1]

Anger is to our lives like a smoke detector is to a house, like a warning light is to a car, and like a flashing yellow light is to a driver. Each one serves as a kind of warning or alarm to stop, look, and listen. They say, "Take caution; something might be wrong."

It is important for us to remember that anger is energy. While we may have minimal control over the fact that we experience anger, we have almost total control over how we choose to express that anger. We can either *spend* that energy or we can *invest* it. We can choose to harness and channel that anger-energy in healthy, positive, and constructive ways.

The energy of anger, when wisely invested, can provide greater focus and intensity and lead to greater productivity. Martin Luther said, "When I am angry I can write, pray and preach well, for then my whole temperament is quickened, my understanding sharpened, and all mundane vexations and temptations gone."

As you learn creative ways to invest the God-given anger-energy, as you develop more effective anger management skills, as you learn how to approach anger from a biblical perspective, you will find one of the most powerful sources of motivation available to humankind.

Constructive Steps for Dealing with Anger

One of the most effective ways to make the emotion of anger work for you rather than against you is to decide in advance that when you experience anger you will choose to invest the anger-energy and express it in a healthy way. When you are angry, the power of that emotion can block your ability to think clearly. Think back to the last time you experienced strong anger. How objective were you? How clearly were you thinking? It is important to develop a plan for dealing with anger before you get angry. Here are some simple steps that you can take to help your anger work for you.

Step 1: Be aware of it.

If you had met Greg at church you would not have considered him to be an angry person. He rarely appears to be angry. One of the many myths regarding anger is that if a person doesn't look or appear on the outside to be angry, then they don't have a problem with anger, and they are clearly not an angry person. While Greg does not appear to be an angry person on the outside, he can be like a battlefield on the inside. When he feels misunderstood by Karen or when she contradicts him in public, his anger is right there. How often are you aware of being angry? What situations do you encounter that might make you more vulnerable to anger? How does your body respond to anger? What are your physical manifestations of anger?

Step 2: Accept responsibility for it.

Someone has said that one of the major effects of original sin is seen in our tendency to blame someone else for our problems. When God confronted Eve in the garden and asked her what happened, she blamed the serpent. When God confronted Adam, Adam first blamed Eve and then he blamed God. When we are angry it is easy for us to blame someone else, to say, "It's your fault; you made me angry." This is especially true in marriage. While it's true that other people can say or do things that cause hurt or frustration, we are responsible for how we choose to respond. If we are angry, it is *our* anger.

Step 3: Determine at the outset who or what is going to have control.

This is a critical step. When we become aware that we are angry, we are faced with a choice. We can either allow the emotion of anger to dominate and control us, or we can, with the help of the Holy Spirit, choose to control the anger and invest the anger-energy in a healthy way. While we can't always control ourselves when we *experience* anger, we can with God's help choose how we *express* the anger. As we take our anger to God in prayer, he will help us find creative and constructive ways to deal with it.

Step 4: Define it! Identify the source and cause of it.

While there is an almost limitless number of situations that can lead to anger, most causes of anger come under three major categories: hurt, frustration, and fear.

Hurt is usually caused by something that has already happened, something in the past. When we are hurt we feel vulnerable and open to more hurt. This is especially true of people who are very sensitive. Believe it or not, even men can be sensitive. For many people anger is an automatic defense mechanism to protect against hurt. When I get angry at someone it tends to erect a wall between us, and then I can hide behind that wall. The unhealthy expression of anger produces distance between individuals, and many feel safer with that distance.

Frustration is an emotion that takes place in the present. We can become frustrated by blocked goals or desires or by unmet expectations. Frequently the things that lead to the greatest frustrations have one main characteristic—they really aren't that important.

In our own marriage, one situation that has frequently led to my (Gary's) expressing unhealthy anger is when I'm trying to communicate with Carrie and she doesn't understand what I'm trying to say. I'm especially vulnerable to frustration when I'm tired, weary, and in a hurry. When she doesn't seem to "get it," I can assume she's not trying, she's not listening, or she just doesn't care. When I let my unhealthy anger take over, I can become sarcastic, cold, and in times past even mean. I'm not proud of it, I don't enjoy it; I've apologized on numerous occasions for it, and I've made great progress with it, but it still happens.

What kinds of situations cause you to become frustrated? Are there any specific individuals that you find more frustrating than others? What situations or individuals have frustrated you this past month? When are you most vulnerable to experiencing frustration? How do you usually respond when you are frustrated?

Fear is an emotion that tends to focus on things in the future. Many people associate fear with vulnerability and weakness. Some people, especially men, find it more comfortable to express anger than fear, and so many respond to situations in which they are anxious or afraid by getting angry. When you are experiencing the emotion of anger and aren't sure where it is coming from, ask yourself, "Is there something that I am afraid of that could be triggering my anger?"

Step 5: Choose your response. Are you going to spend your anger-energy or are you going to invest it?

There are many ways to deal with anger. Some are constructive and some are destructive. Some of the destructive ways to deal with anger

214   The Challenges of Marriage

are to stuff, deny, suppress, or repress. One of the most destructive ways of dealing with anger is to ventilate it or dump it on someone else. The problem is that for most of us the more we talk about it the more worked up we get. Ventilating the anger tends to increase rather than decrease it. Paul Hauck has stated that "attacking someone else is like throwing cactus with your bare hands; they may get hurt but so will you."[2]

When you are angry one of the first steps is to start by asking yourself the question, "Is this really that important?" If it isn't then simply let it pass. If it is important, then ask yourself, "How can I express my anger in a way that is biblically consistent and that will enhance the probability of resolution?"

Take your Bible and look at some of the key passages that deal with anger: Proverbs 15:18; 16:32; 29:11; Mark 3:5; Ephesians 4:26–31; Colossians 3:8, 21. Make sure that you "speak the truth in love." Take the time to acknowledge the other person's opinion and feelings. Be open to an apology or an explanation. Make your primary goal understanding and then work toward an agreement.

Some Final Observations

For many couples both the experience and expression of anger have become a habit. Habits can be hard to change and may take some time. The good news is that with God's help we can change, we can grow, and we can be more than conquerors. As we allow the Holy Spirit to fill us and as we apply promises in God's Word, we can stop the old unhealthy ways of responding and develop new, healthy, and biblically consistent emotional responses.

In Daniel 1:8 we are told that Daniel "purposed in his heart" not to defile himself with the king's meat. And he didn't. We can purpose in our hearts not to allow our anger to control us but rather to put our anger as well as our other emotions under God's control. Again, while we can't always control when or why we will experience anger, we can with God's help control how we express that anger.

David Augsburger offers three helpful suggestions for dealing with anger:[3]

1. Be angry, but beware: You are never more vulnerable than when you are angry. Self-control is at an all-time low, reason decreases, and common sense leaves.

2. Be angry, but be aware: Anger can easily turn to resentment, bitterness, and violence. Anger can become a way of life, making you bitter and joyless.

3. Be angry, but be kind: Only when anger is motivated by love is it constructive and creative anger.

If you have a problem with anger, the problem isn't with the emotion of anger but with your ability to understand and deal with the emotion. Anger is an emotion. Like all other emotions it is not in itself good or bad. There are only good or bad uses of it. Part of what it means to be made in God's image is that we can experience and express the emotion of anger. When we are angry we are energized. We can either control and direct that energy or we can let it control us. We can be conquered or we can with God's help be more than conquerors.

God has given us that choice. We can allow ourselves to be controlled by our anger or we can pursue "quality anger." Quality anger involves open, honest, and direct communication. It involves speaking the truth in love. It involves investing the energy God has given us to declare truth, to right wrongs, and to help ourselves and others "become conformed to the image of His Son" (Rom. 8:29 NASB).

Evaluate Your Anger Expression[4]

Place a check by those statements you believe are true:

Positive Results

_____ 1. My spouse responded better after I expressed my anger.

_____ 2. I felt better after expressing my anger.

_____ 3. I feel my spouse felt better after the interchange. (It would be helpful if you asked him or her about this.)

_____ 4. Becoming angry protected me when my spouse became upset.

_____ 5. My spouse gained a clearer understanding of my position because of my anger.

_____ 6. I feel closer to my spouse because of expressing my anger.

_____ 7. Becoming angry helped solve the problem so we won't need to experience it again.
_____ 8. We felt more loving toward one another because of expressing anger.
_____ 9. My expression of anger involved more constructive statements than provocative.
_____10. We learned from this experience so that our next disagreement should be better.

Negative Results

_____ 1. In expressing my anger, I was so upset that I didn't clarify my position well.
_____ 2. I made statements or behaved in a way that I now regret.
_____ 3. My spouse did not accept what I said.
_____ 4. My spouse had difficulty hearing me because of my anger.
_____ 5. My spouse became upset because of my anger and became very emotional.
_____ 6. My spouse was hurt by my anger.
_____ 7. My spouse is still recovering from my anger.
_____ 8. My anger prolonged the disagreement and hindered us from finding a solution.
_____ 9. Our next disagreement will probably be more difficult because of my anger. We really didn't learn from this experience.

Questions to Discuss

1. Where did you learn about the emotion of anger?
2. What is the difference between healthy and unhealthy anger?
3. Look up the verses referenced that deal with anger, or look up additional verses in a concordance referencing anger. What is one insight or principle that you can pull from each verse?
4. When are you most likely to experience the emotion of anger?
5. What is the primary emotion that most often triggers the secondary emotion of anger for you?

For Further Reading

Paul Hauck, *Overcoming Frustration and Anger* (Philadelphia: Westminster Press, 1974).

Gary and Carrie Oliver, *Raising Sons and Loving It!* (Grand Rapids: Zondervan, 2000).

Gary Oliver and H. Norman Wright, *Good Women Get Angry* (Ann Arbor, Mich.: Servant Publications, 1995).

Gary Oliver and H. Norman Wright, *When Anger Hits Home* (Chicago: Moody Press, 1992).

David Stoop, *Self-Talk: Key to Personal Growth* (Grand Rapids: Revell, 1996).

Glenn Taylor and Rod Wilson, *Exploring Your Anger* (Grand Rapids: Baker, 1997).

Warren Wiersbe, *Angry People: And What We Can Learn from Them* (Grand Rapids: Baker, 2001).

17

Unpacking the Family Baggage

David and Jan Stoop

"Listen to me, all who hope for deliverance—all who seek the Lord! Consider the quarry from which you were mined, the rock from which you were cut! Yes, think about your ancestors."

Isaiah 51:1–2 (NLT)

Remember the old song, "I want a gal, just like the gal, that married dear old dad"? For many of those who grew up in that era, they could have just as easily said, "I want a marriage just like mom and 'dear old dad' had." But times have changed, and most of us today would say, "I want more than what my parents had in their marriage." We may love Mom and Dad dearly, and they may have had a good marriage, but we want ours to be better. And with the increased number of divorces, many of us today are saying, "We want our marriage to be different—we intend for our marriage to last!" But it takes more than good intentions.

I (David) can still see the look on Marian's face. She had been giving me some history about her estranged husband's family. Dan had left Marian about three months before for another woman, and she was trying to understand what had happened and what to do from this point forward. In the course of the conversation, she said that Dan's father had left his mom for another woman when Dan was thirteen, and that Dan had never spoken to his dad ever since that point in time.

I looked back in my notes and then said to Marian, "Isn't that interesting? His father left his mom when he, the oldest in his family, was thirteen. How old is your oldest child?" Without really thinking, she answered, "Thirteen." And then it hit her—Dan had acted out a generational pattern with a frightening precision.

The question being raised in your mind is probably the same one she asked. "Does that mean he was 'destined' to act this out?"

"No," I assured her. "But when we don't look at the baggage from our family-of-origin, it is easy for generational patterns to repeat themselves. Dan's refusal to have anything to do with his father over these years meant he simply had stored away all the baggage from his past and had hoped it would stay hidden in its place."

What Are Generational Patterns?

Generational patterns are the repetition of behavioral patterns from one generation to the next. One of the ways the Bible talks about generational patterns is to call them the "sins of the fathers." We read that God is rich in "unfailing love to many thousands by forgiving every kind of sin and rebellion. Even so I do not leave sin unpunished, but I punish the children for the sins of their parents to the third and fourth generations" (Exod. 34:7 NLT).

An example of repeated generational patterns can be seen in the Book of Genesis, where we have the history of one family over the period of four generations. Let's look at some of the repeated patterns of behavior. The bitter hatred that Joseph's brothers had toward him, which led them to the point of their almost killing him, was part of a larger pattern that had existed over several generations. Joseph was a favored child. Genesis 37:3 (NLT) says that "Jacob loved Joseph more than any of his other children." This favoritism toward one child as opposed to the others was a generational pattern. Genesis 25:28 (NLT) says, "Isaac loved Esau . . . but Rebekah favored Jacob."

And go back another generation: Abraham and Sarah favored Isaac over Ishmael. In addition, in each generation, one son is sent away.

In Abraham's generation, Ishmael and his mother, Hagar, were sent away because Sarah was jealous. In the next generation, Jacob was sent away by his mother because she feared for his life. And then in the next generation, Joseph was sold into slavery because of the hatred of his brothers due to the favoritism shown by their father. And in the family of Jacob and the family of Isaac, the favoritism had a negative effect on their marriage, and even the marriages of their children.

In each generation, marriages were affected as the patterns were repeated. Can you imagine the tension between Isaac and Rebekah as they lived out the tensions of their divided home? What started out as a beautiful love story between these two people turned into a tense, and probably estranged, marriage. And Jacob's tensions started out between his two wives—one of whom he loved and the other whom he merely tolerated. Abraham's tension was resolved by sending Hagar and Ishmael away. Generational patterns are not only seen in parent-child relationships, they have a profound effect on marriage as well.

Unpacking the Baggage—Breaking Free from the Patterns

Ray and Cathy were concerned about breaking the pattern of their parents—both sets of parents had divorced. Ray's parents divorced when he was starting high school; Cathy's parents had divorced when she was five. They were both committed to making their marriage last forever.

Ray commented on how, when his parents divorced, in his anger, he vowed that when he married, he would never divorce. He and Cathy had talked about this prior to their marriage, and each took their marriage vows very seriously as a commitment to stay together until death. But was a vow enough to break a generational pattern? From the experiences of many of their friends, they felt it wasn't. They saw too many of their friends getting divorced in spite of their vows.

I (Dave) suggested that Ray and Cathy look at Isaiah 51:1–2 (NLT). The opening line calls out to what they were desiring: "Listen to me, all who hope for deliverance—all who seek the LORD!"

"That's us," they almost said in unison. "We want deliverance from the past patterns!"

Then they read on. Isaiah says, "Consider the quarry from which you were mined, the rock from which you were cut!" Ray stopped and thought a moment about what he had just read.

"Is that sorta like what my dad's friends used to say about me—that I was a 'chip off the old block'?" Then he answered his own question by reading on: "Yes, think about your ancestors Abraham and Sarah, from whom you came."

We talked about what they had just read. It seemed clear that what Isaiah was suggesting is that if we want deliverance from any problem or situation, we need to understand the beginnings of that problem or situation. In Ray and Cathy's case, they needed to understand what had been going on in their parents' lives prior to the divorces and also what had been going on in the generation that shaped their parents.

The Genogram

One of the most helpful tools we can use to think about our ancestors is called the *genogram*. A genogram is

> a sort of expanded family tree that charts the relational and emotional aspects of a family across several generations. It includes the kind of information that a typical family tree would contain—names, birthdays, weddings, divorces, deaths, and the like. But it also includes brief descriptions of family members, their particular strengths and weaknesses, and aspects of their lives that can have a continuing effect down through the years.[1]

A genogram can help us not only identify generational patterns; it also can give us understanding in three ways. Before we can break the patterns of the past, we must understand what they are. First, we can gain insight into how personal and marital boundaries have been handled. Second, we can identify what types of roles people have had to play in their family. And third, we can articulate some of the unspoken rules we were taught as we grew up.

When working with couples, I always ask questions about their family-of-origin and look for these three things: the boundary issues, the roles people play, and the unspoken rules that form the basis for recurring patterns over the generations. Many times, these couples have said, "This should be required work for every couple before they get married." I don't think they meant that would have changed their choice of whom they married—they were probably thinking instead of all the hassles and frustrations they had encountered that would have been different if they had known what was packed away in the family baggage. Let's look at how we can construct our family's genogram.

Step 1: Gathering Information

You begin by remembering everything you can remember about your family-of-origin. Talking together with your spouse will help refresh your memory. And your spouse can point out things about how your family functions that you cannot see. Then expand on your knowledge by gathering as much information as you can by going back at least two generations. Talk to your parents. Call your grandparents, your aunts, uncles, and cousins. You might especially want to talk with whoever has been labeled the black sheep in your family-of-origin. They usually have some interesting bits of information that are often very helpful.

Step 2: Building Your Genogram

Get a large piece of paper, about the size of the sheets that come with demonstration flip-charts. You'll need the space because you want everything on one sheet so you can look at it as a whole. The husband's family will be on the left half of the paper and the wife's family will be on the right half of the paper. Here are the basic symbols to use in making your genogram. Male family members are represented by squares; females are represented by circles. An "X" is drawn through a square or circle to indicate that the person is deceased. Children are listed with the oldest on the left and the youngest on the right. Marriage is represented by a solid horizontal line connecting the symbols. Two slashes through such a line represents a divorce.

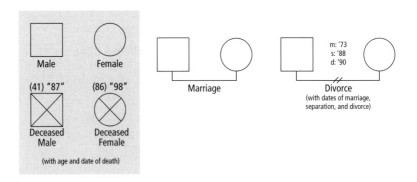

Now let's see how we put together one family:

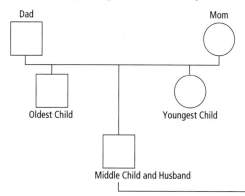

What we have just drawn is the family-of-origin for the husband. We can see that he is the middle child and that both parents are alive and are still married to each other. The line that comes off the bottom of the husband and then goes to the right will connect to the wife's circle, which is drawn within her family-of-origin. We always "drop" the main person being highlighted. In this family, the husband is highlighted, so he is dropped lower on the sheet than his siblings. We would do the same thing with the wife. And when we draw the father and mother's family-of-origin, they will be dropped lower than their siblings so we can see more clearly their relationship with you as a husband or you as the wife. So parents and grandparents are always going to be dropped down a little lower than their siblings.

Let's look at how we might draw it if it were a little more complicated. Let's imagine that your husband's mother died when he was ten, and his father remarried someone who was divorced with two children, and they subsequently had a child together. Here's what that would look like:

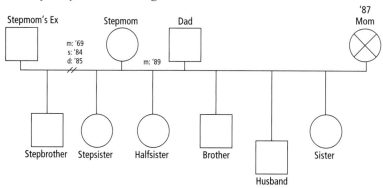

We can see now that the husband has a brother and a sister, a half sister, and a stepbrother and stepsister. We see that his mother died in 1987 and that his father remarried in 1989. His stepmother was divorced in 1985.

Step 3: Flesh Out Your Combined Genograms

Once you've done your research and built your three-generational family tree, go back and add the names of all the individuals and the key dates that relate to them. Then add any other events or issues, such as alcoholism, divorces, deaths, suicides, and so forth, along with a brief description of what that person was like and what their relationships were like. Look at whom they were close to and whom they sought to avoid. Draw a double line between them and the person they were close to and a jiggly line between them and the person they tended to avoid. Or use different color pencils to highlight the straight lines and the jiggly lines. And then look to see what patterns you can identify as repeating themselves both across the generation and down through the generations. You can add any personal touches you want that will make it clearer for you to see the patterns.

Now a word of caution. One doesn't need to become an "emotional archeologist" to do a genogram. Take enough time to be able to see the patterns but avoid the urge to keep searching for every little tidbit of information possible. If you and your partner will work on this together, you should be able to keep a good balance between getting enough information and avoiding the extremes. The idea is not to find out who the villains are in your family. We aren't looking to condemn family members. We want to better understand the "sins of the fathers" over the generations.

And it is important to recognize that we are not trying to blame anyone for whatever problems we might be experiencing. Our goal is to be able to take full responsibility for ourselves and then to find freedom from these generational patterns. We want to learn to respond to what has happened to us in a way that helps us rise above the negative influences and patterns of the past. Once we identify the patterns, we can find this freedom through prayer and forgiveness.

Breaking Generational Patterns through Forgiveness

When dealing with issues of the past, the only way they can be resolved is through forgiveness. That's how God deals with our past—through forgiveness. When told this, people usually have one of two reactions: Either "I've already forgiven them," or "I'll never forgive them!" We need to look at each of these two options.

Forgive?—But I've already forgiven them.

If your response is "I've already forgiven them," no one is going to question that statement, except to ask whether or not you have experienced freedom in your relationship with that person through your forgiveness. One of the pressures we can experience when dealing with issues of the past is that we must forgive quickly. Sometimes we think we have genuinely forgiven someone, but we have been pressured into a "too-quick-forgiveness." Someone may have said to us something like, "You're a Christian—you have to forgive. What are you waiting for?" And so we forgive quickly without working through the emotions and/or the consequences of what we have forgiven.

Quick forgiveness is reserved for minor offenses. More serious offenses take time, and the more serious the offense, the more time it may take. I've found that our wanting to forgive quickly often comes down to wanting to forgive like God forgives. First John 1:9 (NLT) says, "But if we confess our sins to him, he is faithful and just to forgive us and to cleanse us from every wrong." When we ask ourselves, "How long does it take God to forgive when we confess?" the answer is "Instantly!" So that's how we want to forgive.

However, that perspective is only looking at a small piece of the history of God's activities with humankind. We only look at the "post-cross" era. What if we had lived in Old Testament times? If we sinned, we would have to offer either a sin offering or a guilt offering (see Lev. 4–6:7). And every time we sinned, we would have to repeat the sacrifice process, because forgiveness was incomplete back then. Only at the cross was forgiveness complete—finished!

Or take Adam and Eve as they were in the Garden of Eden after they disobeyed God. If forgiveness was instant back then, all they would have had to do was confess and the problem would have been resolved. The opposite was true. They confessed, but their complete forgiveness (on the cross) was still a long way off. One could say that from the garden to the cross, God was in the process of forgiving. In the garden, God made the decision to forgive, but it wasn't until the cross that this forgiveness was completed. In between, he processed his grief and anger at our sinning, at our offense. If God could take all those thousands of years to forgive, what is our rush?

Forgive?—I'll never forgive them!

The other option is never to forgive. Our hurts from our growing-up years may be so deep that the very thought of forgiving is beyond us. But whatever we haven't forgiven from our past is always seeking to express itself in our present. That's part of why generational patterns repeat themselves. There are several misunderstandings we have about forgiveness that keep us from forgiving.

One of these misunderstandings is that if I forgive, I must forget. And then we go to the reverse idea—because I can't forget, I can't forgive. But for human beings, forgiveness has nothing to do with forgetting. Let's define forgiveness. One of the more understandable definitions is that forgiveness means "to cancel a debt." Banks forgive bad loans. They actually say, "The debt has been forgiven." And we know that when a bank forgives a loan, it never forgets it. The bank learned something in that process—whoever's loan was forgiven was obviously a bad risk, and banks will never lend them money again. There are consequences, but the debt has been canceled.

We often think we must forget because God forgives and forgets. For example, God says, "For I will forgive their wickedness and will remember their sins no more" (Jer. 31:34). God can forgive and forget because he doesn't need to learn anything in the process. We forgive and remember because we need to learn some important lessons in the process.

Another misunderstanding that keeps us from forgiving the past is the fear that if we forgive, we will somehow condone the hurt that was done to us. We will make the offense "okay." Forgiveness never makes a hurtful, evil act into something good. The process of forgiving only cancels the debt; it doesn't mean the debt never existed. The act of forgiving must always take into account the seriousness of the offense. Forgiving never erases an evil. Nor does it benefit the other person by letting him or her off the hook. There are still the consequences of what occurred. Forgiving simply frees us from bitterness and resentment and breaks generational patterns.

A third misunderstanding—probably the main thing that keeps people in a bind over forgiveness—is the belief that forgiveness and reconciliation are one and the same. We think if we forgive, we must be reconciled to that person, regardless of what the other person says or does. Forgiveness and reconciliation are two separate and distinct processes. We can have forgiveness without reconciliation, but we can't have reconciliation without forgiveness. Forgiveness requires only my effort to accomplish the task; reconciliation requires that both of us enter into the process. It takes us both working on repenting and forgiving for there to be reconciliation.[2]

Our failure to effectively resolve our past is the fuel that keeps generational patterns at work within our relationships, and especially within our marriages. So what are the steps we can take to lead to forgiveness and freedom? Here are five steps that form what we call the "process of forgiving," or unpacking our family baggage.

1. We begin with the awareness of the patterns and behaviors we don't want to repeat in our marriage or in our family relationships. This is the "truth" step. We need to be honest about what has happened to us. I (Dave) remember, long after my father had died, how I had to come to terms with his temper and abuse. I had blocked it out of my mind soon after he died. But I was also determined that my relationship with my sons would be different than his relationship with me. I found that years later, as my oldest was finishing high school, I had repeated the pattern of emptiness in my relationships with my sons and with my wife. I was my dad all over again. That reality, coupled with some timely statements by my sister, forced me to face the truth about my past relationship with my father.

2. Once I faced that painful truth, I moved into the next step of the process. I finally grieved over my father. When he died some twenty years earlier, I didn't really grieve. I tried, but I wasn't able to. Finally, once I faced the truth, I was able to grieve. I was angry; I was sad. Memories flooded my mind about things I had shut out for years. I came to realize that the ulcer I had at ten years of age was due to the tension of living with his temper. I wept and I raged. I talked with Jan. All the emotion that had

been shut off over the years rose to the surface. It was important that I talked with people I trusted during that time. I needed to express what was going on inside me.

3. If my dad had been alive, the third step would have been to set some healthy boundaries so that he couldn't keep hurting me as he had when I was young. I can't forgive something that is continuing to occur in my life. I need to be able to stop the hurtful behavior before I can forgive it. If I try to forgive without setting healthy boundaries to ward off the hurtful behaviors, I am merely excusing the behaviors, and that is always an encouragement for those hurtful things to continue. So before I reach the step of forgiving, I need to protect myself.

4. Now comes the step of actually forgiving. What has been a process up to this point now becomes a decisive act. I choose to cancel the debt—for me, my father didn't owe me anything anymore!

5. After the forgiving comes the opportunity to consider the possibility of reconciliation. Up to this point, I have not involved the other person in my process. My father was dead at the time, so I couldn't involve him. But even if he had been alive, I would not have included him in steps one through four. Only after forgiving him would I consider involving him, and that is always optional. It's important to do this only after forgiving, for if I have truly canceled the debt, my expectations are minimal, and the risk of additional hurt is limited.

What I found after working through the forgiving of my father was that I was a different person. I truly believe that the generational pattern that I was repeating was broken. Jan says that I not only became more of a father to my sons, I became more of a husband to her. I did feel, and still do feel, an incredible release from the painful repetition of what I had experienced growing up. Forgiveness will break the generational patterns and will bring freedom to your marriage.

Questions to Discuss

1. What are some of the good things you saw in your parents' marriage that you want to include in your marriage?

2. What are some of the ways you want your marriage to be different from your parents'? Could some of these areas be considered generational patterns?
3. Talk together about some of your memories about your "larger family." What were your grandparents like? What was their marriage like? What about aunts and uncles—any of them unusual? Any of them have good marriages?
4. What patterns do you see in your "larger family" that could be considered generational patterns? Talk together about your thoughts and feelings about those patterns.

For Further Reading

Dave Carder et al., *Secrets of Your Family Tree* (Chicago: Northfield Publishing, 1999).

Harville Hendrix, *Getting the Love You Want* (New York: Henry Holt & Co., 2001).

David Stoop, *Real Solutions to Forgiving the Unforgivable* (Ann Arbor, Mich.: Vine Books, 2001).

David Stoop and James Masteller, *Forgiving Our Parents, Forgiving Ourselves* (Ann Arbor, Mich.: Vine Books, 1991).

Sandra Wilson, *Released from Shame: Recovery for Adult Children of Dysfunctional Families* (Downers Grove, Ill.: InterVarsity Press, 1991).

18

Husband and Wife and Baby Make Three

Elisa Morgan and Carol Kuykendall

We were like newlyweds for the first nine years. Then children started arriving, three in four years. Now we struggle to maintain a relationship that is a shadow of what it once was.

An interviewed couple

Children change a marriage. Completely and permanently. They change who we are as individuals and as a couple. They change the way we think and act and relate to each other. They are both an incredible joy and a total distraction as they cause us to redefine ourselves and our relationship. Children throw a marriage out of whack.

Think of a marriage and family as a whimsical mobile. The mobile is first made up of a husband and wife who are tied to each other by their heartstrings at their wedding. For a time they bounce around together as they adjust to each other's personalities and habits, values and expectations. Soon they settle down as they gain a sense of balance in their relationship.

In time, a child is added to the mobile. New strings are added, the original ones are stretched, and the whole mobile wobbles crazily out of whack. This bouncing around increases as a second and maybe a third child is added. Husband and wife have become mom and dad, and they face a critical transition in their marriage. Their challenge is to regain a sense of balance in their relationship within the new configuration of the family mobile.

230

But here's the good news. Couples can grow stronger through this challenge. The way they learn to love each other through this transition will help them maneuver their way through all the other transitions their marriage will face in the future. And there will be plenty. Here are six principal areas of change in a marriage with children.

Regain Balance

Children change a marriage in deeply enriching ways but also in confusing ways that make many couples feel they have lost their sense of balance. Experts identify the birth of a first child as a potential crisis time in a marriage, because a baby changes the roles and responsibilities of both husband and wife. Many couples are surprised by the changes in their priorities and lifestyle and the emotional reactions to those changes. "My wife is so consumed by this baby, she doesn't even know I'm around." "My husband thinks I love my child more than I love him, and fear grips my heart that he might be right."

The way to regain balance is to recognize the imbalance as normal and to realize that healthy marriages are works in progress. A good marriage is always growing and changing; a good marriage is always hard work, and learning to love your way back to balance will strengthen and enrich your relationship.

Recommit Yourselves to Each Other

Children deepen, complicate, and test the "I do's" of marriage. When a couple stands at the altar and makes those vows about "for better or for worse" and "in sickness and in health," they hardly have a clue of what they're saying. But they learn to live out those vows at a deeper level when they begin raising a child together.

Consider, for instance, the "sickness and health" vow. When a husband or wife got the flu before they became parents, the other probably didn't change the day's plan. But when a parent and a small child get the flu at the same time, the other parent must rearrange all plans to care for the sick family members. Before children, commitment only stretches to include another adult. With children, commitment requires greater personal sacrifice.

The over and over again need for commitment is really a *recommitment,* which restores balance to the marriage mobile. Recommitment comes through intentional efforts in four areas.

1. *Sacrifice.* In the 1800s, Ralph Waldo Emerson remarked, "The greatest gift is a portion of thyself." True. Sacrifice is wrestling your body from sleep to care for a crying baby so that your spouse can rest. It's giving up your moment of free time to wash dishes or clothes or cars or babies—even when no one specifically has asked you to do so.
2. *Kindness.* Similar to sacrifice, kindness is simply small behaviors that enhance the life of the one we love. Kindness is bringing a cup of coffee to the bedside of your spouse. It calls up a babysitter and whisks a wife away to an unexpected dinner out. It says "please" and "thank you" and "I love you" in simple actions.
3. *Forgiveness.* Even when he couch-potatoed all afternoon while she cleaned the entire house, forgiveness comes in to smooth out the wrinkles. When she sighs and groans and whines about not having any help, he moves to action without judging her style or emotions. Forgiveness doesn't hold grudges. It aims to move beyond the disagreements. It doesn't major on the minors.
4. *Discipline.* Like any other skill, the habit of love improves with the discipline of practice. You may agree not to retreat into silence during a conflict. You may decide to phone each other when one of you will be more than half an hour late. Discipline takes the smallest of skills and enlarges their effects in a marriage by using them over and over again.

Commitment in marriage is a promise made to another person before God. Commitment is not based on feelings but an intentional act of the will. In marriage, commitment is an over and over again recommitment of those promises, which restores balance to the marriage mobile.

Redefine Yourselves

When a first child is born or adopted, a mother and father are born as well, and this new role causes us to ask: "Who are you and me, now that we are three?" Both husband and wife redefine themselves as individuals and as a couple in this new role. Interdependence is the mixture of the separate and together parts of individuals in a marriage relationship.

Children play a major role in this redefining process, especially as they reveal our original family issues. The way we approach parenting is affected by the way we were raised, but we don't realize how many of those patterns are stuffed into our heads until we become parents. We might discover differences in our expectations about gender roles, such as who changes the diapers or who gets up in the middle of the night to respond to a crying child.

Bringing balance to our interdependence means working together, yet also allowing differences in our style. We need to respect and accept that mommy style and daddy style will not always be the same, but that doesn't mean one is better than the other. Daddy might dress a child differently or play with a child differently than Mommy, but that doesn't mean different is always wrong or better. To check your progress in this earthly endeavor, ask yourself these questions: "Am I helping my spouse to reach his or her God-given potential?" "Is my spouse better because I'm in his or her life?" "How am I encouraging my spouse's uniqueness through our marriage?"

Regaining balance means seeking to understand and respect the way we live out this new role in our lives.

Rediscover Intimacy

All marriages struggle to retain, grow, and enjoy marital intimacy, and children bring a unique challenge to this area of the relationship. First, let's clarify that intimacy isn't all about sex. It really means "into-me-see," and it's about being understood by each other. It's being intentional about maintaining both emotional and physical closeness.

Children can deepen and diminish intimacy. From the moment we receive the news we are going to have a baby, our love takes on a deeper meaning. We suddenly share a new, creative purpose. Then there's the emotional intimacy of sharing the joint project of parenting, which bonds us together as we turn to each other and to God for strength and hope.

As for physical closeness, herein lies the challenge. Children are a distraction. It's been said that "Sex makes little children and little children make little sex." For obvious reasons of exhaustion and lack of time and fear of interruptions, the physical closeness of the marriage relationship undergoes a major change. Couples have to be inten-

234 The Challenges of Marriage

tional about maintaining physical intimacy, which really begins with the emotional closeness that is built through good communication and acts of kindness toward each other. Both emotional and physical intimacy come from teaching children to respect your marriage relationship and your need for privacy.

Several key issues help restore intimacy when children change a marriage.

- *Rest.* Sounds good, but we struggle with the application. Perhaps we make too big a deal of our resting, assuming it has to mean, "getting away from it all." We think we have to spend money or go out of town or somewhere away from home to rest. Try taking Sundays off. Go to church, and then do *nothing.* Be intentional. Mark it on your calendar. Nap when the kids nap. Lie in the grass and look up at the clouds together. Eat finger foods off paper plates. Keep it simple. Rest replenishes our hearts and souls and enables us to have energy to nurture our marriages.
- *Need each other.* Intimacy in marriage is about learning to need each other, communicating that need, and figuring out how to continue to be comfortable with that need. Risky business, yes, but vital to keep connected.
- *Communicate.* Both husbands and wives report that communication is the most crucial ingredient to intimacy in marriage. Remember that this large skill is composed of three essential smaller skills: listening, talking, and fighting fair. Pay attention to where you excel and where you need improvement in your communication skills.
- *Make love.* Sexual intimacy is reached when several other layers of intimacy are in place. Satisfaction is improved when you figure out what works in your busy schedules and as you communicate expectations to your spouse.

Define Your Mission

What makes this family a family? The clear answer to that question defines our purpose and shapes the growth of our family. The lack of an answer keeps our family mobile wobbling out of whack with no stability. Having children forces us to think about what we stand for as a family and what values we want to pass on to our children.

A family mission is formed as we define what we value in our marriage, in our parenting, the making and management of money, work ethic, traditions, relationships with those beyond our family, especially as we reach out to others with the love of Jesus.

To create a family mission, you might consider these questions: What do we value as a family? What does God want for our family? How can we glorify God as a family? What would we like this family to look like in five years? In ten years? What kind of adults would we like our children to become? What are the most important character qualities we hope they will have?

If you're uncertain as to just how to get started in the formation of a mission, consider a resource at your elbow: a mentor couple. Check out marriages that are further along in life in your church, your place of work, or your neighborhood. Observe how these couples handle their children. Watch how they juggle home and work. See how extended family members invest their money and time. Then shape your own family by the good and bad examples you discover.

Identifying a family mission helps you set priorities and make choices that determine how you spend your time and money and what you teach your children. It gives you a purpose beyond your circumstances. A family mission stabilizes and strengthens your family mobile.

Recognize Your Need for Hope

Every marriage needs hope, especially a marriage with children. Hope that's greater than our circumstances. Hope that's greater than the strength we find within ourselves. Hope that helps us see the potential of our relationship. Hope for the future. Hope in God's promises, especially as we face the challenge and task of raising our children.

"Having a child has brought us a much greater understanding of God's love for us; and our child's dependence on us has made us more aware of our dependence on God and our need for hope," one mother said.

Having children helps us recognize who we are; they reveal our inability to be always loving and patient and kind in our marriage and in our parenting. We find ourselves out of balance with no ability to make things right on our own. We reach the end of ourselves and turn to God for help because he is our only lasting source of hope.

Research shows that couples who attend church together as little as once a month increase their chances of staying married for life. As one mom wrote, "Now that we have children, the thing that our marriage needs most is prayer time together. Recently, I was sick and a child was sick. We stopped praying and started whining and were miserable . . . until we realized what we'd done. We started praying again and everything changed, especially our hearts."

We find God's hope through reading the Bible, praying together, going to church, getting connected in fellowship groups with other parents, and finding Christian mentors.

Through the years, every marriage faces changes, but in the midst of the wobbliness caused by these transitions, we discover the importance of attaching our marriage mobile to God. After all, he gave us the gift of marriage and children in the first place, and he provides the love and hope we need to hang in there to find strength and stability.

Seven Ways to Regain Balance in Your Marriage While Raising Children

1. *Spend time with God.* Pray together. Go to church. Get involved in a couples' or mothers' group. If your children are young, find a MOPS (Mothers of Preschoolers) group by checking the web site at www.mops.org or calling 1-800-929-1287.

2. *Create and protect your "together time."* Teach your children to respect your closed door or personal conversations. Establish a date night. You benefit and they benefit by knowing you love each other.

3. *Allow each other some alone time.* You both need a break and an opportunity to pursue the activities or hobbies you enjoyed before children.

4. *Rewrite your wedding vows, now that you have children.* Describe what commitment means now and how it has changed since becoming parents.

5. *Remember who you married.* Remember the reasons you fell in love in the first place, and vow to keep encouraging each other to become all God created you to be.

6. *Find a mentor couple.* Choose a couple older than you who reflect the same values.

7. *Don't let little things grow into big things.* Don't fixate on the flaws. Focus on the overall good and goals of your marriage.

Questions to Discuss

1. What is the most difficult change you've discovered in your marriage since having a child?
2. What has been the easiest wedding vow for you to live out and why? What's the hardest one and why?
3. What did your parents do that you'd like to repeat in your own parenting? What did they do that you'd like to change in your parenting?
4. What are some of the greatest stresses in your relationship and how can you minimize them?
5. What is your family's overall mission statement?
6. What does spiritual intimacy look like in your relationship?

For Further Reading

Henry Cloud and John Townsend, *Raising Great Kids* (Grand Rapids: Zondervan, 2000).

Elisa Morgan and Carol Kuykendall, *What Every Child Needs* (Grand Rapids: Zondervan, 2000).

Elisa Morgan and Carol Kuykendall, *What Every Mom Needs* (Grand Rapids: Zondervan, 1999).

Elisa Morgan and Carol Kuykendall, *When Husband and Wife Become Mom and Dad* (Grand Rapids: Zondervan, 2000).

Les and Leslie Parrott, *Becoming Soul Mates* (Grand Rapids: Zondervan, 1997).

MOPS stands for Mothers of Preschoolers, a program designed to nurture mothers with children from infancy through kindergarten. MOPS groups meet in churches throughout the United States, Canada, and thirteen other countries. The media arms of MOPS include *MomSense* radio and magazine, newsletters, web site, and books. For more information about MOPS and the MOPS to Mom Connection, contact MOPS International at 1-800-929-1287 or www.MOPS.org.

This chapter was adapted from *Children Change a Marriage* (Grand Rapids: Zondervan, 2000) by Elisa Morgan and Carol Kuykendall.

19

Enrich Your Marriage by Loving Your In-Laws

David and Claudia Arp

Life is an opportunity for every person to create a new story that can be passed along by generations to come.

Anonymous

Did you realize that when you married your Prince or Princess Charming, you inherited the king, the queen, and the whole court? In a real sense, you did marry the whole family. Despite all the "in-law/outlaw" jokes, in-laws play a significant role in how your marriage goes.

Healthy in-law relationships are a wonderful blessing in any marriage. Unhealthy in-law relationships can be a continual drain and irritation. So what can you do to build healthy relationships with your in-laws? That's what this chapter is all about. We want to help you evaluate your present in-law relationships and come up with a plan for building better ones in the future. We'll look at what you can do to improve relationships with your in-laws. We'll also consider what you can't do—what is unrealistic in relating to your parents and in-laws and how to handle the reality that some relationships are just closer than others. Then we will give you some tools to help you build better relationships with your spouse's parents and siblings. Let's get started.

Balancing the Generational Seesaw

The more mutual respect and enjoyment you experience with your extended family, the more security and stability you and your spouse will feel in your marriage. Start by looking at your place on the family seesaw. Are you newlyweds just starting out? Or perhaps you have young children who demand your time and energy and you have parents and in-laws who also demand part of your life. You might even have aging parents who are beginning to experience health problems. If you are a blended marriage with his children, her children, and "ours," you could have extended family members all up and down the family seesaw. Wherever you are on the family seesaw, it will be a balancing act. How can you build your marriage and love your in-laws at the same time? Let's start by evaluating your present relationship with your in-laws.

Leaving and Cleaving

In the beginning God created marriage and it was very good. And in Genesis 2:24 he gave three foundational principles for making marriage work. It is not surprising that the first principle deals with in-law relationships. We read, "For this cause a man shall leave his father and his mother, and shall cleave to his wife" (NASB). Why is leaving so important? Aren't we always to love and respect our parents? Absolutely. But we're also commanded to leave.

In Genesis 2:24 leaving is switching our family allegiance. If one mate refuses to realign his or her priority from parents to spouse, that marriage will have problems. When most modern-day couples marry, they physically leave their parents' homes. But they also need to leave on another level—on the emotional level. The realigning of our priorities means we need to move our allegiance from our parents to our partner. We don't stop honoring, respecting, and loving our parents, but they are no longer the number one priority relationship in our lives—or they shouldn't be!

Jeff and Ann

In a recent Marriage Alive seminar for engaged and just married couples, we met newlyweds Jeff and Ann, who were struggling in their marriage. Part of their problem was the misconceptions they brought into their marriage. From day one they struggled with in-laws and other issues. For instance, Jeff just didn't understand why Ann objected to his Wednesday night out with the guys. And Jeff was ticked about all the time Ann spent on the phone with her mom each evening after dinner. Wasn't that supposed to be their time?

We talked to Jeff and Ann about how they needed to reevaluate their marital foundation and make some adjustments. Maybe you do too. It's easy to drift into marriage and, without choosing your own foundation, for your marriage to slip into patterns passed down by your parents and grandparents. Jeff's dad always had his night out with the boys, and Ann's mom checked in daily with her mom when she was younger. But things weren't working well for Jeff and Ann. They were both irritated. We suggested that they revisit the issue and talk about what they needed to do to follow the biblical admonition to "leave and to cleave."

Beth and Jonathan

At the same seminar we talked with Beth and Jonathan, who were soon to be married and were planning to live with Jonathan's parents for a year. Jonathan has one more year at the university, and living with his parents will help them out financially. How does Beth feel about this arrangement? While she thinks Jonathan's parents are great, she seemed to have some apprehensions. Clearly, it will be harder for Jonathan to "leave his parents" if they are living under the same roof.

Our advice? Do with less and find a small apartment near the university. We realize in some circumstances and in some cultures it's necessary for several generations to live together, so leaving is much more than physical separation. It's an attitude of refocusing on each other and making other people and things less important. Jonathan and Beth may find this is more difficult to do if they are living with his parents.

When we were first married, we spent two years in Germany with the U.S. military. Physically we were thousands of miles away from our parents, and as much as we loved our family, we really benefited from this time apart from them. We had the opportunity to work out our own problems and develop our own style of marriage.

Ralph and Carla

Ralph and Carla weren't so lucky. They came to us in a last-ditch effort to save their marriage. As they told us their story, it was obvious they had violated the basic principle of leaving. Ralph was still so emotionally attached to his mom and sisters that Carla was convinced he loved them more than he loved her. When Ralph had choices as to how to spend his time, he chose his mom and sisters instead of Carla. Holidays *had* to be celebrated with *his* family.

Do you identify with any of these couples? Before you can really love your in-laws, you need to make sure you are following Genesis 2:24. From the backdrop of having a high-priority marriage where your mate comes first, you can then really love your spouse's parents. After the process of "leaving" or reprioritizing your relationships, you have the challenge to reconnect with your in-laws on an adult level.

But what about the parents who don't want to let go of their adult children, who want to be in control of the extended family? While you can't change another person by direct action (and this includes your in-laws), you can change your own attitudes and actions. And amazing as it seems, sometimes others will change in reaction to your own adjustments of attitudes and actions. You can be the catalyst to better in-law relationships. Being willing to be the one who takes the initiative to change is demonstrating an unconditional kind of love that can also be a transforming kind of love.

Understand What You Can and Can't Do

We like to say, "You can do what you can do and that's what *you* can do." We might add "that's *all* you can do." Maybe you are blessed with parents and in-laws who are positive and loving. Or you might be in a more distressing situation, and your parents and in-laws are negative and critical. Whatever the situation, whether your extended family has a positive or negative effect on your marriage depends more on you than on the situation. A negative situation can bring you closer together as a couple as you seek to find a solution you can all live with. One couple in our survey decided to turn down an offer of financial help from their parents because it was perceived as a means of control. They would rather be poor than manipulated by their parents.

Also, we need to face the fact that some extended families are just closer than others. Your extended family will not be as close as your nuclear family, nor should it be. Everyone struggles with family relationships. And the older we get, the more complex family relationships become. Also, we assume that if we had a close-knit family growing up, that closeness will remain when we add in-laws. But having a great nuclear family doesn't translate automatically into a great extended family.

Evaluating your own unique situation will help you understand what is and what isn't realistic to expect from your in-law relationships. Stop for a moment and think about the following questions:

- What is the best aspect of my relationship with my in-laws?
- What is the major tension with my in-laws?
- What is the best way to communicate with my in-laws?
- What kinds of things pull us together as an extended family?

In the following pages we want to share with you some of the answers we received from couples in a survey we conducted about how they were attempting to love their in-laws, and also share with you some practical suggestions that will help you do what you can to build better relationships with your own in-laws.

Appreciating the In-Laws

Realizing what you can and can't do is the first step. The second step is to work at better understanding and appreciating your in-laws. When you identify specific areas you need to address, you must come up with your own game plan.

Relationships are fluid and ever-changing. We hope the following suggestions will help your in-law relationships change for the better. Positive change can begin in several ways. It can begin with a new idea, and we want to suggest several new ideas for loving your in-laws that maybe you haven't considered before.

Change can begin with a change in attitude, and change can also occur through actions, so we'll tell you some practical things you can do right now to really love your in-laws.

Find the Comfort Zone between Intimacy and Distance

When we asked, "What is your best advice for building healthy in-law relationships?" we received the same answer from four different countries! Two simple words, "Stay away!" This wasn't the answer we were expecting, but it gave us a clue to one big dilemma in in-law relationships. In-laws have difficulty finding the comfort zone between intimacy and distance.

Picture a seesaw with intimacy on one end and distance on the other. What you want to do is find the appropriate balance in your relationship. It is a continual balancing act, and it's easy to get off balance. The many changes in life create the need to continually adjust that balance. Some families enjoy getting together each Sunday for dinner, while others say, "Isn't it great that we get to see our parents and in-laws several times a year?"

There are so many factors: where you live, children, jobs, and financial resources. This is one area where you simply have to find what works for you. The more in-laws you add, the more complicated relationships become. You can't be as intimate with everyone as you can with your own spouse and children.

Then you need to evaluate your expectations. Susan, a new mom, told us how she felt when she was in the hospital when her first child was born. She loved all the attention she received during her pregnancy. Then the baby arrived. It was great fun when all the family came to the hospital to visit her and to see the baby, but then they all said good-bye and went out to eat together. She was left alone in her hospital room with her new baby while everyone else was celebrating at her favorite restaurant! She felt more distance at this point than she wanted to feel. Then, in the following weeks, both her mother and mother-in-law were continually around to give a helping hand. Their motives were great, but at this point Susan just wanted a little space. It's hard to find the balance.

How can you find the appropriate balance between being too involved and not being involved enough? And how do you deal with a mother-in-law (sorry, not trying to pick on mothers-in-law, but this is an occupational hazard for mothers who love and care for their adult kids and spouses) who wants to be overly involved in your life? Here are some suggested ways to find that comfort zone:

- Think about the past. How did your parents or in-laws relate to their own parents and in-laws? Was their style to hover or to ignore, or was it somewhere in between? They simply may be repeating the pattern that was modeled for them.
- Talk it out with your parents and in-laws. One couple asked each set of parents, "What does it take to make you feel comfortable with us?" One mother-in-law answered, "I need to feel included." Another said, "I need some time alone away from people."
- Share your own feelings. Talk openly about holidays and try to work out a compromise beforehand that everyone can live with.

Realize You're Not in the Same Season of Life

To simply admit that you are in different seasons of life is a great starting place for better understanding and appreciating your in-laws. Try to look at life from your parents' and in-laws' perspective. Your goals are probably very different. Nowhere does this manifest itself more than in family-owned businesses. The younger generation is ready to dig in, work hard, and invest in the future by expanding the company's base of business. The older generation's desire may be to wind down, take the profits, kick back, and enjoy life. You may not be involved in a family business, but you may find your goals are just as different as those who are. It helps to try to understand both sides—your situation and that of your parents and in-laws. Work at developing the attitude, "I will seek to understand my parents' and in-laws' goals and try to understand life from their perspective."

Here are some ways to understand your different seasons of life:

- Intentionally look at life from your parents' or in-laws' point of view.
- Don't complain about how hectic your life is. Believe me, it's all relative.

- Become educated about your parents' or in-laws' new challenges. For example, when a parent or in-law is retiring or changing careers, take an interest.

Find Things in Common

To help develop a sense of belonging, look for things you have in common. Everyone has to eat, so food is one shared interest. One daughter-in-law shares her experience:

> When my mother-in-law came to visit I didn't know what to do since we really don't have very much in common. So I suggested that we learn a new recipe together. (She loves to cook so that seemed to be a natural.) Together we made a casserole, and it was a total flop. I learned how clever my mother-in-law was. To make the dried-out rice and vegetable casserole edible, she simply melted a stick of butter and poured it over the casserole. Voila! It tasted great! Since then I've resorted to the butter treatment for turkey dressing that's too dry. It definitely improves the flavor!

If only all in-law relationships could be improved by melting a stick of butter. Unfortunately, it's not that simple, but you can look for things you have in common or *could* have in common. For instance, years ago when our boys were growing up, one Christmas we all got Austrian wool bedroom slippers. They were so toasty and warm that we continued the tradition over the years. When one pair wore out, we simply replaced them with a new pair. We gave them to our parents for Christmas one year, and when one of our sons was married in Austria, the tradition was extended to our daughters-in-law. It's nice to know our feet all look alike.

Another time I (Claudia) gave each couple as well as our parents a homemade cookbook of our family's favorite recipes, including Grandmother Arp's pumpkin pie, my mom's molasses cookies, Aunt Myrtle's coconut cake, and my favorite cheese fondue recipe.

Whatever your interest, whatever the interest of your parents and in-laws, look for commonality. It will enhance your relationship.

Here are some ways to develop a sense of belonging and a sense of commonality:

- Host a dinner party together. It's fun to cook together. Try new recipes.

- Choose a family project, at your house or theirs, such as wall-papering a room or putting up shelving in a closet. Do it together.
- Take a vacation together. Once we went to Disney World with Claudia's parents. It wasn't their first choice of places to visit, but the grandkids loved Disney World and getting to experience it with their grandparents. We all built great memories.
- Play games together. Some of our favorites are Scattergories, Balderdash, Trivial Pursuit, and Pictionary.

Plan Realistically for Family Visits

Each year we get several Christmas cards from families who look like they are right out of the "Super Family Fairy Tale." Everyone is dressed alike and everyone is smiling. We admire them, but a picture like that just isn't realistic for us. Everyone in our family is so different, we would never agree on what to wear!

Even if we could pull off such a picture, it wouldn't reflect reality. We're just happy when we get together and there are no major crises. Please don't misunderstand. We love it when we all can get together, especially when we resist adopting unrealistic expectations!

So before your next family get-together, evaluate your expectations. One survey participant wrote, "When I go home I feel like I'm fifteen years old again and must comply with my parents' wishes even at the expense of my relationship with my spouse."

From the parents' side, we can tell you from our own experiences in the early days of adjusting to in-laws that it was easy for us to land back in the "parent" slot—suddenly it was as if we had teenagers again. So it works both ways. One mother-in-law wrote, "When our married kids come back to visit, we're all adults for the first fifteen minutes. As the visit progresses, they regress, and we get put back into the parent role. Not fun!"

When you get together, ask, What's the lowest common denominator? Then adjust your expectations.

We also have discovered over the years that when we are together as a big extended family, we tend to talk more about the children and surface issues. So we don't go with big expectations of deep conversations. Instead, we reserve those times for when we are with only one family. So we suggest developing the attitude of willingly putting aside your expectations and looking for ways to enhance your time together with your extended family.

Whatever your situation at family get-togethers, there will be some things that never change and other things that over time can improve. It helps tremendously if you can have a more realistic and accepting attitude toward these family times. There are so many variables and so many personalities involved, often you just have to go with the flow. Realize it's okay to have some conflict, disagreement, and expression of feelings, but there are some things you can do to cope.

Here are some ways to facilitate happy family gatherings:

- Consider a neutral location. Suggest a cabin in the mountains or a condo at the beach.
- Spend time beforehand thinking through the upcoming time together.
- Make a list of things you can do ahead of time.
- Cook ahead.
- Realize that you can't control other people.
- During the family get-together, take time for yourself. Read a book. Take a nap.
- Get away from everyone for a couple of hours—it will help your perspective!
- Get some exercise. Walk around the block.
- Let everyone help out in the kitchen. Ask for help if no one volunteers.
- Be ready with family activities for those who want something to do. Plan a hike or a golf outing, rent a couple of favorite black-and-white videos or DVDs, or pull out some puzzles or a few fun favorite games.
- Give up any expectations of a perfect time together.
- Choose to serve your parents and in-laws. They will love you for it!

Stay in Touch

Keep in touch through letters, videos, e-mail, and phone calls. One extended family adopted a family web site where each family could post and download pictures. One survey participant wrote, "E-mail works really well—everyone gets the same message at the same time." Another participant responded, "We publish a humorous biweekly family newsletter. Contributions are solicited from all. It is called *The Latest Dope* and has a 'Latest Dope Award' in each issue." Another person wrote, "My first cousin compiled a book of family stories. Everyone who wanted to could submit stories. Then he printed out a copy for each family."

A tip from grandparents: Grandparents love getting artwork from grandchildren or newspaper clippings about special awards, and, of course, we all love getting pictures—you simply can't send too many! If your parents and in-laws have voice mail, when they aren't available to answer the phone, encourage your children to leave personal messages. We kept one message from a three-year-old grandson on our voice mail for weeks. Each time we listened to his robust laugh, we laughed and felt loved!

Here are some ways to stay in touch:

- Pick up the phone and call to say hello.
- Send e-mails and pictures.
- Encourage your children to stay in touch with their grandparents.
- Start a family web site or a family e-mail newsletter.

Remember That You Have at Least One Thing in Common

One daughter-in-law related how she tried for twenty years to relate to her mother-in-law but never felt accepted or respected. After twenty years, her mother-in-law finally began to come around, and today they have a pleasant relationship. If you are the daughter-in-law struggling with a mother-in-law who is totally different from you, you can help build mutual respect by remembering what you do have in common— you both love your spouse—and it won't take twenty years to build a relationship. Then look for other things you have in common. You may be surprised by what you find. Remember that whatever your differences, you both love the same person. Let us encourage you to concentrate on what you have in common, not on areas where you disagree.

It's your choice. You can concentrate on the positive things you see in your in-law, or you can dwell on the negative. Why not take a few minutes and make a list of all the positive traits you can think of that describe your in-law. You may even admire some of the ways he or she is totally different from you. Each person is unique, and it's up to you to appreciate that uniqueness, especially when it comes to your in-laws.

Here are some ways to build respect and find things in common:

- Compliment your in-law in the presence of your mate.
- Make a list of your in-law's positive qualities.
- Make a list of ways you are different that give variety to your family tree.
- List your spouse's good qualities he or she got from your in-laws.

Accept Love Where You Find It

With your in-laws learn to accept love where you find it. Not all grandparents are "grandchildren friendly." Not all in-laws look for ways to encourage you in your marriage—like offering to keep the kids. Not all relatives are sensitive to your needs. So give up expectations and accept love in whatever form it is offered. When the phone rings, whether it's that long-awaited call offering to keep your kids for a weekend for your getaway or a call telling you they've booked a cruise for themselves, accept them and love them. You can always be thankful if your parents and/or in-laws are still married and love each other enough to cruise together!

Again, to really love and appreciate your in-laws, expect nothing and accept love where you find it. Oh yes, one other tip: Start your own list now of how you would like to relate to your children as adults—and to your grandchildren. And don't forget that occasional cruise just for the two of you!

For Further Reading

David and Claudia Arp, *Love Life for Parents* (Grand Rapids: Zondervan, 1988).

David and Claudia Arp, *The Second Half of Marriage: Facing the Eight Challenges of the Empty Nest Years* (Grand Rapids: Zondervan, 1996).

David and Claudia Arp, Scott Stanley, Howard Markman, and Susan
    Blumberg, *Empty Nesting–Reinventing Your Marriage When the
    Kids Leave Home* (San Francisco: Jossey-Bass/John Wiley & Sons,
    2002).

For information about Marriage Alive seminars or other Marriage Alive
resources, visit www.marriagealive.com, e-mail mace@marriagealive.org,
or call 1-888-690-6667.

20

When a Crisis Hits Home

Paul and Jan Meier

People are born for trouble as predictably as sparks fly upward from a fire.

Job 5:7 (NLT)

I (Paul) sat in my car, parked in our driveway, sobbing profusely while listening to the song "Little One" by Chicago—a song about the singer apologizing to his daughter for being gone too much. Our own youngest daughter, Beth Ann, had run away from home a few weeks earlier and was still gone, and we had no idea where she was. We had a private detective looking for her, following her credit card trail until she quit using it. She was only fourteen years old, so I begged God to protect her, but I honestly thought there was a pretty good chance she had been raped or killed or both by now with her overly trusting spirit.

Jan and I both knew she had been a little down in the dumps and irritable before she ran away, but we didn't know at the time that she had been clinically depressed, even though we are both therapists. We believe we did the right things to handle this crisis. We prayed a lot. We told all our friends and colleagues about it, even though we were embarrassed. We saw a Christian counselor for professional advice and to help us with our own grief process. We wept—a LOT! We appreciated our friends and associates for comforting us, encouraging us, praying for us, and giving us some hope. Dr. James Dobson gave me his home telephone number and told me to call him or Shirley as soon as we got word about her.

Finally, the phone call came. It was from a pastoral counselor from a Baptist church in Kentucky (we lived in California at the time, working as partners with Drs. Dave and Jan Stoop). He said our daughter had come to his church and sought him out for counseling and was staying at his home with his family. She had been there a few days, but he had waited to call me until she trusted him enough to give him permission to do so. We were greatly relieved that she was fine and hadn't been raped or killed and was in safe hands. But I was already a little mad at the counselor for not calling us right away since she was so young and we were so painfully worried. He asked if Jan and I could fly there right away and meet with him and Beth Ann at 9:00 Saturday morning. He told us he had figured out what I had done wrong to contribute to her depression and that we could take her home with us if she said okay and if he felt comfortable with the situation. I sweetly replied, "Sure, we'd be glad to come"—then hung up after getting the address.

I was furious now at him and at Beth Ann. Doesn't he know that I'm Paul Meier, the Christian psychiatrist, a great dad, and the author of some really good books on childrearing? What an insult. And how could she possibly be blaming me for her depression and running away? I always listened to her, went to her activities, drove her carpools, gave her lots of hugs. After all, there are three things that determine how our children turn out: genes, environment, and personal choices. Beth Ann had the best possible genes and home environment, so she must be depressed because of her own lousy choices. Why couldn't that pastoral counselor figure that out and convince her to accept her own responsibility in all this! *Oh well,* I thought, *I guess it's because of his inferior training.*

We flew to Kentucky on Friday and checked in at a hotel. I lay in bed that night trying to decide what to say at the counseling session Saturday morning. I just knew I hadn't done anything wrong as a father, and I didn't want to lie and act like I had just to appease Beth Ann and the counselor. But I wanted very badly to get her back home so I could take her to a good counselor who would straighten her out. But if I told them the truth, that I didn't make any significant mistakes as a father, they would think I was defensive and arrogant.

I fell asleep that Friday night praying that God would give us, especially me, the wisdom to be able to speak the truth in love. And he did—in a dream in the middle of the night—a very intense dream. Jesus was actually in my dream, and he lovingly leaned over and cupped his hands and spoke softly in my ear, but the only thing he said was "Matthew seven, three through five; Matthew seven, three through five; Matthew seven, three through five."

I woke up terrified, realizing that this was much more than a normal dream. I didn't want to wake Jan up, so I quietly climbed out of bed and got a Gideon Bible out of the hotel room drawer and went into the bathroom to look up that passage of Scripture to see what it said. I was stunned when it basically said that I was being hypocritical and that I needed to get the log out of my own eye before I got so mad at my daughter for having a toothpick in her eye. Being a psychiatrist, I knew this verse was talking about the phenomenon of projection. In other words, I instantly realized that Beth Ann was a lot like me—artsy, craftsy, impulsive, forgetful, attention-seeking, and sometimes selfish. I also realized for the first time that I had been picking on her a lot verbally in recent years without ever realizing that it was because she was unconsciously reminding me of my own faults that I was too arrogant to see in myself. I sat there in that hotel bathroom and wept bitterly and apologized to Jesus for that habitual sin and promised Jesus that I would confess this sin to Beth Ann and the counselor, regardless of whatever faults the counselor happened to think I had.

I went back to sleep and woke up the next morning, feeling forgiven by God and ready to confess. But I didn't tell Jan about the dream. I decided to wait until our family session to tell everyone at once about what God had shown me.

The counselor introduced himself and informed us that he had actually met me thirty years earlier, even though I didn't remember him. We sat down on either side of Beth Ann, and I was about ready to apologize to her. But before I could, the counselor opened his desk drawer and reached for his Bible. He asked me if it would be okay for him to read me a passage of Scripture in order to explain to me what he thought I was doing wrong. I told him that would be fine, but that

I also had a passage I wanted to share with him that showed what I thought I was doing wrong.

He opened his Bible and began reading Matthew 7, verses three through five, and I immediately began sobbing. He asked me why I was crying, so I told them all how Jesus had shown me that very passage six hours earlier in a dream. We all realized this was a very significant event, and I hugged my daughter and apologized to her. We have been very close ever since, and as I write this chapter, she is studying in graduate school to get her doctorate in social work.

How to Face a Crisis

So why are we sharing this very embarrassing moment with all of you? Well, the answer is quite simple. That was the most painful crisis in our lives, and if we can share anything with you that will help you avoid the horrible pain we felt or to get through your pain sooner, then our personal pain will have been worth it! So from the bottom of my sometimes naïve and narcissistic heart, the following advice is what I would tell you if you were my patient—or if you were my very best friend.

Crisis Is Inevitable

First of all, you *will* have crises in your marriage, in your family, in your church, in your personal life, in your health. As the terrorist acts of September 11, 2001, showed us, life is uncertain, and suffering from time to time is certain. The Bible tells us that many are the sufferings of the righteous and that we all fail in many ways. Everyone Jesus healed of a disease two thousand years ago eventually died of some other disease or accident. Death is certain. Suffering is certain. Losses are certain. Grieving is certain. If you are married, you are married to a sinner, and so is your mate, so marital conflicts are certain. But as a Christian psychiatrist, I am also certain that much of the suffering we go through is totally unnecessary. The purpose of this chapter and this entire book is to save you lots of unnecessary suffering through practical education and life-changing decisions you will make as a result of reading this timely book.

Don't Face It Alone

Second, the happiest and most productive people on this planet are people who have an intimate connection to Jesus and who are in intimate, honest relationships with family members and friends who know all their secrets and love them in spite of their failings. No man is an island. No man can stand alone. People who need people are the luckiest people in the world. My wife and I have been hanging out with the same couples for more than twenty years now. We laugh with them, cry with them, pray with them, vacation with them, go to church with them, play games with them, go out to eat and to the movies with them, and go to the same weddings and funerals they go to.

In our crisis with Beth Ann, our friends were lifesavers. I had a prayer partner also, a fellow psychiatrist who did his psychiatry training as a classmate of mine at Duke Medical Center; he died in March 2002. If I was struggling with my anger or greed, I confessed to him and to my wife and to my friends and they prayed with me. If I was struggling with some lustful thoughts that day or week, my wife would rather not hear about them, so I just told my prayer partner and we praying for one another. I wrote a book several years ago entitled *Don't Let Jerks Get the Best of You.* When doing research for that book, I discovered that a majority of people admit that they would lie to you and steal from you if they knew they wouldn't get caught. So we have to be careful who we develop intimate friendships with. But we have to have relationships in order to maintain sanity and minimize suffering. A shared burden is only half of a burden.

Protect Your Thoughts

Third, don't *catastrophize.* We tend to have a crisis and think that all is lost, life is meaningless, we (or someone else) are *all bad,* and that the pain will never go away. But none of these is true. Some of the best and most valuable lessons I have learned in my fifty-six years of life are the direct result of crises I have had. I wouldn't want to go through any of my past crises again, but I am very thankful that I have grown as a person from every one of them.

Stop and think about it. Ninety percent of the things we worry about never come true. And the ten percent that do come true help us grow, even though they are very painful at the moment. I don't worry much about the terrorists. What's the worst thing that can happen? They could kill me and my family and my friends today, and you know what? If they did, we would be in heaven together today, laughing and hugging each other.

An Experiment to Help You Be Prepared

Finally, I have a very unusual request for you to experiment with during your next crisis. I would like for you to pretend that you are outside yourself, prayerfully observing yourself and whoever else you are having the crisis with. You will be amazed at how quickly and objectively you can resolve your crises if you can do that and not take your crises so personally. I do this all the time. For example, I may get into an argument with my wife. After all, she isn't always right! (Just kidding—she's right more than I am.) But just when I feel like saying something I will regret, I stop and pause for a moment to get outside myself psychologically and analyze what is happening. Then I will discover and share with my wife something like, "Can you believe what I was just doing? We have been getting along great and feeling so close for the past few days that I think I am looking unconsciously for something to get mad at you for to back you off to a level of intimacy that I feel more comfortable with."

I have used this technique for years with my patients at my Meier New Life Day Program, where they come (alone or with their mate) for three weeks of individual and group therapy for seven hours a day, five days a week. Whenever they have an argument or have any crisis, they stop and pray for insight and try to calmly analyze the best they can what is really going on and what beneficial things they can learn from that crisis. After all, most marital crises are merely repetitions of the crises we saw our parents experience when we were growing up. The sins of the parents are passed on as habits to three or four generations.

Will you decide right now to be smarter and more spiritual and self-protecting than the last three or four generations of your ancestors? It will take a lot of humility, insight, confession, community, and maybe even professional counseling for several years in some cases, but you can do it. And I hope you do. After all, I feel awesome when I think I am saving someone from some of the horrible, unnecessary pain that I myself have felt from time to time in my own life.

Questions to Discuss

1. Do all couples eventually have crises? Why or why not?
2. Can we survive our crisis without God and friends? Why not?
3. What wonderful things happened to the USA after the terrorist attacks of 9-11-01?
4. What wonderful things can happen to your marriage as a result of your most recent crisis?
5. Since we all tend to react (and overreact) the same ways we saw our parents react to marital crises, how can we "stand outside ourselves" and analyze our situations and solutions maturely?

For Further Reading

Paul Meier, *Don't Let Jerks Get the Best of You* (Nashville: Thomas Nelson, 1995).

Les and Leslie Parrott, *When Bad Things Happen to Good Marriages* (Grand Rapids: Zondervan, 2001).

Beverly and Tom Rodgers, *Soul Healing Love* (San Jose, Calif.: Resource Publications, 1998).

21

Special Tasks
in a Second Marriage
Jim Smoke

It is far more difficult to create a second marriage than a first marriage when children are involved . . . and it is more important to succeed. The stakes are higher. The risks are greater. And everybody involved knows it.

Judith S. Wallerstein, *Second Chances*

There are always warning signs when a second marriage is in trouble. One either pays attention to those signs and takes action or denies they exist and does nothing. Denial may not mean the imminent failure of that marriage but may cause the participants to don their combat uniforms and spend most of their time in the remarriage battle zone.

Many men and women enter second marriages by a process I call emotional collision. Struggling with the pain of a primary marriage failure, they reach out for anyone who can rescue them from their suffering and make their pain vanish. Shortly after their divorce is finalized (or even before), they are already attached to a new person who can usher them to a very premature second marriage.

The "quick fix" route leaves no time to heal the hurts of a first marriage termination, to learn what caused it to happen, or to rebuild a broken family and lay plans for the future. Personal growth is short-circuited, and unresolved issues are subliminally transferred to the second marriage only to eventually reappear and cause ongoing conflict in that new relationship.

If that sounds like a scenario in your present situation, one of the wisest things you can do is seek counsel from a family therapy specialist. All the other issues I will speak about in this brief chapter can be fueled by not doing your homework when a first marriage ends. Ghosts that remain from a first marriage can haunt a second marriage for years to come.

Areas of Conflict in Second Marriages

There are nine basic areas that can cause ongoing conflict in a second marriage. I have watched them contribute to numerous second-marriage failures over the past twenty-six years as I have worked in the field of divorce and remarriage. Look at them carefully and ask yourself if they are warning signs in your current situation.

Unrealistic Expectations

Most people get in trouble when their expectations are either too high or too low. When a first marriage ends and your expectations about that marriage go down the drain, how do you realistically form solid expectations you can live out in a second marriage? It is easy to compile a long list of what did not happen in a prior marriage and expect your new list to be fulfilled in the first three months. Hope often lies in your new spouse doing all the things that your former spouse did not do: namely, fulfill all of your new expectations. Here are a few realistic expectations for your new spouse and for your marriage.

1. My new spouse has a character and personality that was formed before I appeared on the scene. I will love and accept him or her as is.
2. My new spouse is not responsible for my happiness but can greatly contribute to it.
3. My new spouse will do things that will disappointment me. I accept that because we are both human, and I will learn to practice forgiveness.

4. My new spouse will not be the instant relief I need to put my first marriage to rest. He or she can contribute to my healing process, but that process is basically my responsibility.
5. My new spouse may have different styles and standards of child discipline than mine. I will seek to blend mine with his or hers and have a good blend that will work in our family.
6. I realize that a second marriage will be tougher to build than a first marriage.
7. I can expect it to be a slow building process.
8. Blending families is hard work and will take time to accomplish.
9. I can expect to want to run from it every now and then, but I won't.
10. I can expect my new and enlarged family tree to snarl me in its branches often. I will want to take a chain saw to that tree and use it for firewood, but I won't.
11. I can expect to have days when I *win* and days when I *lose*. I will try to keep them in balance.
12. Those happy blended families you see on television only exist on television. Mine will be very real with all its twists, turns, discouragements, frustrations, and celebrations.

Everyone has expectations. Healthy people keep them tied to reality.

When the Children Have Taken Over

I have a friend whose favorite saying is, "Never surrender leadership!" Many parents living with blended families would do well to remember that. Lack of a coordinated discipline standard, indecision in resolving family disputes, and the inability to give consistent and good direction for the family are three reasons parents lose their leadership roles in second-marriage blended families. When the children question who is in charge and everyone and no one appears to be, the children often take over and do as they please. The war of "my kids" versus "your kids" can quickly escalate into open hostility, and the parent leadership that gets lost often cannot be reclaimed.

In a second marriage where children are involved, there will always be some form of leadership seesaw between primary parents and new stepparents. It is hard work to work together and get good results.

Often an absentee parent will lose his or her leadership voice while a resident parent assumes it. When leadership is lost and the children take control, the seeds of marital destruction take root and second marriages teeter on the edge of destruction.

Children will always test the waters in a second marriage to see who is really in charge. They soon decide how to use one set of parents against the other to achieve their own goals.

Uniform standards of discipline, house rules, general behavior, and an absence of favoritism will go a long way to bringing peace and harmony within the walls of a second marriage. Remember, you don't wait until the game is well in progress to set the rules. By then, the players have set their own rules!

It is a rare blended family where children act, look, and think like the old Brady bunch. Most blendings are complex and will take a huge amount of love and patience to achieve a healthy and balanced family system. It also takes time!

When It's Déjà Vu Time

When you come to a moment when your second marriage begins to take on the appearance and similarities of your first marriage, look out and wake up! When you revert to handling things the same way you did in your first marriage, your train may be running off the tracks. Growing feelings of sameness can indicate that your marriage may need some repair work. When in discussion and arguments you begin to use the same words, actions, accusations, and attempted resolutions from your first marriage, trouble may be brewing. Watch for developing patterns that are unhealthy and get the help you need to break them—fast!

I remember two people in my office a while back who felt that the new spouse was the reincarnation of their former spouse. Both had been previously married to highly dysfunctional people that they happily escaped from. The problem was that they were both using methods on each other in their new marriage that they had used on their former spouses to stay semi-sane. Those old survival tapes were so entrenched in their brains that they were now being used against each other. Once they could admit what they were doing, they were able to begin to change the old tactics.

Many long-term first marriages are ending today. Many of those entering a second marriage are carrying years of ill-conceived coping mechanisms into a new relationship. It is hard to realize that your second marriage is vastly different from your first and should be treated differently. A second marriage and a blended family come with a full set of history books from the prior marriage. Healthy people learn from their history. They don't just go out and repeat it.

A friend recently told me that the most hurtful words her new spouse would say to her were "What you just did [or said] reminds me of my first wife." That could well be the most demeaning statement in the land of second marriages. Who wants to be compared to someone's former whatever? No one I know, so be very careful here.

In a second marriage, spend more time and energy looking ahead than looking back.

Frayed Finances

Money, or the lack of it, still seems to be at the heart of most marital problems whether it be a first, second, or third marriage. Second marriages and blended families cost more than first marriage because there are incredible carrying charges. Financial resentments toward primary family financial responsibilities can become so large that they become overwhelming burdens to a growing second marriage family. When you need the money that is going elsewhere and the money you should receive from somewhere else is not coming in, tensions and pressure will follow. As many blended family adults have told me, it is easy to end up in a good guy/bad guy financial war that goes on year after year. Court appearances and lawyer fees to find answers usually cost far more than the amount of money being fought over. As one person stated recently, the only winners in the money battle are the lawyers.

I always ask couples considering second marriage and family blending if they really can afford their proposed union. They usually laugh and tell me that love will win out over money, and they are not worried. A year or two later they end up in my office because they are in a financial mess trying to keep up with their responsibilities.

Different money-management styles often enter into the second-marriage mix. This seldom appears when two people are dating. It doesn't take long after a second marriage begins for the couple to wake up and realize that one might be a spender while the other might be a saver. I deal with this problem constantly with men and women in second marriages. By the time they get to me, credit cards are maxed out, the house has a second mortgage, the cars are in disrepair, and the bill collectors are calling.

One of the ways to avoid this problem is to take some premarital counseling and testing before the second marriage begins. When money problems arise after the fact, you should still seek counseling and work with a credit counseling firm. It's never too late to learn how to manage money.

Some of the couples in my church who have entered second marriages and formed blended families have told me that four and five years into their new marriage, they are still wrestling with money issues created by their divorce.

When it comes to money in a second marriage, you will need to do your homework. Many have resolved the issue and are able to celebrate their new happy union.

Growing Apart or Growing Together

It is relatively easy for two people to live together and grow apart. Many first marriages terminate for that reason. By the time the divorce happens, there is little feeling involved, because both parties have spent years distancing themselves from each other.

In today's culture, drifting apart is a simple process that does not demand a whole lot of effort. When both adults work different jobs and even have different social commitments, and have children with similarly full agendas and responsibilities to primary parents, there is little time left for bonding and growing closer to each other. It is like sitting on a raft when the tide is going out. Suddenly, you are a long way from shore, but you have not noticed the distance or even felt the movement.

The partners in a second marriage can grow apart very quickly. There are more demands and divisions of time. There are more people involved and demands are heavy on everyone's time. When the emotional space between two people remains empty, one of two things will happen: Either the space will become larger and the new partners will settle for less than what they desired, or someone else will fill it.

Growing apart is almost a silent cause of death in a second marriage. The only prevention is spending quality time together and scheduling time for it every week on your calendar. The same principle applies to the children within that family structure. Quality time, quality sharing, quality family planning and sharing, and quality conversation all go together. When those things are not happening, the warning lights are on!

When Your Former Spouse Hasn't Moved to Another Planet

Someone has said, "The only difference between death and divorce is that in divorce you have to keep dealing with the corpse." I am certain that some second marriages have been destroyed by the hovering specter of a former spouse wreaking havoc on one's new household. I always ask these questions of anyone thinking of remarriage when they have a troublesome former spouse still roaming the landscape:

1. Can you live comfortably with your new mate's former spouse just over the horizon?
2. Will having that person around the edges of your new marriage affect your new family and you in a negative way?
3. Will he or she keep grinding your new spouse down with problems that will never be resolved?
4. Will he or she constantly disrupt the lives of your children or stepchildren?
5. Are any of you in danger in any form from that former spouse?

You are probably well into your second marriage at this time and the questions are a little late in coming. They are, however, subject to review by you and your family if that person is still throwing rocks in your direction. I have personally watched the rocks fly for years after a marriage ends and a new one begins. For some, there is no end to the revenge and the feeding of a bitter spirit through acts of reprisal. There is nothing that will cause more unrest in a second marriage and blended family than a vindictive spouse using various forms of crazy-making.

One of the most common ways you can deal with a vindictive former spouse is to obtain a restraining order from your local police department. It usually sends a clear message that your life space will not be continually invaded by someone out to disrupt the daily flow of your life and the life of your family.

I have watched some blended families I have worked with over the years decide to relocate in another state to prevent the constant verbal harassment by a former spouse. That might seem like giving in to someone who won't go away, but sometimes drastic measures must be taken to allow your family to live in peace.

On the other side of the vindictive spouse syndrome is the happy, cheerful, "he or she just won't leave us alone" harmless former spouse. This rare soul wants to be included in all family events and would probably move into your house if allowed. They don't cause dangerous chaos. They just won't leave you and your new family alone.

A final hook that some former spouses hang onto is constant calling and demanding that their former husband or wife help them out with a wide assortment of needs. That list goes from needing additional money to fixing things in their house or apartment or running errands all over town for them. They often add to that list extra demands that you, the former spouse, fulfill some of the responsibilities in the children's lives that they alone can fulfill.

I have collected hundreds of former spouse stories over the years. Tragically, most of them fall into the "bad" category. My one strong word of advice is to take all threats seriously and do everything you can to help your new family live in a stress-free world.

Conflict in Family Structures

If a former spouse can affect the outcome and happiness of a second marriage, the former spouse's family may not be far behind with their own devious plans. The rising issue of grandparents' rights alone can put pressure on the newly blended family. The more involved the remarriage is structurally with former spouses' families, the more people there will be vying for the children's time and offering their varied advice on your family matters.

Add the elements of birthdays, holidays, special school events, sports events, and vacations into this family mix, and you will soon find yourself wanting to run away from the demands that are being made on you and your new family.

The acceptance or rejection of your new spouse by your own family of origin can also be crucial to the growing success of the life you are trying to rebuild. When your family rejects your new spouse while your former spouse is still accepted, you will experience some rough relational times.

A great deal of the possible conflict in a second marriage can come from the extended family forces. The pressure they exert can become unbearable, and they can easily destroy the foundation of a second marriage. Moving away from family forces is sometimes the only salvation. One should not have to run from family, but when they cause constant conflict in your remarriage, you had better call the movers!

Family structures are as intricate as emotions in individuals. Some are exclusive while others are inclusive. Some are more accepting while others are rejecting. Some are loving and some are cruel. Family structures, like children, are part of the carrying charges in a second marriage.

Many sons and daughters want to defend their primary family unit to the death, regardless of what you do, think, or say. When that is done to the exclusion of your new spouse, he or she will not be around for too many family gatherings. If this lack of acceptance occurs before the second marriage, there is no guarantee that person will be more accepting after the marriage takes place.

You may have to take some tough stands to preserve your marriage, and outside guidance can help firm up that stand. Toxic interpersonal family dynamics can choke the life out of a second marriage very quickly. There are usually too many people to deal with, and when they are all on the other side, you may be tempted to run away and hide.

New family structures seldom blend easily. It takes work, time, understanding, and patience. Remember, they have had many years to perfect their idiosyncrasies prior to your arrival. Good ones will enhance your marriage a thousandfold. Bad ones will either scuttle it or send you looking for a private island in the Caribbean with a NO VISITORS sign out front.

Sweeping Away Yesterday's Cobwebs

The crisis of divorce often brings the past into focus. Some problems were inherited; some were created. Both need to be dealt with to set the person free and allow wholeness in his or her life. Increasingly, counselors and therapists are discovering that dysfunctions in birth families are often passed along through members to new families. Dysfunction that has been repressed and not dealt with for many years often becomes manifested in the new family. Fortunately, once these dysfunctions surface and are acknowledged, help can be received. At any point of major change in your life, it is always wise to take a long, hard look at yourself. Ask yourself the following questions:

- Who am I now?
- What caused me to be who I am?
- To the best of my knowledge, what have I been living with that is unhealthy?
- How can I begin to resolve these old issues in my life?
- How do I get rid of the excess baggage I have been carrying around for many years?
- How do I process healing and forgiveness?
- Is it time to face my issues and find answers?

Those are hard questions to ask yourself and harder still to begin working on. But if these and similar questions are not faced when one marriage ends and another is about to begin, you may simply transfer the past dysfunctions in your life to a new stage surrounded by a new audience. If these dysfunctions contributed to the failure of your first marriage, they may perform an even quicker execution of your second marriage.

Wholeness in another person cannot be discerned by some emotional x-ray process. People with severe dysfunction may appear whole, hold responsible jobs, make healthy salaries, and speak intelligently. Some dysfunction is buried only inches below the surface and appears at very unexpected times. Other dysfunction is buried deep and remains hidden from view.

When you have lived with another person's dysfunction, you can easily become suspicious of every person you meet. None of us is responsible for fixing another person, even though frequently we would like to try. We are only responsible to fix ourselves and discover who we really are under the layers of our protective armor. That's our best protection.

Dysfunction in families always involves unhealthy relationships. If those relationships continue to be unhealthy, they will be perpetuated in a continuing string of families. The ones you lived through came from somewhere, and the danger is that you may take them down the road with you. Dysfunctional chains must be broken if there is to be health in a second marriage. Counseling and therapy are often needed to assist in severe situations. Remember, the word is *resolution*, not *transfer!*

Help! I Lost My Space

For most people, remarriage means changing living situations. Some people with children marry others with children. Some without children marry others with children. Some without children marry others without children and give birth to new children. Still others have grown children out on their own and marry someone with children still living at home. The blended family can involve all these varied mixes. On a very basic level, it can mean new and different living conditions with numerical changes in the people living with you. Few blended families live in as much harmony as the fictitious *Brady Bunch*. Whenever I watched that show and saw the apparent size of the house they lived in, I wondered where they all slept, ate, and played. They always appeared crowded but blissfully happy.

What happens in a second marriage when you wake up one morning and realize either you have lost your space or your space has been invaded? You may begin to resent the new way you have chosen to live. If your children leave for a weekend with their other parent while your new spouse's children invade your home for two days of chaos, you may find yourself sneaking away to the crawl space above the garage just to have some space to yourself.

Having a place of quiet and privacy is important to the balance in all of our lives. It is little wonder that older people, who have served in the trenches of parenthood for many years, relish the joys of peace and tranquility in their homes after the children leave.

It is in our "space" of quiet and seclusion that we find the strength to eventually walk back into the daily combat of life. We read in Psalm 46:10 (RSV), "Be still, and know that I am God." David the psalmist found that God is most often present when things are quiet.

There are many forms of being crowded in life. We each need our space from that crowdedness. Second marriages are no exception. Many of my second-marriage friends have confessed their need for and struggle to find some space for themselves in their new marriages.

That does not mean the marriages are falling apart. It just means that we need to give each other the gift of space to regroup and return to the front lines each day.

When claustrophobia strikes in a second marriage, seek a place of renewal and sanctuary. The place of peace is a gift that everyone in the family needs from time to time. Sometimes closing the door to your room can afford the peace you need. At other times it will be sending the family off on a camping trip while you enjoy the solitude at home. For a husband and wife, it may mean a trip to an out-of-town hotel for the weekend.

Silence, solitude, and seclusion are always gifts that renew and refresh us. From them we gain the strength to go another mile in the journey through life.

Words of Hope

My contribution to this book has been aimed at carefully examining various conflicts that can occur in second marriages and blended families. If your second marriage is free of any of the struggles I have mentioned here, I applaud you and encourage you to keep building a healthy, well-balanced new life for you and your family. If you need help in resolving some of the issues mentioned, contact a family therapy specialist in your area and ask for help.

Throughout the past twenty-six years, I have personally performed second-marriage ceremonies for hundreds of men and women. I have watched families blend, stretch, struggle, and grow healthy. Some of those marriages are now more than twenty-five years old and thriving. Families were successfully blended, and the children are healthy and whole.

I believe the promise found in Jeremiah 29:11: "'For I know the plans I have for you,' declares the LORD, 'plans to prosper you and not to harm you, plans to give you hope and a future.'"

I encourage you to wrap that verse around your second marriage and blended family and look for God to bless your life.

Questions to Discuss

1. What warning signs that something might need attention have you noticed recently in your second marriage?

2. What do you think you need to do to resolve these impending issues?
3. Would your children say that they live in a happy, well-adjusted blended family? If not, what needs to change?
4. What personal goals and dreams do you both have for your future in your second marriage?
5. What family goals and dreams do you have for your blended family?

For Further Reading

Helen Hunter, *Remarriage in Midlife* (Grand Rapids: Baker, 1991).
Les and Leslie Parrott, *Saving Your Second Marriage Before It Starts* (Grand Rapids: Zondervan, 2001).

Part 4

Keeping Love Alive

22

How to Divorce-Proof Your Marriage

David and Jan Stoop

We only regard those unions as real examples of love and real marriages in which a fixed and unalterable decision has been taken. . . . If men or women contemplate . . . an escape, they do not collect all their powers for the task. In none of the serious and important tasks of life do we arrange such a "getaway." We cannot love and be limited.

Alfred Adler, *What Life Could Mean to You*

I (Dave) have never met a couple that got married in order to get a divorce. There are some, I am told, who will marry to get citizenship, and once the time limit has passed, they get a divorce. But that's not really a marriage; it's an arrangement. Whenever a couple enters into a real marriage, hopes and expectations are high, and they have every intention of staying married. But good intentions are not always enough. In spite of the best of intentions and desires, all too many couples today end up divorced. Fortunately, there has been some great research that helps us identify some key danger signals that warn us when we are off track and need to get back on track. In this chapter, we want to identify these danger signals.

Three Relationship Truisms

Here are three principles I try to teach every couple that comes to me for counseling. They are simple statements, but we often overlook the truth found in them. Even when we see the truth in them, our behaviors show that we all too often ignore these principles. Here they are.

Principle 1: Trying harder only gets you more of the same.

There must be something about human nature that sets us up for this one. Often we operate on the belief that if something doesn't work, we just need to try harder to make it work. If we are in an argument with our spouse, and he or she is not listening to what we are trying to say, we think we need to try harder to get him or her to listen—we talk louder. When that doesn't work, we talk even louder, until we are shouting at each other.

Teachers have learned the truth of this statement. When their class starts to get rowdy, instead of shouting at the children—which would be an example of trying harder—they start to talk more softly. And to their amazement, when they do the opposite of trying harder, they get the desired response. Their class quiets down. Can you imagine what would happen if in the midst of an increasingly loud argument with your spouse, you suddenly started to talk softly? I can. I've seen it work. When one starts to talk softly, the other starts out at the same loud volume they have been using, and then they are suddenly startled by the loudness of their voice, and they immediately start talking softly as well.

When something isn't working in your marriage relationship, instead of trying to do the same things that haven't worked before, only trying harder to do them better, why not do something totally different. Do something unexpected, and watch the change that takes place.

Principle 2: When a discussion becomes emotional, facts are totally irrelevant.

Men don't usually like this truism, for one of their supposed strengths in an argument is their ability to marshal the facts. But if they were to stop and think about past experiences in which they have masterfully listed the facts, invariably the facts proved to be irrelevant to the argument.

Couples tend to have arguments because they are operating with different sets of facts. Your set of facts will not convince me, nor will my set of facts convince you, especially once our emotions get involved. Now sometimes, there is a missing fact that will change my perception of the situation, but if that is the case, why wait to bring it up until after the discussion has become an emotional argument. Point it out early in the discussion.

Another reason facts become irrelevant when emotions get involved is that our emotions tend to stop, or at least slow down, our ability to listen. Many of the things couples argue about, even in the best marriages, never get resolved. Some of them never get resolved because we know what the other person is going to say, and we stop listening. Instead of listening, we begin to marshal our own set of facts, knowing that the other person has stopped listening as well.

Once a discussion becomes emotional, take a time-out and talk about what you are each beginning to feel. Are you feeling unheard, devalued, misunderstood, or simply overwhelmed? Talk about that until the emotions have calmed down, and then come back to the discussion. Or take a time-out, as the Tirabassis suggested in their chapter, and agree to come back to the discussion after you both have cooled off.

Principle 3: There is no such thing as "constructive" criticism.

We get a lot of arguments about this one. Most of the arguments involving "constructive" criticism boil down to the idea that if I can't criticize you, how can I get you to change your behavior. The fact is not very many things get changed in a partner's behavior through the medium of criticism.

Many years ago, I asked Jan to critique me every time I spoke or preached. I asked for "constructive" criticism. The first time she did it, I regretted asking her. I felt attacked, even though I had invited her to tell me! I was wise enough not to shut her down, and over the years she has learned that what we both thought was criticism that was supposed to be helpful really was damaging to our relationship. It has never gotten any easier; I still tense up inside when she forgets and "constructively" criticizes what I have said or written.

I believe my experience is pretty normal. If we have a hard time even receiving criticism that is invited, how much more difficult it is for us to hear criticism that is being offered without an invitation.

Criticism's Cousins

In the groundbreaking research by John Gottman at the University of Washington, he found that one of the most destructive behaviors we do in our marriage is to criticize. It's interesting that he found that it is usually the wife who initiates criticism. Her reasons for doing so are not evil. She usually will try to use criticism as a means to bring about positive change in the relationship. Whereas husbands are typically content to leave things as they are relationally, the wife wants things to improve, and so she raises the issue with her husband. Even if she tries to avoid criticizing and protests that she is only expressing her concerns, her husband will usually hear her concerns as criticism. And his response is a close relative to criticism. He becomes defensive.

Defensiveness

If the first destructive behavior is criticism, then the second destructive behavior is defensiveness. When anyone is feeling criticized, he or she will respond defensively. To this day, I become defensive when Jan offers her invited critique of my speaking or writing. It's like a natural reaction: Criticism will invariably lead to my defensiveness, and Jan always gets defensive in return. That's why we need to avoid criticizing our spouse.

Sometimes we forget what the term *defensive* means. Defensiveness is our attempt to defend ourselves in some way because we perceive ourselves to be under attack. And our usual defense is a good counterattack. If Jan criticizes the way I am drying the dishes, I may point out to her the defects in the way she is washing the dishes. There doesn't need to be any relationship to what she is criticizing me about—I could criticize her about anything. In doing so, I am counterattacking whatever it is that she is saying to me. When I am defensive, my goal is to get the focus off of me and back on her.

Remember now, the wife usually starts the cycle because she wants to deal with some issue in the marriage or in the family. But the husband, in becoming defensive, basically refuses to take any responsibility for what is going wrong. Defensive behaviors are basically a denial of responsibility, which sets in motion a vicious cycle of criticizing and defensiveness. As the spiral goes downward, eventually we get to another relative of criticism: contempt.

Contempt

Eventually, someone becomes so frustrated that he or she, or both marriage partners, begins to feel and act contemptuous toward their spouse. The difference between criticism and contempt is this: Criticism is an attack on the other person's *behavior*. It includes statements such as: "I can't believe you said such a terrible thing, how could you?" Or, "I don't know why, after all these years, I still have to ask you to take the trash out. Can't you do anything without being asked?"

Contempt, on the other hand, is an attack on the *person*. It is usually accompanied by feelings of disgust, being fed up, or even being repulsed by the other person. It includes statements such as: "You are disgusting! How could you be so stupid?" Or, "You make me sick the way you acted tonight. I could throw up." Contempt can be expressed through hostile humor or through sarcasm. It can also be seen on the face when we curl our upper lip and roll our eyes. When the interactions of a couple reach this stage, the couple is in trouble and usually in desperate need of professional help. It's hard to break the cycle at this point, and the combination of criticism, defensiveness, and contempt will quickly lead to the fourth destructive behavior, where one of the partners uses the tactic of stonewalling.

Stonewalling

Husbands are typically the stonewallers. It is a withdrawal tactic. Basically, when a husband is stonewalling his wife, she knows it. To her, it feels as if she is talking to a stone wall. He goes silent. You can almost see him pull the shades down behind his eyes; he's no longer present, even though he is still physically there. None of the verbal or nonverbal cues that indicate listening are present.

Obviously, at this point, communication has stopped. And like contempt, this can be a very destructive behavior. When your partner is stonewalling, he or she has gone silent. You don't know what they are thinking or if they are even still involved in what you have been arguing about. And it is hurtful because it feels very rejecting. The person who is being stonewalled is thinking, *You don't care about what we've been talking about, and worse, you don't even care about me.*

It's interesting to note what happens to a man physiologically when he is feeling overwhelmed by the emotions being expressed. His heart rate soars. Once his heart rate goes over one hundred beats per minute, he is flooded emotionally and unable to respond in an appropriate way. He is not rejecting what is being said. Instead, he is typically thinking to himself in his silence such things as, *This is terrible. I've got to figure out something to do to calm this down. I better not say anything, because I'll only make things worse.* Or, *What am I going to do? I need to think this through.*

Antidotes to Criticism and Its Cousins

If we find ourselves using any of these negative, destructive behaviors, what can we do to change the cycle? It's interesting that the antidote to criticism is to complain. When I complain, I am not attacking you or your behavior. I may say something such as, "I'm tired of having to take the trash out! You said you would do it. Why aren't you?" "I get so embarrassed when you talk like that. You really hurt my feelings." Or, "I need your help with the kids, I can't do it alone."

The obvious antidote to defensiveness is to take responsibility for one's own part of the problem. When your wife says she's tired of taking the trash out, acknowledge the fact that you have let her down by not keeping your part of the bargain. Or when she complains about some of the things you said at the party, acknowledge the fact that you were not being sensitive.

If we can stop criticism and defensiveness, we usually won't get to contempt, but when one partner is feeling contempt and disgust, it's probably because the other partner has been stonewalling. The stonewaller needs to describe what he or she is experiencing emotionally and ask for some time to think. Slowing down the conversation, using some soothing words, or acknowledging how overwhelmed the other person may feel can help them continue the conversation.

If we are feeling contempt and disgust, we need to cool off and back away from the problem so we can regain control of our emotions. Usually contempt is the result of a long pattern of conflict, and especially of being stonewalled by our partner. We may need some help from a professional to reverse this pattern before it is too late.

The real antidote to any of these destructive behaviors is to limit their use and to have enough positive behaviors going on in the marriage so that we can offset the effect of the negative behavior. Gottman found in his research that one negative behavior needs to have at least five positive behaviors to offset its negative effect on the marriage. When a marriage had a five-to-one, or better, ratio of positives to negatives, the marriage succeeded. When the ratio fell below that level, the marriage was in serious trouble. Positive behaviors include knowing and talking more about our partner's needs and desires, affirmations and praise, affection, admiration, date nights, a daily ten-second kiss—all the things we loved to do while courting each other.

Three Critical Periods in the Life of a Marriage

We all know only too well the divorce statistics in our culture. Unfortunately, the statistics are pretty much the same for Christians as for our culture as a whole. There appear to be three critical periods in the life of a marriage when we are most vulnerable to divorce, and there are two styles of marriages that spell trouble.

The Volatile Couple

More than half the number of divorces occur within the first seven years of marriage. The typical pattern of behavior that leads to divorce in this early stage of marriage has been identified. Couples who divorce during these early years are usually volatile couples who never learn how to deescalate tension and argument in their relationship. Conflict simply continues to escalate over time.

What typically happens with these couples is that they never learn how to dialogue about their problems and the resulting conflicts. When they encounter a problem, they will fall into the criticism/stonewalling cycle, anger increases, and they do not know how to break the destructive cycle. Attempts to repair the conflict are halfhearted and noneffective. So the hurt, resentment, and contempt grow rapidly, eventually leading to the couple withdrawing from each other and then to the eventual breakup of the marriage.

Couples who effectively learn how to navigate these early years have learned skills that allow them to repair conflict to some degree. Two skills are especially important for this to happen. The wife needs to learn how to soften her approach to her husband when addressing a problem, and the husband needs to allow himself to be influenced by what his wife is expressing. These two skills can quickly reverse the destructive cycle and create an atmosphere of hope and caring.

In the beginning of the marriage, a couple will typically learn to do these things after an argument. As they revisit the issue, the wife softens in the way she expresses herself, and the husband allows himself to take in what his wife is saying to him. He doesn't just become a puppet, he simply opens himself to the broader picture of what is being discussed. After some time, it is hoped that the couple can actually make these changes in the midst of the conflict, adding a sense of humor to what is going on, allowing the repair of the relationship to take place.

When one takes into account the fact that most issues couples fight about are never resolved even in the best marriages, one can see that resolving the issue isn't what makes the difference. Rather it is how the couple handles the conflict that makes the difference. Couples that succeed in their marriage find ways to hold on to each other as they work their way through the problem. Having a dialogue about the problem is just as effective in providing repair in the relationship as solving the problem.

The "Perfect" Couple

I remember well the first "perfect" couple I met in my counseling office. They had been married almost twenty years and were on the verge of signing the final papers for their divorce. They thought they would give counseling one more try before ending their marriage. I asked them some questions about their marriage, and they made it clear that there were no problems in the marriage. They were quick to assert that they had never had a single disagreement in all the years they were married. They liked each other and still enjoyed traveling together.

When I asked them why they were getting a divorce, they said, "We've just grown apart, and in many ways, we no longer know each other. We both feel that if we met each other today, we wouldn't consider the other person as a potential marital partner."

Their friends were shocked when they heard they were divorcing, for they seemed the perfect couple. There was never any conflict, and they appeared to be perfectly adjusted to each other. They were both successful in their own right, and there was no obvious reason to divorce. But they fit the second cause of divorce "perfectly." This couple was totally disengaged from each other emotionally. There was no bond that ever developed between them. When they tried to find the balance between togetherness and separateness, they both settled for separateness. And then, over the years, they lost touch with each other until one day they woke up and no longer knew the other person in bed with them.

Couples like this will typically divorce sometime between the sixteenth and twentieth year of marriage. Perhaps they were frightened by potential conflict in the early years of their marriage, and both made the choice to back away from the conflict situation. Or perhaps they were both so shut down emotionally before they were married, that after the courtship, they went back into emotional deadness.

Sometimes these couples will make it past the twentieth year—in many cases because of the children. But then sometime after the thirty-year mark, when the children have left home and established their own lives, the emotional emptiness coupled with the empty nest is more than the couple can bear, and they divorce. There is nothing more tragic than for a long-term marriage to end in divorce. And the cause is usually not based on continuing conflict but rather is based on the emotional emptiness of the relationship that has been there for years. Now it became unbearable for at least one of the partners, and they end up divorced.

Hope for the Future

Fortunately, research has shown us the danger signs we need to heed in our marriage. It has also shown us the positive things we need to be continually working on in our marriage. Much of what we can do is articulated throughout this book. But here are three things to keep in mind. (1) Don't be afraid of conflict in your marriage. It is healthy, *if* you learn how to talk about what you can't agree on. Dialogue is more important even than resolution. (2) Focus on what your partner needs in any given situation. Turn toward them, both physically and emotionally; don't turn away from them or close down. And (3) Don't be afraid to seek help when you get stuck. Marriage is a lot of hard work, but nothing we ever do in life can be as rewarding as a satisfying marriage relationship.

Questions to Discuss

1. What are some of your patterns of conflict on those issues that never seem to get resolved? Who does the criticizing? Who does the stonewalling?
2. Describe a time when as a couple you got caught in the criticism/stonewalling cycle. How did you break the cycle?
3. Discuss together how each of your parents handled conflicts. What are some of the ways they handled conflict that you want to repeat? What are some of the things they did that you want to avoid? Talk about why.
4. Discuss the things you and your spouse do that build the positives in your marriage relationship. What are some things your spouse could do for you that would increase the positives in your marriage?

For Further Reading

John Gottman, *Why Marriages Succeed or Fail* (New York: Simon & Schuster, 1998).

John Gottman and Nan Silven, *The Seven Principles for Making Marriage Work* (New York, Three Rivers Press, 2000).

Howard Markman, Scott Stanley, and Susan Blumberg, *Fighting for Your Marriage* (Somerset, N.J.: Jossey-Bass, 2001).

M. McManus, *Marriage Savers* (Grand Rapids: Zondervan, 1995).

23

Keeping Passion Alive

Michael and Karen Sytsma

The passion of love bursting into flame is more powerful than death, stronger than the grave.

Song of Songs 8:6 CEV

Jim and Susan have been married for almost five years now. They were a passionate couple who deeply enjoyed their time together and had wonderful plans for their marriage. They knew they'd have some problems, but they thought their marriage would be more like the passionate couples they saw in the movies. By now they have experienced some of the typical struggles of early married life. They have also learned that they can deeply wound each other in frustration, retaliation, or sometimes through simple things that aren't meant to hurt at all. They are continuing to learn more about each other and themselves in this relationship and how to manage their differences. Most important, despite the presence of the inevitable problems, they still believe they will be together forever.

Quietly, however, they are aware that the passion they had for each other early in the relationship is not as strong. They don't experience the same excitement they used to feel when thinking of each other. They notice that the intensity they used to feel when making love is not as consistent. Much of their relationship, including their lovemaking, seems to have become routine. They both wonder if this is a danger sign for their marriage and if they can find again the passion that drew them together.

The answers are simple. No, noticing a waning in passion is not a danger sign, and yes, there are important things they can do to keep the passion alive in their relationship. Jim and Susan are experiencing a normal stage in the growth of their marriage. It's okay to be there, but it's not healthy if they get stuck.

Passion draws us together. Early in a relationship, just being around our partner excites us in some way. Science tells us this is the result of a powerful chemical present in our bodies when our partner is present. We feel excited, attracted, loved, and in love. We enjoy this feeling and want to be near the person who sparks that feeling in us. In some ways, we expect we will always feel this good when around our partner. But science also tells us that this passion chemical begins to fade and becomes replaced by a comfort chemical as our relationship becomes more committed. This chemical helps us feel connected, comfortable, and relaxed, like we "belong" with our spouse. While not as exciting, this change is important in the relationship. It is a natural part of the development of our marriage. It doesn't mean, however, that we must give up on passion in our marriage.

There are many things that can be done to keep passion alive. Much of the passion in marriage is focused on and experienced in the couple's sexual intimacy. Therefore, the focus of this chapter is on sexual passion. This doesn't mean the tips to keeping passion alive are all in the bedroom. As the adage states, "Great sex begins in the kitchen." Following this principle, the first steps to keeping the passion alive start outside the bedroom.

Keep Focused on What's Great

Couples begin their relationship focusing on what they like in their partner. We view the expanse of the relationship as great. Sure, there may be some patches of weeds in the garden, but overall the garden is beautiful. We decide we can live with the few weeds we spot, or we believe they will be eliminated after marriage.

As the relationship grows we begin to turn our attention to the weeds in the garden of our marriage. Not that we don't appreciate the beauty of the garden, but we'd really like to get rid of the weeds. There are those few weeds we knew about before we got married, but we've also found new patches since the marriage began.

Susan knew Jim was a bit distracted at times. When dating he would lose focus on her if the football game was visible on the television at the restaurant. He seemed to fade away sometimes in their conversations, but she explained this away in her mind. He was always gracious and apologetic when she would call his attention to it. Now, he is less gracious. She's also seeing the same characteristics in other areas. It really bugs her, for example, that he can't seem to remember to do some of the tasks needed at home. Susan feels more and more like the only responsible one in the house, and she seems to spot additional examples of undone tasks every day.

If Susan keeps focused on these "weeds" in the garden of their marriage, it won't be long before she will think that the garden is full of weeds. The patches of weeds will become the focal point of her perspective, and she won't see the beauty in the flowers (all Jim's positive characteristics) surrounding the weeds. God knows our human tendency is to focus on the negative, and so he gave us powerful instruction to use in marriage: "Whatever is true, . . . noble, . . . right, . . . pure, . . . lovely, . . . admirable—if anything is excellent or praiseworthy—think about such things" (Phil. 4:8).

We all have rough edges, and some of our partner's negative characteristics need changing and maturing. However, we can't allow those characteristics to become the center of our focus. Susan married Jim for many noble and admirable traits. Jim married Susan because she was lovely and true. If we focus on the negative, then it is almost impossible to passionately connect with our partner. We don't want to have passionate, deeply connected sex with someone we don't like. If we can keep focused on the good, it's easier to want to connect. Not that we ignore the weeds, they just don't become the defining characteristic of our marriage garden. You will find that celebrating the flowers of your lover's skills and beauty will nourish and strengthen what you love in them and increase your passion for each other.

Learn to Extend Grace and Forgiveness

Conflict is *inevitable* in intimate relationships. Even if we handle the conflict as healthily as possible, we will still feel and inflict pain. When we feel hurt, the only passion we typically want to share is the passion of anger. To keep negative passion from crowding out the desirable passion, we must learn to extend grace and forgiveness to our partner.

Grace is often defined as extending unmerited favor. The reality is that many of Jim's and Susan's negative characteristics are unacceptable. Neither should have to live with them. In reality, many of those negative characteristics will take a lifetime to grow and may never be fully eliminated. Having a great marriage will require that they extend grace to each other.

God extends enormous grace to us when we fail. He understands our humanness and challenges us to reflect him in being gracious to each other. "Be completely humble and gentle; be patient, bearing with one another in love" (Eph. 4:2). "Bear with each other and forgive whatever grievances you may have against one another" (Col. 3:13).

When teaching this concept in marriage workshops, I give several exercises to help couples begin to extend grace. One of my favorites involves helping couples see the strength behind their partner's weakness. I have them write down several of their spouse's character traits that really bug them. Then I challenge them to find the strength behind that weakness and write it beside the weakness.

If Susan views Jim's inability to get things done around the house as laziness, then it's really tough for her to be passionate and love him. It's tough to love a lazy individual. However, if Jim can learn to grow out of that weakness, he would still be a laid-back individual. Being laid back is a more positive and admirable personal characteristic. Susan can really love that in Jim. Extending grace is Susan choosing to see his behavior as laid back while Jim continues to rein in his weakness, so it better reflects the strength Susan sees in him.

The corollary of this is in learning to extend forgiveness. While grace tends to cover the ongoing failings, forgiveness allows us to heal the wounds we incur in the relationship. There are many great resources that will give couples guidance on applying this. Remember that in forgiveness, justice is not being served. You are pardoning an offense, like a governor pardons a murderer. You are graciously choosing to clean the slate and keep no balance of hurtful behaviors. Love "keeps no record of wrongs" (1 Cor. 13:5). The couple who fails to learn to deeply forgive will never keep deep, intimate passion alive in their marriage.

Grace and forgiveness are powerful in the bedroom also. We all bring some level of sexual baggage into the relationship. We don't handle our sexual intimacy with a high level of emotional or physical skill at first. Demandingness, withdrawal, pushing comfort zones, critical statements, and many other negatives are common parts of early sexual experience for couples. In many subtle and nonintentional ways, we damage our sex lives from the start. Many times couples tell us of damage that happened on the honeymoon that triggers hurt they can still feel intensely. Keeping the passion alive means forgiving and moving past these legitimate hurts and barriers. It also means extending grace while we continue to put pressure on our marriage to grow out of these destructive behaviors.

Grieve the Loss of Your Fantasy

It doesn't take long in most marriages to learn that your partner is not your fantasy prince or princess. In keeping with the above points, if we keep demanding our spouse become who we wanted them to be, we will effectively squash passion in our marriage. In his excellent book *The Heart of Commitment,* Scott Stanley encourages couples to grieve the loss of what they will never have in their relationship.

As an example, Jim always dreamed of a wife who would be outgoing and love to party. While dating, it seemed like she did. Now he realizes that she is an introvert and what she enjoyed while dating was being with him, not being at the parties. Introversion and extroversion are characteristics that don't change much. While Susan can stretch herself to continue to enjoy parties because they are important to Jim and she enjoys being with him while he's having fun, Jim needs to grieve the loss of a party animal for a wife. Letting go of this dream allows him to move beyond it and be passionate for what she does provide in the relationship.

While this principle is important outside the bedroom, it is also important in our sex life. Depending on where they learned about sex, many people develop unrealistic fantasies about what their sex life will be like. At some point in the marriage, couples learn that their partner doesn't work the way they do. Sometimes they find their dreams unappealing or even offensive to their partner. Letting go of those dreams may be an important step in moving forward.

Push Yourself to Grow

Immature lovers are passion killers. It's tough to be passionate when your partner is whining, screaming, pouting, throwing a tantrum, or otherwise acting like a child. One of the greatest aphrodisiacs is a lover who is pushing himself or herself to grow personally. I've heard many wives say their passion was renewed when they watched their husbands get involved in an accountability group that pushed them to be the best they could be. None of us wants to be the maturity police for our spouse.

Work to identify and grow up your fears—fear of rejection, fear of losing yourself in your partner, fear of sparking past memories, fear of losing control, fear of losing your partner. Addressing and growing these core issues helps you be a whole individual, allowing for the potential of a whole marriage. Some of the best money you spend on your marriage may be in counseling to help you grow personally. Passion grows when we take responsibility for ourselves and see our spouse do the same.

Again, this fits in the bedroom in a powerful way. Jim came into the marriage with some bad information about how women worked sexually and had an insecure tendency to take things personally. He believed, for example, that women should desire sex as aggressively as men do. When Susan wasn't as sexually aggressive as he thought she should be, it would have been easy to blame her and make it her problem as he withdrew into his hurt and insecurity. Instead, he did some research and found that normal sexual desire in women is receptive, not aggressive. He realized what he was asking wasn't realistic for most women, including Susan. Jim also sought some counseling to learn how to stay calm and present in the face of conflict. They can now coach and explore each other with greater confidence. In pushing himself to grow, he became a more informed and better lover.

Make Your Couple Time Sacred

Growing up in a conservative Christian home, we never discussed whether we would go to church on Sunday morning. Church attendance was a given. If something came up at school or in the community that was going to occur on Sunday, I didn't even need to consider it. Sunday morning was sacred. It was set apart for one thing only—corporate worship of the Lord. Setting time aside to fulfill our commitment to our marriage is also sacred, one that we carefully honor.

Early in a relationship we fight for time together. We will go out of our way to be together for even small amounts of time. Once we get to the point where we are coming home to the same place and sleeping together every night, we tend to stop fighting for that connecting time. To keep passion alive we must continue to fight for time together.

We encourage couples to make their relationship a high priority in their lives by establishing some kind of couple time and making it sacred. If it's sacred:

- No reason is good enough to disrupt your time together.
- There's no discussion on *if* it happens, only *how* this particular time will look.
- As with worship, you seek to remove any barriers that would distract you from your sacred time together. These might be kids, phone, pager, television, or unresolved anger (Mark 11:25).
- It's a time that you honor your spouse and your relationship and seek to make the experience great.

As you begin to get the analogy, you can continue the list for how you would want this time to look for you as a couple. The main point is to take it seriously and fight for that deeper connecting time. Don't let anything, even your frustration or hurt, keep you from connecting with your partner.

Sometimes couples get frustrated with the assignment to schedule their sexual connecting time. "Sex should be spontaneous, not scheduled," they complain. At the same time, they discuss how they are so busy they can't seem to find time to connect and are frustrated with how that's impacting their marriage. I quickly point out that scheduling a sacred connecting time does not prohibit spontaneity within the time they have sacredly saved for lovemaking.

Get Comfortable with Your Own and Each Other's Bodies

One of the great deathblows to passionate sex is when one partner (or both) is uncomfortable with their own or their partner's body.

Women state that one of the main barriers to great sex is the discomfort they have with their bodies. Nurturing a passionate sexual relationship requires an increasing comfort with ourselves—inside and out. We need to take care not to accept society's unrealistic ideal. Instead, we can push ourselves to accept what we cannot change and work to see ourselves as sensual, erotic creatures.

Not that we allow ourselves to relax and demand that our spouse accept the worst in us. This is childish and destroys passion. Instead we need to allow our best to be enough. I will often ask couples what it would take for them to be comfortable dancing naked before their spouse. Not that I'm asking them to do it, but what would they need to do internally to get comfortable enough with themselves that they could be "naked and unashamed" with their spouse? Once this internal hurdle is identified, they can begin the process of attacking it.

Getting comfortable with your partner's body is the flip side of this. The reality is that you will never be the expert your partner is on his or her own body. As much as you might think you know what *should* feel good to them, you don't. Their body is different from anyone else's body. Make yourself a student of theirs in learning about their body. What do they enjoy? What feels good to them when? Get comfortable with each other's nakedness and explore. Work to be naked and unashamed when looking at and being looked at.

As with many things in this chapter, these skills and attitudes don't develop overnight. For many, achieving a stable comfort in this arena is a lifelong process and not something accomplished in the first five years of marriage. Be patient with yourself, but keep pressing forward.

Find Ways to Be Playful with Each Other

One of the basic instincts in humans and animals is that of play. Neuroscientists have discovered that play is just as encoded in our brains as anger, fear, lust, and other basic responses. Many couples play well together when they are dating but forget to continue that process after they have been married for a while. This is sad in light of a recent study that showed that couples who actively played together on a date had a greater passion for their partner than those who did nothing together or those who spent a quiet, relaxed date together.

Push yourself to get in touch with the playful side in you and create some playgrounds together. There's something about being intense and excited together that keeps the passion burning. Find pleasurable and exciting hobbies or pastimes that you can share together. Get excited about life together, and it's easier to be excited about each other. Jim and Susan found that making out in the back of an almost deserted theater and whitewater kayaking together were two very different ways they played passionately together.

Each couple and individual is different, so you may need to spend some time exploring, but fight for it. Find out what's fun and play together.

Embrace Your Sensuality

A large part of passion is purely sensual. Some couples err in making passion solely about the sensual. Others have a tendency to shut down the sensual. God created sex to be a sensual experience. Even a brief read of Song of Songs illustrates the erotic and sensual nature of sex as God intended it. The writer of Song of Songs speaks of tastes, touches, smells, sounds, and sights as the couple delights in each other.

A powerful way to keep passion alive is to continue to drink in the sensations of each other. Experiment with your senses together. Focus on ways to engage all senses during your connecting time.

- Look at each other as you get aroused and enjoy the other's passion through their eyes. It is said that the eyes are the windows to the soul. Learn to communicate love and sexual arousal with just your eyes. Vary between drinking in how your partner looks and connecting deeply as you allow him or her to look into your soul through your eyes.
- Lay your hand over your partner's heart. Tune in to their heartbeat and breathing. Look deep into their eyes and allow yourself to be profoundly aware of their life and presence as you connect with each other.
- Learn to give a sensuous massage to each other. This is not a grabbing, kneading touch, but one that really feels and is felt. There are a number of sources for instruction in this skill, but it takes practice to really learn.

- Create your own aromatic massage oil. Start with a basic massage oil and add the aromatic scents you like best. Experiment and create a unique scent for your marriage.
- Light some candles. Candles not only add an alive, natural, and sensuous light, but they also come in a wide variety of scents. Explore together to find scents that enhance your sensual sexual play.
- Have your partner gently stroke your skin with a variety of materials (fur, silk, feathers, etc.). Close your eyes and soak in the feeling. Share your experience with them and switch places to explore their experience.
- Make noises as you verbally and nonverbally delight to sounds. Play some music—both loud and soft.
- Redecorate your bedroom with the focus on an atmosphere you both find sensuous.
- Try new sexual positions.

There are many more ideas out there. The main point is to allow yourselves to explore and tune in to the power of the sensations God gave you. He truly did intend sex for pleasure. Take advantage of it. It's a key part of maintaining passion.

Use a Variety of Lovemaking Styles

Each couple tends to find a sexual routine that is comfortable for them. This lovemaking style is important. It is often very safe, predictable, and fosters a connectedness that only the tried and true can give. Some meaningful positions of intercourse, proven ways to produce orgasms, and types of initiating will be enjoyed again and again. On the other hand, Proverbs 5 likens our lovemaking to running water and a fresh spring. These are never the same and forever fresh, exciting, and playfully varied.

There is value in spicing up your sexual style by regularly adding in other styles. Plan for a few gourmet sessions that take all afternoon. Make love in the shower. Plan a lunch break rendezvous. Doug Rosenau's book *A Celebration of Sex* lists a variety of sexual styles and techniques (chapters 11–14) you can use as idea starters.

It is important that you proceed *together* in this. There may be some styles you are uncomfortable with. Talk about it. Don't try to force your partner, or you will kill the passion you are trying to nurture. Many times as couples grow and get more comfortable with each other, their comfort with experimentation grows also.

Make Room for Each Other to Say No and Learn to Coach

We all want to be desired. We also want to be desired in *our* way and in *our* timing. In reality, our spouse will not always love us in our way and in our timing. If we don't allow them the space to say no to our advances, they don't really have the freedom to say yes.

Men and women are very different, but neither want to be involved in "duty sex." It's difficult to be passionate about a duty. Lovemaking should never be a chore but an activity both can initiate and refuse graciously. Each must take responsibility for his or her sexual enjoyment and arousal within the mutual process.

If you are the more consistent "no" spouse, you need to do what was recommended above in pushing yourself to grow. The scriptural principle not to withhold yourself from your spouse (1 Cor. 7:3–5) is important, as we become "yes" mates within our own unique preferences and delights.

Both of you, including the more consistent "yes" spouse, need to improve your coaching skills. If you don't take the courage to coach your partner on what you want and need, you will stay unhappy. Learn to talk, challenge, and understand each other in your sexuality. This needs to happen in and out of the bedroom. Some of the heavy coaching should be done while fully clothed across the breakfast table. Other coaching happens best when you are helping your partner learn what feels best to you in the moment.

Coaching is an important skill to learn to give and to receive. Many couples sabotage their sex life because they fail to receive coaching from their spouse. Work on not giving or receiving coaching as criticism. Remain present (physically and emotionally) and learn from it. Withdrawing in a wounded or punishing spirit or escalating and screaming at your partner strangles the passion and growth.

Respect the Critical Boundaries

A final reminder that is most important is to respect critical boundaries in your sex life. I've heard several theologians state there is a close link between the sexual and the spiritual parts of us. Our sex life is very central to who we are, and damage in the sexual arena is often deep damage. For this reason alone, couples must fight to protect the sanctity of their sexual life.

Scripture is very clear on some sexual boundaries. If you or your spouse feels something is against God's direction for your marriage, spend time talking about it and steer clear of it. The risk is too great.

Instead, keep focused on protecting and exploring each other's heart. True passion in a relationship can continue to grow as we express ourselves sensually while connecting spiritually and emotionally. We can quickly push the boundaries in what is okay sensually. Spiritual and emotional connectedness is a deep well that can continue to be explored.

Dream Together

God has a plan, a wonderful vision, of what your marriage and sex life can be. "'For I know the plans I have for you,' declares the LORD, 'plans to prosper you and not to harm you, plans to give you hope and a future'" (Jer. 29:11). I am convinced that his vision for your sex life goes beyond your dreams.

When you were a teenager, you had dreams of what marriage and making love would be like. You carried these great visions into courtship and the beginning of your marriage. A few years into marriage you have learned they need to be adapted, but keep those hopes alive and flourishing. Fight for what is good and beautiful.

Take the time to create a vision statement for your sex life. Dream together and then do the tough work of what each of you would need to do to accomplish this. God has given you a blessed gift. A few years into your marriage you still have no idea how great your marriage can be after thirty, forty, or fifty years. Some research tells us that couples report their best sex happens after thirty years of marriage when they've really learned to implement some of the points we have discussed.

Keeping the passion alive in your marriage doesn't happen naturally—it must be fought for. Keep the vision alive and don't let your own immaturity, woundedness, anger, or hopelessness get in the way. Get help when needed and keep pressing on. It's a worthy fight.

Questions to Discuss

1. What did you do when you were dating that was fun and exciting? Are you still doing that?
2. Is your focus on the weeds or the flowers in the garden of your marriage? What flowers can you celebrate with your spouse today?
3. Are there any personal, relational, or sexual problem areas you need to talk about or get help with?
4. Of the more specific bedroom ideas in this chapter, which one would you like to try with your spouse today?
5. Share something new about your body with your spouse.
6. Share your vision for your sexual life with your spouse. What do you envision it looking like five, ten, twenty-five, and forty years from now? Remember to include the relational, connected, style, and sensual aspects.

For Further Reading

William Cutrer and Sandra Glahn, *Sexual Intimacy in Marriage* (Grand Rapids: Kregel, 2001).

Clifford L. Penner and Joyce J. Penner, *52 Ways To Have Fun, Fantastic Sex* (Nashville: Thomas Nelson, 1994).

Clifford L. Penner and Joyce J. Penner, *Men and Sex: Discovering Greater Love, Passion and Intimacy with Your Wife* (Nashville: Thomas Nelson, 1997).

Clifford L. Penner and Joyce J. Penner, *Restoring the Pleasure* (Dallas: Word, 1993).

Scott Stanley, *The Heart of Commitment* (Nashville: Thomas Nelson, 1998).

24

Finding a Mentor Couple

Les and Leslie Parrott

We loved you so much that we were delighted to share with you not only the gospel of God but our lives as well.

1 Thessalonians 2:8

Tom and Wendy were the typical newly married couple. Now in their mid-twenties, they had dated for nearly two years before getting engaged. They had a great deal in common, and both of them had recently landed pretty good jobs. Tom was the assistant groundskeeper at a local golf course, and Wendy just got her first job as a school-teacher. They had the blessing of their parents, attended premarital counseling, and were on their way to living happily ever after—or so everyone thought.

But marriage for Tom and Wendy, like for many newlyweds, wasn't everything they dreamed it would be. Each of them, for different reasons, felt a bit confused or even disappointed. It wasn't that they thought they had made a mistake, they just knew they had some issues (managing money, for example) to work through. But they didn't feel comfortable talking to their parents or friends about them. Unlike many couples, however, Tom and Wendy sought help. The expectations they had for marriage were not getting met, and they were determined to do something about it. So on a chilly January day, four months after their wedding, Tom and Wendy came to see us.

Bundled up against the cold, they came into our office and began to shed their coats. We could see immediately that they were in love but struggling to overcome some very predictable struggles. As Wendy sipped hot coffee to thaw out, she said, "We have talked a little to friends and family about what is going on, but we both decided we needed more objectivity—we needed somebody who would take us seriously."

Tom joined in: "Yeah, everybody who knows us just says 'give it time' or something like that." Tom went on to say that their marriage was not suffering a major trauma; no major overhaul was needed, only, as he said, "a little realignment." Besides money-management issues, they were struggling with their personal schedules. Tom was a night owl while Wendy was an early riser. It was these kinds of issues that they simply wanted to get ironed out.

We met with Tom and Wendy for nearly an hour, listening to their experiences. We gave them a couple of exercises to help them explore their misconceptions and myths about marriage. We gave them a brief personality test to help them recognize their differing styles and approaches to things. As we were wrapping up our session together, we also recommended a few resources we thought might help them.

"Is this it?" Tom asked. "Are we going to meet with you again?"

"We have a better idea," Leslie said. "We think you could really benefit from being with another couple who are not professional therapists."

"Oh, you mean my parents," Wendy cracked.

"No, we mean marriage mentors."

"What's that?" they both asked.

We told them how meeting from time to time with another married couple, who was more experienced and more seasoned, could give them a sounding board and a safe place to explore some of their questions about marriage.

"Marriage mentors," we explained, "will do something far different for you than seeing a counselor. You don't need a marital overhaul.

You need, well, you need what Tom mentioned earlier in our session: a realignment."

Like most newly married couples we talk to, Tom and Wendy were intrigued by the idea of finding such a couple. After a bit of discussion, they suggested a married couple they both admired in their church.

"Nate and Sharon are pretty cool," Tom told us. "They have a couple of little kids, and they seem like pretty good parents too."

Neither of them knew the couple very well, but they admired their marriage relationship from afar and thought Nate and Sharon would fit the bill. After a couple of phone calls in the days that followed, and a little more exploration, we made the connection for Tom and Wendy. Over the course of the next several months, they met several times with their mentors, and their marriage took a dramatic positive turn.

Tom and Wendy have been married more than five years now. They know their relationship is not perfect, but they are madly in love and happier than they ever imagined they could be. Here is a portion of a letter they wrote to us:

Dear Les and Leslie,

How can we ever thank you for helping us find a marriage mentor couple. Before coming to you we had never even heard of such an idea. But needless to say, our mentoring relationship with Nate and Sharon ended up being the most important thing we have ever done to build up our marriage. It was so nice to have another couple know what we were going through and remain objective at the same time.

We have since moved to another state, but on our wedding anniversary, Nate and Sharon always give us a call to celebrate our marriage.

Anyway, we are writing to say thank you and to say that you should tell more people about the benefits of marriage mentoring. Someday we hope to give back the gift that Nate and Sharon gave to us by mentoring some newly married couples ourselves. We think every couple just starting out should have a mentor.

That's not a bad idea. Marriage mentoring is one of the most significant helps we know of in building a lifelong marriage. We have seen hundreds of couples strengthen their new marriages through mentoring relationships, and we know firsthand the difference it can make.

Today's Need for Marriage Mentors

Let's be honest. The "till death do us part" section of the marriage vow rings increasingly ironic. We all know the tragic statistics. Suffice it to say that for far too many couples, marriage has become "till divorce do us part."

After working with hundreds of engaged couples, however, we are finding that the lost art of mentoring just may be the key to turning around the divorce rate.

Throughout human history, mentoring has been the primary means of passing on knowledge and skills. In the past, mentoring took place in the university where a student learned in the home of the scholar. It took place in the studio where the artist poured himself into the formation of his protégés. The Bible is certainly filled with examples of mentoring (Eli and Samuel, Elijah and Elisha, Moses and Joshua, Naomi and Ruth, Elizabeth and Mary, Barnabas and Paul, Paul and Timothy). Up until recently, mentoring was a way of life between the generations. But today, mentoring is in short supply. In our modern age, the learning process has shifted. It now relies primarily on computers, classrooms, books, and videos. In most cases today, the relational connection between the knowledge-and-experience giver and the receiver has weakened or is nonexistent, especially in the early years of marriage.

What Is a Marriage Mentor?

"What I need is someone to talk to who has walked down the path I'm just beginning," said Lisa, a few weeks into her new marriage. "Whenever I go to my mom or dad with a situation, they end up parenting me or teaching me something I don't really need to learn."

Lisa, like most newlyweds we have met, needs a mentor. Mom and Dad certainly serve a helpful function in the life of a new bride and groom, but they cannot usually offer the distance and objectivity that a mentor gives. For this reason, it is important to first realize exactly what a mentor is not.

- A mentor is not a mother or a father.
- A mentor is not automatically a pal or a buddy.

- A mentor is not "on call" for every little crisis. Mentoring time may be limited to discussion about major situations, not just the minor ones.
- A mentor is not necessarily committed long-term. The association has a natural cycle of its own and is not always predictable.
- A mentor is not a teacher.
- A mentor is not a know-it-all.

We've helped coordinate hundreds of marriage mentoring relationships, and after years of following these couples we have come to believe that there is no single way to be a marriage mentor.

We define a marriage mentor as a happy, more experienced couple who empowers a newly married couple through sharing resources and relational experiences.

It's a broad definition because there is no one right way to mentor. Each mentoring relationship takes on its own style and personality. The amount of time couples spend together and the content they discuss can rarely be prescribed. However, we recommend a minimum of three meetings throughout any given year for the first few years of a marriage. The first year of marriage is especially ideal and when this is the case, we suggest a meeting at three months, another at seven months, and the final one around the one-year wedding anniversary. Of course the meetings don't need to be limited to just these three meetings. These times provide the skeletal structure upon which additional meetings, other meals, phone calls, and so on can occur.

Finding a Marriage Mentor

Several years ago in Seattle, we started something we call The Marriage Mentor Club. We now have more than a thousand members in our city and several thousand across the country. The idea of marriage mentoring is so simple we're amazed that more couples don't do it. Mentoring begins by asking a seasoned, experienced, happy couple (not related to you) to come alongside you and invest in your relationship during the first few years of your marriage. It doesn't have to be a big commitment. You may only meet with them a few times. And you'd be amazed at how willing and honored a couple like this is to be invited to mentor you.

You might be wondering what a mentor couple can do for you. The answer is plenty. With years of experience, marriage mentors serve as a sounding board to help you navigate predictable passages such as setting up your home, managing your finances, negotiating your different roles, managing conflict, dealing with in-law relations, preparing for holidays, and so on. Don't think of them as counselors. Mentors are more like your personal consultants or coaches. They will show you what's worked and what hasn't worked for them—so you can learn from their mistakes instead of making your own. Most couples being mentored learn more by example than by any other method. Hearing your mentors' stories about how they goofed up their finances early in their marriage and how they got back on track will stick with you much longer than reading about how to set up a budget. You can't help but remember the lesson when it is attached to real-life people who care about you and your marriage.

Maybe you had excellent premarital counseling and expect to sail through your first years without a hitch. Maybe you will. But in our years of doing premarriage work with countless couples, we've discovered an experience that is almost predictable. We call it the "threshold phenomenon." It has to do with how different things look to a newlywed couple once they are actually married. The skills and techniques we taught them before they crossed the proverbial threshold seem to have vanished. Actually, they probably never really took root in the first place. Why? Consider this analogy: If someone teaches you how to use a computerized spreadsheet when you have no reason to use it, you will probably tune out within the first few seconds. It's not relevant. However, once you take a job that requires you to use that same program, you are ready to learn. The same is true in the first year of marriage, and a mentor couple can help you put into practice the things you already learned but have forgotten.

We know of few experiences that can help you more in your first married years than having a seasoned couple come alongside you and allow you to peer into their relationship so that you might lay a solid foundation for lasting love. If you would like to explore more seriously this idea of finding another couple to mentor you, begin by contacting your local pastor. The church you attend or one near where you live may have a mentoring program you can plug into. If not, you might ask the church to consider starting one. They can contact us to learn more about how to do this, and we will send them the information about our *Mentoring Engaged and Newlywed Couples* video kit. Have them write to: Drs. Les and Leslie Parrott, Center for Relationship Development, Seattle Pacific University, 3307 Third Ave. West, Seattle, WA 98119.

A Little Secret Mentorees Need to Know about Mentors

"I don't know how much we helped Doug and Sarah," Joan told us, "but *we* sure got a lot out of it." Joan laughed as she was telling us about being a marriage mentor couple along with her husband of eighteen years, Larry. "Helping a young couple seemed to spark a lot of things in our own marriage that we had neglected," Larry added. Joan and Larry agreed that the benefits of being marriage mentors went both ways, to mentorees, of course, but also to mentors. It's what we've come to call the marriage mentor boomerang effect. That is to say the couple who is mentoring you will be benefiting from this experience as well.

The report Joan and Larry were relaying to us has been repeated time and again with the marriage mentors we have observed. Almost mystically, something wonderful happens when a more mature couple reaches out to a new couple. By helping another couple form and live out their dreams, one's *own* dreams for marriage are reawakened and fulfilled.

Perhaps the most common aspect of the boomerang effect we discover is satisfaction. As mentors, you will enjoy the satisfaction of work well done. When a married couple successfully works on any project together—wallpapering a room, raking autumn leaves, and so on—there is a sense of satisfaction that results. And when a couple works on a project that has lasting value, even eternal significance, such as marriage mentoring, there is an overwhelming sense of having done good, of helping a new couple build a love that will last a lifetime.

In the ancient Greek epic *The Odyssey,* the hero, Odysseus, had an elderly friend and adviser named Mentor. Before Odysseus went to fight in the Trojan War, he made Mentor the guardian of his son, Telemachus. This is where we get the term for mentor, and it demonstrates the meaningful value mentors can bring to our lives.

We have a dream that a network of healthy marriage mentors will rise up to become the guardians of the next generation of marriages, ones just like yours. So help us build this network by initiating a relationship with some marriage mentors yourselves. We're convinced that you'll be glad you did.

Questions to Discuss

1. What do you think about the way this chapter defines a marriage mentor? Do you agree with the definition? How about its delineation of what a mentor is not?
2. What, if anything, attracts you to having a personal marriage mentor couple who would walk alongside you? What might keep you from having a marriage mentor couple?
3. If you had a marriage mentor couple in your lives right now, what is one of the specific topics you would want to explore with them and why?
4. Would you like to have a mentor couple relationship? If so, what are the concrete steps you can take to make this happen?

For Further Reading

Les and Leslie Parrott, *The Marriage Mentor Manual* (Grand Rapids: Zondervan, 1995).

Les and Leslie Parrott, *Mentoring Engaged and Newlywed Couples* (Grand Rapids: Zondervan, 1997).

Les and Leslie Parrott, *Questions Couples Ask* (Grand Rapids: Zondervan, 1996).

25

Experiencing God Together

David and Jan Stoop

> Your marriage is more than a sacred covenant with another person. It is a spiritual discipline designed to help you know God better, trust him more fully, and love him more deeply.
>
> Gary Thomas, *Sacred Marriage*

What makes your marriage Christian? I mean distinctly Christian? Imagine that you are good friends with another couple who have a very strong, solid marriage. But they make no claim to have an interest in being Christians, or in having a Christian marriage. Perhaps they go to church with you on Christmas or Easter, but that's the extent of their interest in spiritual things. Over the years, you've watched them, and you know they have a great marriage. They also have high moral standards, and they live by their values. You claim to have a Christian marriage, but how is your marriage different from theirs?

There are a number of good responses that are true and important but don't really answer the question. For example, you might say, "Our marriage is different because we have Christ at the center of our lives." That's extremely important, but how does that make your marriage different—in a practical sense? Or you might say, "We attend church and are active in its ministries." You're getting closer, but again, how does that affect your marriage—in a practical sense? Now you say, "Well, my partner and I both have a great relationship with the Lord. He's very real to us and he affects the way we live our lives." Nothing is more important in our lives than our relationship with the Lord, but again, how does that affect your marriage—in a practical sense?

How about an answer that says, "We experience incredible intimacy with God as a couple"? After all, we're looking at spiritual intimacy in this chapter. But now we come to an even more difficult question: How do we experience intimacy with God as a couple? When we look around for help, there isn't much available. There is no end to the number of books on how we can experience God as an individual. Sermons and Sunday school lessons abound to help us in that task. But very little is available to help us learn how, as a couple, we can together experience intimacy with God.

To better understand what we mean by experiencing intimacy with God as a couple, it helps to go back to the Garden of Eden as it was experienced in Genesis 2—before sin entered the picture. We can imagine that in the absence of fear and shame, Adam and Eve experienced a wonderful openness with each other. In addition, they shared the same openness with God. We can infer from Genesis 3 that in the cool of the day, God would come and walk with Adam and Eve through the garden. As they walked together, they probably shared their day with God, and they experienced a special closeness, an intimacy with each other and with God.

Based on the emphasis we have on individual spiritual growth, it would almost be like God came to the garden in the cool of the day and asked, "Okay, whose turn is it to go first?" And then either Adam or Eve would walk alone with God and share an intimacy alone with God. But the sense of the passage is that Adam and Eve shared this time together with God. As a couple, together, they shared an intimacy with God. The openness they shared with each other and the spiritual intimacy they shared together with God was the way marriage was intended to be. That was God's perfect design!

But sin entered the picture as Adam and Eve rebelled and were disobedient. We read, "The fruit looked so fresh and delicious, and it would make her so wise! So she ate some of the fruit. She also gave some to her husband, who was with her. Then he ate it too. At that moment, their eyes were opened, and they suddenly felt shame at their nakedness" (Gen. 3:6–7 NLT). In addition to feeling shame, they also felt guilt and fear, for they hid themselves, not wanting to walk together with God that evening. In their discussion with God about what they had done, they were for the first time defensive, blaming each other for what each had willfully done.

Now, instead of openness, Adam and Eve experienced shame, guilt, fear, and defensiveness in their relationships with each other, and in the spiritual intimacy they had enjoyed with God. Because of these negative factors that affect all human relationships, but especially the marriage relationship, Paul Stevens notes a number of writers who think that marriage is too complicated a relationship for spiritual intimacy to take place.[1] Perhaps that's why so little is available to help us in this area.

We have found that part of our purpose as believers is to begin to restore some of what was lost when Adam and Eve sinned. In other words, as a Christian couple that is seeking to have a genuine Christian marriage, we will do things that seek to restore to us as a couple what was lost at the fall. That includes confronting our shame, defensiveness, and fear, which every couple has to do to build a healthy marriage. And then we need to begin to repair the brokenness we experience as a couple in our relationship with God.

What makes a marriage truly Christian, then, is that we *as a couple* are seeking to restore in our lives part of what was lost in the Garden of Eden. We not only strive to become more whole as an individual, we want our marriage to be more of what God intended marriage to be—a complete, satisfying union of two people with God—intimacy together with each other and together with God. Unless our search for spiritual intimacy with God is part of our behavior as a couple, there is little else that distinguishes a marriage as being truly Christian. So the question still remains—how do we do it?

Facing Fear and Resistance

I (Dave) remember my first reactions to Jan wanting us to experience spiritual intimacy. I was frightened! Physical intimacy was wonderful. Emotional intimacy was a challenge. But spiritual intimacy—

that was a little too deep for me. I was still struggling with developing my own individual relationship with the Lord. I couldn't imagine trying to develop that area with my wife. I wasn't sure I wanted to be that vulnerable. And over the years, I've found that my fearful resistance was quite common among men (and some women, as well). Our differences as male and female, along with our personality differences, make emotional and spiritual intimacy huge roadblocks in the development of our marriage relationship, and this was especially true for me.

Our fears are often hidden, even from ourselves. We have three basic strategies for coping with our fears. We either move toward our partner but in the wrong way, we move against them in anger and hostility, and/or we move away from them. Here's how each works:

1. *We move toward our partner but in the wrong way.* The insecurity we experience because of our fears will lead us into behaviors that actually work against the intimacy we want. For instance, we can try to cover up our insecurity with perfectionism. A couple talks together about developing a closer relationship with God and about doing this together. They really want this. But fear invades their desire, creating thoughts like, "We must become better, either as a person or as a Christian, before we can really get serious about this." Or, "We tried this, but it didn't work like we expected, so we aren't sure we want to try again." Or, "We need to analyze how best to do this—we want to do it right." And we never really develop our spiritual intimacy together.

2. *We push against the other person through anger or hostility.* Often our anger isn't overt. It's much more subtle. I remember one husband who said he couldn't pray with his wife because he was still angry with her over something that had happened years before. When I asked his wife about this, she said, "We've been over that so many times, and each time I ask for his forgiveness. But anytime there's something he doesn't want to do, he brings that up again." In talking with the husband more, it became obvious that he was holding on to his hostility as a protection against having to do something that was frightening for him. Sometimes the anger takes the form of irritability and restlessness. I used this one with Jan. Whenever she'd talk about pray-

ing together, I would get restless and get up and walk around, and then get irritable.

3. *Fear moves us away from our partner, separating us emotionally.* Our fear leads us to withdrawing, emotionally and/or physically. It can be as subtle as "pulling the blinds down behind our eyes," where we are still there physically, but we've checked out every other way. Sometimes we withdraw with busyness. Other times we just go silent or get lost in the television.

As we've said in an earlier chapter, the only way we can overcome our fear is to face it. I remember well the day I decided to "bite the bullet" and agree to begin to pray with Jan. I was surprised at how easy it was. And our developing the habit of praying together daily for over thirty years has been one of the strengths of our relationship.

How Do We Begin?

We understand the importance of developing spiritual intimacy, and we're ready to face our fears and begin. What do we do now? There are a number of things that couples can do together to begin to develop spiritual intimacy as a couple, but it's important to start small. Sometimes we feel that we have grown a lot individually in our walk with the Lord and that all we need to do is transfer some of that maturity into our marital walk with the Lord. But when we make the attempt, we fall flat on our face. And then we give in to our fears again. We've found in talking with couples that our own individual maturity in the Lord doesn't cross over into our walk as a couple. We need to start small and lower our expectations.

Praying Together

One of the important things a couple can do together spiritually is to pray together on a regular, daily basis. But rather than beginning by having long prayer sessions together, start small. Aim for five to ten minutes at the most. In the beginning, pray together silently, holding each other's hands so that when you are finished you can squeeze your partner's hand, and when they finish, they can squeeze back.

After praying silently together for a while, you can get bolder, and while you squeeze your partner's hand, you can say "Amen" out loud. We've found that praying together is one of the most powerful things we can do to develop spiritual intimacy as a couple. Prayer is an important part of spiritual warfare. And we know that marriage is a battle zone for the enemy of our souls. Prayer is one of the weapons we have as we battle "the evil rulers and authorities of the unseen world . . . mighty powers of darkness who rule this world" (Eph. 6:12 NLT). Following this description of our enemy, Paul encourages us to "use every piece of God's armor to resist the enemy" (v. 13 NLT), and finishes that passage by urging us to "pray at all times" (v. 18 NLT).

To pray together is not just a simple activity we add to our day; it is an act of aggression against spiritual forces, and the enemy will resist our efforts. As you begin to pray together, realize that some of the difficulty you may experience is due to this invisible spiritual battle. But be encouraged by knowing that you are entering into God's unseen activity, which is going on all around us. So what can we do?

1. *Pray Scripture for each other.* One of the things Jan and I do is find different prayers in the Bible that we can pray for each other. One of our favorites is Paul's prayer in Philippians 1:9–10. We often use this prayer as our theme verse for couples' retreats. You may want to pray this prayer for each other:

> And this is my prayer: that your love may abound more and more in knowledge and depth of insight, so that you may be able to discern what is best and may be pure and blameless until the day of Christ.

Find other prayers in Scripture and pray them for each other. If you are just beginning to pray together, you can combine Bible study with your praying by individually finding prayers in Scripture that you can then pray together for each other. Other examples include Ephesians 1:18–20 and Romans 12:5–6.

2. *Write out prayers and then share them.* Another way you as a couple can begin to pray out loud together is first to write out a short, simple prayer that is meaningful to you. Then come together and read your prayer out loud. After you finish, you may want to discuss your positive responses to what each other prayed, and how it felt to talk out loud to God together.

3. *Pray as you talk.* After you have been praying together daily for a while, you may find that it is a natural part of your conversation together for one to stop and say, "Let's pray about that," and then you pray together. It becomes an acknowledgment that God is a part of not only your lives together but your conversation as well.

Twice a year we get together with four other couples for a long weekend. We've been doing this for years. We know each other well, and we care about each other, our children, and grandchildren. Often during the weekend, one couple will be talking about some situation in their family, and someone will say, "Can we pray about this right now?" One or two will pray and then we move back into conversation. We've learned to acknowledge God's presence in our conversation.

We've all heard that "the couple that prays together stays together." It's true. Praying together does more than bring two people into the presence of the living God, as powerful as that is! It also knits two hearts together. We've worked with couples with all kinds of problems. We ask each one to commit to praying together daily, regardless of the issues. We've found that those couples who follow through communicate better, work through their issues more efficiently, and become more aware of God's activity in their marriage.

Bible Study Together

I really don't know any couples that can handle doing a formal Bible study together, where one is the teacher and the other is the student. The hierarchical arrangement of teacher-student isn't conducive to the development of spiritual intimacy. Both partners are the learners and the Holy Spirit is the teacher. When we as a couple can come to the Scriptures together as equals before God, in much the same way we do when we pray together, we are in the presence of the living God through his Word.

I was talking with a couple recently that was having a very difficult time in their marriage. The husband was willing and hopeful, but the wife was so fed up that she was even resistant to the counseling. They came in for their session and the wife's attitude was completely changed. I asked her what had happened. She related that one night she had trouble sleeping and for some reason picked up her Bible and started reading. God spoke to her through a specific passage that she had turned to, and she was deeply moved by the Holy Spirit to look at her own life. In the morning she shared her thoughts with her husband, along with the passage. They read it together and then discussed what struck them in the passage. It marked a breakthrough in their relationship as they, each day, had read a passage to each other and then discussed its personal meaning to each of them. They had refused to pray together, but God led them to meet him together through his Word, and healing in their marriage started to take place.

Some couples find that reading a devotional book together on a daily basis is meaningful. One will read the devotional to the other, and then the other reads the relevant passage of Scripture. Then they talk a bit about what they've read, and then they have a short time of prayer together. Again, part of the armor we put on as believers is "the sword of the Spirit, which is the word of God" (Eph. 6:17).

Marriages never stand still, even though they may feel that way at times. Either a husband and wife are growing closer together spiritually, or they are drifting apart. Either they are getting healthier, or they are getting more and more unhealthy. To grow, a marriage needs nourishment, and the Word of God is food for the soul of a marriage.

Other Activities to Do Together

Perhaps you're beginning to see that what marks a marriage as distinctly Christian is that we, as a couple, are doing things together that non-Christian couples don't do together. While nonbelieving people may pray at times, and may even read the Bible for comfort at times, it is not a regular habit they are doing to nurture their marriage. Reading the Bible together and praying together on a regular, daily basis are the foundation stones for building spiritual intimacy in a marriage. George Barna's surveys found that the divorce rate for couples who read the Bible together daily is only 1 out of 1,100.[2] Another statistic we found was that couples who pray together on a daily basis have a divorce rate of 1 out of 1,200.[3] These are unbelievable statistics in light of the divorce rate in the general population being one out of two marriages. Reading the Bible together and praying together are strong divorce-prevention behaviors, but their primary purpose is to develop spiritual intimacy together as a couple.

Another activity we did together that was very meaningful was to go away for a three-day silent retreat. Silent retreats are usually done alone, but we wondered what would happen if we did it as a couple. We decided to make reservations at a retreat center in the high desert for three days. When we told our couples Bible study what we were going to do, one of the women said, "Oh, we have one of those every weekend around our house. He never says a word, just watches TV." We laughed together and then promised to report back what we experienced.

We were totally surprised by what happened to us. We expected to have an incredible time with the Lord. We spent time meditating on Scripture, journaling, walking together in the foothills of the desert, and just being silent. When we were finished with the three days and could talk again to each other, we were both amazed at the sense of intimacy we experienced with God, but even more amazed at the sense of intimacy we felt with each other. God met us in a special way as a couple together.

Later on, one of the couples in our Bible study decided to do the same thing. They went to a different retreat center for a long weekend. When they came back to the group, they reported the same experience—an incredible sense of intimacy together as a couple with God.

Talk about ways to make your weekly worship experiences more of a couples event. How can you prepare for worship as a couple? What can you do after worship to bring more of a sense of "coupleness" to your time of worship? All too many of us arrive at church all frazzled by the kids, or getting a late start, and don't have, or don't take the time to prepare our hearts as an individual, let alone as a couple. Making sure you have time to prepare together is a part of using the time of worship to build spiritual intimacy together. Or if you are involved in some type of ministry, either together or separately, how can you share your experience more meaningfully with your partner? How can you pray for each other in the work you are doing? How about a time to share what God is doing in and through your acts of ministry?

Spiritual intimacy in our marriage means that we are developing a shared inner life together. While this may sound like a frightening, huge task, remember, we begin with a few simple things. Don't rush the process, but don't fail to get started either; or if you've already started, don't fail to add new ways to experience God together in your marriage.

Questions to Discuss

1. What are some of the ways you've tried to develop spiritual intimacy together in the past? What was difficult for you in that process?
2. If you've tried and failed, talk about a first simple step you can take to begin again. Why do you think you failed in the past? Make a commitment to each other to stick with it this time.
3. What are some of the ways you enjoy reading the Bible? What would you enjoy doing together with either the Bible or a devotional book?
4. What are some of the other things you would like to do together in the future to build spiritual intimacy in your marriage? Talk about ways you could plan some of the activities.

For Further Reading

Paul Stevens, *Marriage Spirituality* (Downers Grove, Ill.: InterVarsity Press, 1989).

David and Jan Stoop, *When Couples Pray Together* (Ann Arbor, Mich.: Vine Books, 2000).

Gary Thomas, *Sacred Marriage: Celebrating Marriage as a Spiritual Discipline* (Grand Rapids: Zondervan, 2000).

Dallas Willard, *The Spirit of the Disciplines* (San Francisco: Harper, 1988).

Notes

Chapter 3

1. Archibald Hart, *Me, Myself and I* (Ann Arbor, Mich.: Vine Books, 1992), 171–72.

Chapter 4

1. J. H. Larson, "The Marriage Quiz: College Students' Beliefs in Selected Myths about Marriage. *Family Relations,* (1988): 37, 3–11.
2. 1997 Gallup poll by the National Association of Marriage Enhancement in Phoenix, Arizona.

Chapter 6

1. These rules, along with the "Intentional Listening" material, are expanded on in our book *Let Love Change Your Life (Nashville: Thomas Nelson, 1998).*
2. Mary E. Donovan and William P. Ryan, *Love Blocks: Breaking the Patterns That Undermine Relationships* (New York: Penguin Books, 1991), 325.

Chapter 16

1. Harriet Lerner, *The Dance of Anger* (New York: Harper & Row, 1985), 1.
2. Paul Hauck, *Overcoming Frustration and Anger* (Philadelphia: Westminster Press, 1974).
3. David Augsburger, *Caring Enough to Confront* (Glendale, Calif.: Regal Books, 1980).
4. Gary J. Oliver and H. Norman Wright, *When Anger Hits Home* (Chicago: Moody Press, 1992), 174–75.

Chapter 17

1. David Stoop and James Masteller, *Forgiving Our Parents, Forgiving Ourselves* (Ann Arbor, Mich.: Vine Books, 1991), 101.
2. These steps are expanded upon in David Stoop, *Real Solutions to Forgiving the Unforgivable* (Ann Arbor, Mich.: Vine Books, 2001).

Chapter 25

1. Paul Stevens, *Marriage Spirituality* (Downers Grove, Ill.: InterVarsity Press, 1989), 42.
2. Reported in *Focus on the Family Newsletter,* based on research by George Barna.
3. Based on research by Gallup and noted in chapter 4.

THE COMPLETE PARENTING BOOK

Practical Help from Leading Experts

- Parent the strong-willed child
- Work through anger and loss
- Encourage a practice and love for prayer
- Nurture your child's unique personality
- Discipline with sensitivity and awareness

Dr. David Stoop & Dr. Jan Stoop, editors

The Complete Parenting Book collects insights from more than twenty Christian parenting experts on everything from ADHD and education options to spiritual and physical development.